I highly recommend this thoughtful exploration of contemporary bioethical debates. Prof John Wyatt combines well-informed analysis with the empathy of a fellow Christian who never forgets how difficult the challenges of life can be. This book will be of assistance to both health-care professionals and those in the wider church who seek to honour God with their choices.
Dr Megan Best, Bioethicist and Palliative Care Practitioner, Sydney, Australia

This is one of the most important books I have ever read. It's a tour de force, dealing with life issues from conception to the end of life. Every Christian should read and inwardly digest this masterpiece; its content affects us all profoundly. Powerful, pastoral, pertinent and professional – written by the most qualified author.
Lyndon Bowring, Executive Chairman of CARE

John Wyatt offers a clear, authoritative, and highly intelligent account of some of the greatest issues confronting the human race – at the confluence of new technology and changing mores. With few exceptions (mainly on abortion), Christians have bizarrely not shown much interest. The future of the species is at stake; so I hope this excellent book will make a difference.
Professor Nigel M. de S. Cameron, Founding Editor, Ethics and Medicine

Professor Wyatt debates the ethical dilemmas that surround, in his own words, the twin 'edges of life': its beginning and end. His experiences and examples as a practitioner, his Christian commitment and his own personal integrity challenge us to look at complex issues and examine our attitudes and actions.

He highlights the stark realities on both sides of the arguments. We live in a world with more choice, and alongside that, greater responsibility.

As a Christian, nurse practitioner and pastoral care worker, this resourceful book equips me to think through tough real-life issues – not simply things 'out there'.
Ruth Coffey, SRN, Adjunct Tutor, Moorlands College, Dorset

Professor John Wyatt has produced a book that addresses hugely difficult issues with sensitivity, humanity and Christian charity. It is a book that guides by example. It challenges the reader to face the reality of human suffering in the context of medicine. The aim of a guide to ethics is not to provide easy answers but to help us become the kind of people who can see clearly and can act virtuously. I am sure any reader will find some point on which he or she would take issue with the good professor. Nevertheless, I can think of few better guides for someone intent on seeing clearly and on acting virtuously in the life and death decisions of medical practice.
Professor David Albert Jones, Director, Centre for Bioethics and Emerging Technologies

The experience of shrill headlines and some scientists' over-reaching claims can be bewildering at the best of times. But when that feeling is coupled with the vague unease that ethical boundaries have been crossed, it is a profound relief to know that wise guides like John Wyatt are at hand. I am immensely grateful for the new edition of this book. Skilfully combining the insights of a scholar, the compassion of a practising doctor and the nuanced convictions of a mature Christian, Wyatt is uniquely qualified to write it. His style is readable and fluent, but never superficial or sloganeering.

Because he takes care to tackle difficult ethical questions head-on, applying biblical wisdom and drawing on a wide range of case studies (some of which derive from his own professional experience), I cannot recommend this book enough, to medical professional and concerned onlooker alike.

Mark Meynell, Senior Associate Minister, All Souls, Langham Place

I am so grateful for John and this book. Medical issues cannot be avoided today; they are frequently in the media, most people have an opinion to express or a question to ask, some face the agonies of the decisions they demand, and all the time they reveal the often hidden assumptions that frame our worldviews. These are issues that provide priceless opportunities to think and talk about life and what it means to be human. John's book is a great guide as he faces up to some of them with a warmth and realism born from experience both at the medical and ethical coalface, and shows us how to engage the ideas with the Scriptures. Essential and valuable reading for all of us who want to think and speak Christianly and relevantly.

Hugh Palmer, Rector, All Souls Church, Langham Place, London

Prof Wyatt is one of our most popular guest lecturers. He speaks and writes from a rare combination of personal and clinical experience of suffering, a wealth of research, original thought and a commitment to live as a Christian in twenty-first-century medicine.

The value of this wonderful book as a course text is attested by the fact that copies worn out from sheer overuse have to be replaced at regular intervals. I have no doubt that this second edition, which retains all the highlights of the first, but adds extra up-to-the-minute case illustrations and key references, will prove even more invaluable.

Dr Trevor Stammers, Lecturer in Healthcare Ethics, St Mary's University College, Twickenham

It is most gratifying to see this fine book available in a fully revised and updated form, which takes into account some of the most recent developments in the medical sciences – some of which hold enormous potential for the good of humanity, and some of which are personally, socially and ethically disturbing, often in paradoxical ways. Professor Wyatt shows, however, that we are not just talking about 'medical facts and procedures', but about profound underlying worldviews, in which there have been major shifts in medical consensus, public policy and popular perception – shifts that leave Christians often marginalized in the argument and counter-culturally unpopular. This book explains both the science and the worldviews with admirable clarity and provides biblical foundations for Christian responses that are Christlike by being 'filled with grace and truth'. Few professions more than John Wyatt's world of neo-natal care give their practitioners daily reason to 'rejoice with those who rejoice and weep with those who weep'. It is clear that John Wyatt does both in life and in this book, which is filled with compassion and empathy, written out of a clear head and a warm heart.

Christopher J. H. Wright, International Director, Langham Partnership International Author of Old Testament Ethics for the People of God

Matters of

To Celia, JJ, Tim and Andrew

Matters of
Life &
Death

Human dilemmas
in the light of the Christian faith

John Wyatt

INTER-VARSITY PRESS
Norton Street, Nottingham NG7 3HR, England
Email: ivp@ivpbooks.com
Website: www.ivpbooks.com

First published 1998
New edition 2009

British Library Cataloguing in Publication Data
A catalogue record for this book is available from the British Library.

ISBN: 978–1–84474–367–4

Set in Monotype Garamond 11/13pt
Typeset in Great Britain by CRB Associates, Potterhanworth, Lincolnshire
Printed in Great Britain by Ashford Colour Press Ltd, Gosport, Hampshire

Inter-Varsity Press publishes Christian books that are true to the Bible and that communicate the gospel, develop discipleship and strengthen the church for its mission in the world.

Inter-Varsity Press is closely linked with the Universities and Colleges Christian Fellowship, a student movement connecting Christian Unions in universities and colleges throughout Great Britain, and a member movement of the International Fellowship of Evangelical Students. Website: www.uccf.org.uk

The Christian Medical Fellowship was founded in 1949, has around 4,000 doctors and 1,000 medical students in the UK and Ireland as members, has long been associated with the Universities and Colleges Christian Fellowship, and is linked with some 100 similar bodies worldwide through the International Christian Medical and Dental Association.

Members are united by their faith in Jesus Christ, their belief in the Bible as God's word, and their calling in healthcare. One aim is 'to promote Christian values, especially in bioethics and healthcare, among doctors and medical students, in the church and in society'. In fulfilling this, John Wyatt has chaired CMF's Medical Study Group since 1994.

Website *www.cmf.org.uk*

John Wyatt is Professor of Ethics and Perinatology at University College London. He has engaged in clinical practice as a neonatologist and academic researcher into the prevention of brain injury in newborn babies for more than twenty-five years. He is now engaged in research and teaching on ethical and philosophical issues raised by modern medical practice.

The London Lectures in Contemporary Christianity

This is an annual series of lectures founded in 1974 to promote Christian thought about contemporary issues. Their aim is to expound an aspect of historical biblical Christianity and to relate it to a contemporary issue in the church in the world. They seek to be scholarly in content yet popular enough in appeal and style to attract the educated public; and to present each topic in such a way as to be of interest to the widest possible audience as well as to the Christian public.

Previous Lectures:

1997 'Matters of Life and Death: Contemporary medical dilemmas in the light of the Christian faith', *Professor John Wyatt* (published by IVP in 1998 as *Matters of Life and Death: Today's healthcare dilemmas in the light of the Christian faith*, and in 2009 as *Matters of Life and Death: Human dilemmas in the light of the Christian faith*)

1998 'Endless Conflict or Empty Tolerance: The Christian response to a multi-faith world', *Dr Vinoth Ramachandra* (published by IVP in 1999 as *Faiths in Conflict: Christian integrity in a multicultural world*)

1999 'Justice That Restores', *Charles Colson* (lectures not delivered, but published by IVP as *Justice that Restores*)

2000 'The Incomparable Christ: Celebrating his millennial birth', *John Stott* (published in 2001 by IVP as *The Incomparable Christ*)

2001 'Moral Leadership', *Bishop James Jones* (published by IVP in 2002 as *The Moral Leader: For the church and the world*)

2002 'Moving Genes: Evolving promise or un-natural selection?' *John Bryant* (published by IVP in 2004 as *Life in our Hands: A Christian perspective on genetics and cloning*)

2003 'Can Christianity and Islam Co-exist in the 21st Century?' *Professor Peter G. Riddell* (published by IVP in 2004 as *Christians and Muslims: Pressures and potential in a post-9/11 world*)

2004 'Spirituality, Christianity and the Future of the World', *Dr John Drane*

2005 'Disciples and Citizens', *Bishop Graham Cray* (published by IVP in 2007 as *Disciples and Citizens: A vision for distinctive living*)

2006 'Redeeming Family', *Revd Andrew and Revd Lis Goddard*

2007 'Redeeming Creation', *Peter Harris and Revd Dr Chris Wright*

2008 'Christian Approaches to Armed Conflict', *Peter Dixon* (published by IVP in 2009 as *Peacemakers: Building stability in a complex world*)

The London Lectures Trust

The London Lectures in Contemporary Christianity are organized by the London Lectures Trust, which was established as a charity in 1994. The committee represents several different evangelical organizations.

CONTENTS

We invite you to visit our website: www.ivpbooks.com/mattersoflifeanddeath. This symbol 🖥 in the text indicates further information and resources relating to a topic or topics which you may wish to explore.

FOREWORD

What is so impressive about Professor Wyatt is that he combines within himself three persons. First, he is a trained and well-informed scientist, with an extensive knowledge of medicine, biology, genetics and reproductive technology. He writes, not as an armchair theorist, but as an experienced practitioner. He takes readers into his confidence, shares his expertise with them, and expects them to make up their own minds on each issue.

Secondly, he is a Christian, who stands firmly in the tradition of historic Christianity. His well-grounded Christian faith informs all his thinking, as he seeks to relate his biblical worldview to the complexities of the modern world.

Thirdly, he is a human being with all the vulnerability that this entails. He sees in the incarnation the perfect model of empathy, of entering deeply into other people's experience of pain. As a neonatologist, he has the grievous responsibility of telling parents that their baby is dying. Then he weeps with those who weep.

John Wyatt's personal integrity shines through this book from beginning to end. He makes no attempt to conceal disturbing facts, or to hide his own struggles and uncertainties. He ducks no questions and offers no glib solutions to complex contemporary problems.

Nor does he underestimate the seriousness of the current liberal assault on traditional Christian doctrine and ethics, not least on the sanctity of human beings, made in the image of God. He has read (and debated with) many of the principal professional assailants. The names of Peter Singer, Richard Dawkins, Ronald Dworkin and John Harris keep recurring. Their arguments are summarized and John Wyatt begins to formulate a reasoned response to them.

I find him at his most fresh and imaginative when he develops his analogy of God as the artist and of the human being as his 'flawed masterpiece'. Each person is a masterpiece of divine creation, reflecting the divine image, and so possessing incalculable value. Yet evil has spoiled God's creation. A quotation will give readers a flavour of John Wyatt's skill:

> The original masterpiece, created with such love and embodying such artistry has become flawed, defaced, contaminated . . . the reflection of God's character is distorted and partially obscured. But through the imperfections, we can still see the outlines of the original masterpiece. It still inspires a sense of wonder at the underlying design.

'The task of health professionals,' he continues, 'is to protect and restore the masterpieces entrusted to our care, in line with the original creator's intentions.'

John Stott
Rector Emeritus of All Souls Church, Langham Place, London, and
President of the Institute of Contemporary Christianity

ACKNOWLEDGMENTS

This book would not have been possible without the support and encouragement of many friends. I am particularly grateful for the support and patience of my family – Celia, JJ, Tim and Andrew, and to my parents-in-law, Malcolm and Anne Richard, who provided hospitality and seclusion on several occasions while I was writing the manuscript. I owe a unique debt to John Stott for his friendship, wisdom and encouragement over more than thirty years, and I am very grateful that he agreed to provide a Foreword. I continue to be grateful to the members of the Study Group of the Christian Medical Fellowship for many stimulating discussions, especially Peter Saunders, Andrew Fergusson, Caroline Berry, Duncan Vere, David Jones, Charles Foster, Eldryd Parry and Mark Campbell. Mark also provided particular assistance in researching case histories. I have learnt a great deal from the wisdom and insights of many other friends, including Steve Beck, Brian Brock, Nigel Cameron, Phil Clarke, Mary Evans, Rob George, Janet Goodall, Mark Greene, Roy McCloughry, Pete Moore, David Zac Niringiye, Oliver O'Donovan, Elaine Storkey, David Turner and Vinoth Ramachandra. I'm grateful to Christopher's parents, Alan and Verity, and to Ruth, who allowed me to tell their stories, and to Dave and Sue Ryan who also provided hospitality while I was completing the manuscript.

The first edition of this book was based on the 1997 London Lectures in Contemporary Christianity and I am grateful for the support and encouragement of the committee members of the London Lectures Trust, and for the assistance of Nick Page, Sue Radford, Richard Bewes and Diane Baird. I am indebted to Eleanor Trotter, Brian Wilson and Barbara Ball of Inter-Varsity Press who provided invaluable advice and editorial guidance and for a number of readers who provided feedback on an earlier draft of the manuscript. Of course I retain responsibility for any errors and inaccuracies which remain. Finally I want to record my debt to my parents, John and Grace Wyatt, now deceased, whose love and example of Christian service was profoundly formative both for me and for many others.

INTRODUCTION

When I was a medical student in London in the 1970s, I received just one lecture on medical ethics in my six years of undergraduate professional training. I was taught that all the practising doctor needed to know about the subject could be summarized under five A's: Abortion, Adultery, Alcoholism, Association (with non-medically qualified physicians or 'quacks') and Advertising. Of these evils, which the General Medical Council was dedicated to stamping out, it was widely held that the most objectionable was Advertising.

But the world has changed. Medical ethics has been transformed from an obscure and unimportant branch of professional practice into a high-profile media activity. 'Shock horror' tabloid journalism and highbrow television documentaries have brought the issues to a world audience. A single medical case can now achieve the same media prominence as the latest disclosure about the British royals or a soap opera scandal.

What are the underlying forces behind the modern transformation in medical ethics? And how can people who wish to be faithful to the historic Christian faith respond to the challenges and the opportunities of recent and dramatic medical progress?

This book attempts to formulate a Christian perspective on a number of central ethical dilemmas raised by modern medical practice. While writing from my individual perspective as a practising clinician and Anglican layperson, I have tried to reflect a broad theological position of historic or 'foundational' trinitarian Christianity, a theological position which takes a high view of Scripture and of the doctrines of the ancient creeds and councils of the Early Church. I am not a professional philosopher or theologian. For most of my professional life I have been a practising paediatrician and a Christian believer who has had to face some of these agonizing dilemmas as part of my daily medical practice. What I do have to offer is a view from the coalface. It is a view which has been created in my personal struggle to understand what is going on in the world of modern medicine and the attempt to develop an authentic Christian response.

These questions are not just matters for an interesting academic debate, of the sort that philosophers, ethicists and students love to engage in. These dilemmas touch us at the most intimate, painful and vulnerable part of our lives. Many of the people who read this book will be carrying secret sorrows which they cannot share with others. The statistics show that more than one couple in seven will suffer from some form of fertility problem, and many will never be able to have children naturally. Some parents who pick up this book will have watched their child struggle and die, or will have given birth to a stillborn baby. Some will have had an abortion, although even their closest friends and relatives may not know. Some will have watched a close relative die in pain or emotional distress. A few will know that they suffer from a major genetic disorder which is likely to curtail their life, and they are wondering how they and their families will cope with the future. Many more of us are unknowingly carrying genes which may result in major illness, disability and death later in life: diseases such as Alzheimer's, stroke or breast cancer. Virtually all of us are carrying the genes for devastating illnesses which we might pass on to our children. Many people who pick up this book, for instance, will be carrying the gene for cystic fibrosis, though they are completely unaware of it.

So these are not just ethical issues 'out there': they touch us at the core of our being. Nobody is immune: we all share in a common humanity, a physical nature which is painfully vulnerable and deeply flawed. As you read the following case histories, you may well find them disturbing and painful, as indeed I have done. A French philosopher of the Enlightenment once said that 'death, like the sun, should not be stared at'. Yet that is precisely what we shall be doing in this book: staring at death and at the questions and fears that it raises.

The vision behind the London Lectures in Contemporary Christianity is the Christian task which John Stott has termed 'double listening'.[1] First, our task is to listen to the modern world in order to try to understand the real issues. Next, our task is to listen to the unchanging historic Christian faith in order to develop an authentic Christian perspective. Finally, our task is to build a bridge which spans these two foundations: the modern world and the authentic biblical

Christian faith. The task of biblical Christians is to understand the modern world in the light of the Bible, and to understand the Bible in the light of the modern world. Unless our bridge is securely rooted in both foundations it will be unable to bear the weight demanded of it.

Of course, bridge-building is a perilous art. My father was a structural engineer, and I have a vivid memory of watching with him as a child while a concrete bridge he had designed was being tested by huge weighted lorries. I embark on my process of bridge construction with due trepidation. I have made no attempt to be exhaustive, as I lack the expertise and the experience to span the vast range of ethical issues raised by modern medical practice. Instead, I have concentrated on the ethical dilemmas surrounding the twin 'edges of life': the start of life and its end.

These are not easy matters. I have no simple answers – indeed, there are no simple answers. Yet I do have a deep conviction that the historic Christian faith, the faith of the Bible and of the Church Fathers, gives us a way forward as we approach these agonizing dilemmas. It is a way forward that is intellectually coherent and satisfying, and also immensely practical and down to earth. The historic Christian faith does have something vital to say to the world of the Human Genome Project, the intensive-care unit and the palliative care specialist. As I have researched and written this book, I have had a continuing sense of optimism, hope and confidence in the answers which the Christian faith provides.

To set the scene, I will outline a number of important and influential medical cases which have hit the headlines. My purpose is to illustrate some of the technical possibilities and human dilemmas which modern medical technology has created, before we attempt to analyse the fundamental trends and social forces which underlie them.

Mary and Jodie: conjoint twins

In May 2000, Michaelangelo and Rina Attard travelled to the UK from their home on the Maltese island of Gozo. Rina was pregnant with twins, and an ultrasound scan had shown that they were physically joined at the lower half of the body – an extremely rare condition. Further scans in the UK revealed that the twins faced considerable medical difficulties. The twins, known publicly as Mary and Jodie, were delivered by Caesarean section in a Manchester hospital. It rapidly became clear that Mary's condition was extremely poor and that her body was being effectively supported by Jodie – the two aortae were connected. The doctors were of the opinion that if the twins were surgically separated,

Jodie had a good chance of survival, although Mary would die as soon as the arterial connection was severed. If there were no operation, both twins would weaken and eventually die. The medical team wanted to perform the surgical procedure, but after prolonged discussion the parents refused to give permission, arguing that the doctors were 'playing God'. The case was referred to the UK courts. The parents had engaged the help of the publicist Max Clifford, and the case was thrust into the crucible of worldwide media debate.

One of the judges, Lord Justice Ward, describing the case as 'excruciatingly difficult', said: 'In this case the right answer is not at all easy to find. I freely confess to having found it truly difficult to decide – difficult because of the scale of the tragedy for the parents and the twins, difficult for the seemingly irreconcilable conflicts of moral and ethical values . . . The parents cannot bring themselves to consent to the operation. The twins are equal in their eyes and they cannot agree to kill one even to save the other. As devout Roman Catholics they believe that it is God's will that their children are afflicted as they are and they must be left in God's hands. The doctors are convinced that they can carry out the operation so as to give Jodie a life which will be worthwhile.'[2]

Ultimately, both the High Court and the Court of Appeal held that it would be lawful for the doctors to separate the twins. In November 2000 a 20-hour procedure was performed at St Mary's Hospital in Manchester. Mary died but Jodie survived, and after six months of convalescence was able to return home to Gozo. In a subsequent interview Mrs Attard said, 'We were upset that we lost the case because we always thought we should have the right to say what was best for our children and that the taking of life was wrong. The decision was taken out of our hands in the end but we are happy that the decision to separate was taken by the judges.' The money obtained from media interviews, some £350,000, was put into a trust to pay for the medical care that Jodie is likely to need during her lifetime.

Was it right for the courts to overrule the sincere convictions of the parents? Did Jodie's right to life trump Mary's interests? Were the doctors and the law courts 'playing God', or acting responsibly?

Dr Anne Turner: a case of assisted suicide

Anne Turner was a retired doctor from Bath in the West of England. She had watched her husband die slowly from a tragic, degenerative medical condition, and now she herself had been diagnosed with a rare incurable neurological disorder, progressive supranuclear palsy. The condition was slowly progressing, and by January 2006, Dr Turner had slurred speech and difficulty in swallowing.

She was unable to drive or take a bath without assistance. Although she was likely to live for several more years, she feared the coming deterioration and said to her children, 'I don't want to be remembered by you as being totally incapacitated.' Dr Turner had talked of suicide and in October 2005 she made an unsuccessful attempt to kill herself with sleeping tablets, antidepressants and a plastic bag. Now she requested the help of her family in ending her life. In the UK, assisting in a suicide is a serious offence. So Dr Turner chose to travel to the Dignitas clinic in Zürich. She said she was angry that she was forced to go to Switzerland to end her life, but was convinced it was the right thing to do. 'I am not looking forward to it, but at the same time I am. I had this awful fall last night and could not get up. I thought then that this really demonstrates that what I am going to do is right. Doctors should be able to help people to die. I always quote the fact that I had a cat, and I had him put down because he was riddled with cancer, but we cannot do that with humans now.'[3]

Her son Edward expressed the anguish of the family: 'It's the hardest thing I have had to face. I have a very close relationship with my mother; she is one of the people I love most in the world. So when your mother suddenly tells you that she has a terminal illness and is planning to take her own life, it is extraordinarily hard. Until the suicide attempt we had probably been in denial . . . Everybody had always told her not to go ahead with it because there were so many reasons to stay. It was only when she went ahead with the failed attempt that we thought there is no point in messing around; let's do it properly because it's just too cruel to do it any other way.'

The case was taken up by the UK Voluntary Euthanasia Society (now renamed Dignity in Dying), who were campaigning for the legalization of assisted suicide in the UK, and the issues were debated across television, internet and media outlets. In the glare of the media Dr Turner travelled with her three children to Switzerland, where the final arrangements were made in an anonymous Zürich apartment. The family chatted together, sang some songs, and then Dr Turner drank the lethal mixture of barbiturates, leading to coma and death within minutes. She was the forty-second Briton to die at the Dignitas centre.

So was Dr Turner's way of death a model for modern people? Is this the best way to die? Should the law be changed to allow medically assisted suicide? Is the prohibition of medical killing an outdated taboo from a previous era?

Joanna Jepson – late abortion and the law

Joanna Jepson was a theological trainee in the Church of England. Whilst reviewing officially published abortion statistics, she became aware that in 2001 a late abortion had been performed on a <u>fetus</u> diagnosed with bilateral <u>cleft lip</u> <u>and palate</u>. Although the clinical details of the case have never been made public, the abortion was performed under Clause E of the Abortion Act, allowing an abortion if *two doctors conclude in good faith that there is substantial risk that if the child were born he or she would suffer from such physical or mental abnormalities as to be seriously handicapped.*

Miss Jepson herself was born with a facial deformity and had a brother with <u>Down's syndrome</u>. She was concerned at the way that the Abortion Act was being interpreted by doctors when there was a fetal abnormality. Lawyers representing Miss Jepson wrote to the Commissioner of the Metropolitan Police to make them aware that the procedure in question had been carried out at twenty-eight weeks of gestation (6½ months) and to ask them to investigate the matter. A police review was carried out and concluded that no offences had been committed and that the doctors involved would not face prosecution in the criminal courts. In December 2003, the High Court gave Miss Jepson permission to proceed with a legal challenge against West Mercia Police Constabulary for its decision not to prosecute the doctors. In particular, Miss Jepson asked the High Court to declare that cleft lip and palate did not constitute a 'serious handicap' in the context of the Abortion Act.[4]

The case led to public debate and discussion about the practice of late abortion where there is evidence of fetal abnormality, but after some delay the Crown Prosecution Service announced that the legal proceedings would go no further. Many obstetric specialists were relieved that the legal threat to their clinical autonomy was averted. But the case raised deep and unsettling questions about the working of the Abortion Act, and the fact that private decisions made by doctors and parents could not be exposed to scrutiny. Under what clinical conditions should a late abortion be carried out, and what does the practice say about our attitude to the disabled children and adults in our society?

Ms B – the right to refuse medical treatment

In August 1999 Ms B, a 41-year-old social worker, suffered a spontaneous haemorrhage into the spinal cord in her neck. After a number of investigations, she was advised that she was at risk of further bleeding that could result in severe disability. Around this time she made a '<u>living will</u>' stating that medical treatment should be withdrawn if she were to suffer from a life-threatening illness leading to permanent mental impairment or permanent unconsciousness. However, her medical condition improved and she was able eventually to return to work.

At the beginning of 2001, there were signs of progressive weakness, and Ms B was readmitted to hospital. Examination showed that she was now becoming paralysed from the neck down. Because of increasing breathing difficulties she was transferred to the intensive-care unit, and life-support treatment with artificial ventilation was commenced. A neurosurgical operation was carried out to relieve pressure on the spinal cord, but there was little improvement and she remained dependent on the mechanical ventilator. Miss B repeatedly asked the doctors caring for her to switch off the life-support machinery so that she could die. However, the medical team insisted that it was their professional duty to preserve her life.

In the months that followed, Ms B was assessed by several psychiatrists to determine whether she was mentally competent to make a decision which would lead inevitably to her death. Various treatment options were raised but Ms B remained adamant about her choice. The case was referred to the High Court and, in a remarkable precedent, the Court held part of its proceedings within the intensive-care unit so that Ms B could give evidence in person. Dame Elizabeth Butler-Sloss, the presiding judge, expressed her admiration for Ms B's courage, strength of will and determination: 'She is a splendid person and it is tragic that someone of her ability has been struck down so cruelly. I hope she will forgive me for saying, diffidently, that if she did reconsider her decision, she would have a lot to offer the community at large.'[5]

Dame Butler-Sloss concluded that Ms B did indeed have the mental capacity to refuse treatment, and that the hospital, by continuing to treat her with ventilation against her wishes, had acted unlawfully: 'One must allow for those as severely disabled as Ms B, for some of whom life in that condition may be worse than death.' Ms B was moved to another hospital where, shortly afterwards, intensive treatment was withdrawn at her request and she died.

The case was seen as a landmark in English law, confirming the right of competent patients to refuse life-sustaining treatment. But did this judgment, in effect, lead to the legalization of euthanasia in England? Were the doctors who switched off the life-support machinery responsible for her death? Why should Ms B have a right to die whereas Dr Turner, who also wished to die, could not be assisted?

Zain Hashmi – the hope of a saviour sibling

Zain is the fourth child of Raj and Shahana Hashmi from Leeds in the north of England. He was born with a serious congenital blood disorder called beta thalassaemia major. This is a lifelong condition requiring frequent blood transfusions. Sadly, because of the complications of repeated transfusions, there is a high risk of progressive organ failure and early death. Zain's best chance of a cure was the transplant of bone marrow cells from a donor with a matching tissue type. However, none of his three siblings or other close family members had a suitable tissue match. His parents decided, therefore, to have another child in the hope that he or she would be a suitable donor. When prenatal genetic testing showed that this child too would develop thalassaemia, Mrs Hashmi chose to have an abortion. A fifth healthy child was born but again there was no suitable match for Zain.

Mr and Mrs Hashmi applied to the Human Fertilisation and Embryology Authority for the right to test embryos created in the laboratory to find a suitable tissue match, so that they could have a child who could act as a donor for Zain. In 2002 the HFEA granted a licence for this procedure, leading to a national debate about the use of reproductive technology and embryo screening.[6] The case was challenged in the courts, but HFEA's decision was ultimately upheld in the final court of appeal, the House of Lords. In 2005 it was reported that the Hashmis had undergone six attempts at in vitro fertilization (IVF) which were all unsuccessful, and at the time of writing no suitable tissue donor for Zain has been created.

Diane Pretty – the right to die

Diane Pretty was diagnosed with motor neuron disease in 1999 at the age of forty. Her condition deteriorated rapidly, and in the following year she was confined to a wheelchair. By the beginning of 2001 she was paralysed from the neck down and being fed with a tube, although she was still able to breathe by herself. Mrs Pretty realized that she was continuing to deteriorate, and she feared a slow and painful death. She decided that she would end her life when the suffering became too much, but because of the muscular paralysis she needed assistance to end her life. Her devoted husband, Brian, was prepared to help her die, but he risked prosecution and imprisonment. Under the Suicide Act it is a criminal offence to assist suicide even from compassionate motives. Diane Pretty sought an assurance from the legal authorities that her husband would not be prosecuted if he were to assist her death. The case went ultimately to the House of Lords and then to the European Court of Human Rights in Strasbourg. But after prolonged legal argument, Diane Pretty's case failed.[7] The courts, whilst acknowledging her 'frightening ordeal', refused to give her husband immunity from prosecution if he assisted her death. The case was taken up by the Voluntary Euthanasia Society, and caused headlines around the world.

Hospice care was repeatedly offered, but Diane Pretty steadfastly refused help until near the end. In May 2002 her breathing difficulties worsened and she was admitted to a local hospice. She passed into a coma and died shortly afterwards. Brian Pretty expressed his frustration to the world's media: 'Diane had to go through the one thing she had foreseen and was afraid of – and there was nothing I could do to help.'

Tony Bland and the persistent vegetative state

On 15 April 1989 Tony Bland, a seventeen-year-old football fan, went to Sheffield to see his team, Liverpool, play Nottingham Forest. He was caught in the tragic Hillsborough Stadium disaster as thousands of fans pushed to get into the ground. Like many others, his body was crushed against the metal perimeter fences, leading to severe oxygen starvation. Over ninety fans died on that afternoon, but Tony Bland survived. At least, his body survived. Tragically, his brain had been severely damaged, leading to the profound coma known as the persistent vegetative state (PVS). He was alive and the basic bodily functions remained intact. He could breathe, and digest food. His eyes were open at times, and the lowest part of the brain, the brain stem, was functioning at a rudimentary level, but there was absolutely no evidence of conscious awareness of, or responsiveness to, his environment. The cerebral cortex, the brain region essential to normal conscious activity, was irretrievably damaged. His life was maintained by an artificial pump which passed liquid food via a tube into his stomach. For more than three years, Tony Bland existed in this twilight state, as his devoted parents waited and hoped against hope for any flickering sign of improvement. Eventually, Tony's family and his doctor, Dr J. G. Howe, applied to the High Court for permission to stop the feeding. There was worldwide media interest. 'Let poor Tony die,' proclaimed one newspaper headline.

The case went ultimately to the House of Lords. The legal debate turned on the question, 'What course of action is in the best interests of the patient?' In a landmark decision, the Law Lords agreed that, as Tony Bland was not consciously aware of his surroundings and as there was no realistic chance of an improvement in his medical condition, the treatment that was sustaining his life brought him no 'therapeutical, medical or other benefit'.[8] They agreed that artificial feeding should be withdrawn. Tony Bland died some days later.

Many have argued that this was a commonsense development of medical practice in response to an intolerable problem. But others have suggested that the Bland case marks the point at which the British courts ceased to respect the traditional principle of the sanctity of human life.[9] For the first time, the courts accepted as lawful a course of action whose sole purpose and intention was the death of an innocent human being.

As Christians we must never reduce medical ethics to cold theology and unfeeling moral principles. We must never forget the human pain that lies behind every ethical dilemma. Anne Turner and Diane Pretty facing a lonely and agonizing decline into dependence and death. Ray and Shahina Hashmi and their desperate attempt to find a tissue donor for their son. Miss B finding herself being kept alive against her will by life-support technology. Mary and Jodie's parents, facing the intolerable decision of whether to end one daughter's life in order to save the other. The tragic destruction of Tony Bland's young life and the agony of loving parents who wait in vain for recovery.

Before everything else, our first duty is to empathize, to enter into the experience of human pain, despair and perplexity. We must wrestle with these ethical dilemmas not with anger, hatred or judgment in our voices, but with tears in our eyes. For empathy is the way of Christ.

We shall return to each of these case histories in the course of this book. But before we can attempt to formulate an authentic Christian response, we need to reflect on the fundamental trends and developments which have brought us to the current position. How on earth did we get here? What are the underlying forces in science, in technology and in society which have brought us to this point?

1. WHAT'S GOING ON? FUNDAMENTAL THEMES IN HEALTH CARE AND SOCIETY

In this chapter I shall highlight five fundamental themes, or trends, which seem to lie behind the controversies and developments of the last few years. Although the list is not exhaustive, these seem to me to be some of the most significant trends of the last three decades which have brought us to our current position. This chapter may seem rather academic, theoretical and hard-going to some, and you may wish to jump to the next chapter and come back to this one at a later stage, but I believe these themes are significant and important.

Theme 1: Progress in human biology and the triumph of scientific reductionism

The period from the 1980s onwards has seen the spectacular and unparalleled success of a scientific reductionist methodology applied to human biology. 'Reductionism' is a term that is frequently bandied around, often as a term of abuse. But what does it actually mean?

As a scientific method, reductionism can be seen as a way of investigating and understanding processes from the bottom up. As I type this sentence on my computer, I am watching words appear on the monitor screen in front of me. I can analyse the sentence in terms of language, vocabulary and grammar. But those images, which appear to be words that I can recognize, are in fact constructed from a screen display which is generated and regenerated many times per second. The screen display is produced by thousands of tiny semi-conductor devices which are emitting photons according to the fundamental physical laws of quantum mechanics. The images on my screen can be analysed at a number of different levels, each more fundamental than the previous one. Reductionism is the name for a description of processes at the most fundamental level possible, in order to provide the most detailed and comprehensive understanding of which we are capable.

This analogy may be helpful because it illustrates the fact that the appropriate level of analysis depends on the question being asked. If I ask, 'Why are the words at the edge of my screen distorted?', the answer may well depend upon a detailed understanding of the processes of photon emission. But if I ask, 'Why is this sentence written in English and not in Chinese?', an answer in terms of photons is not going to be helpful. The level of explanation required is completely different.

Much of modern biological science is reductionist in the sense that it depends on the progressive breakdown of awesome complexity into relatively simple fundamental cellular and molecular mechanisms. As a way of tackling scientific and medical problems, reductionism applied to biology has been remarkably successful.

The area of molecular genetics is just one example of the success of reductionist biology and the resultant growth in scientific knowledge about ourselves. The sequencing of the entire human genome, recently completed following a massive coordinated research enterprise, has led to a mass of new information about our genetic make-up. We now know much more about the variations in DNA between different human beings, and we are able to compare our genetic code with that of other species. We have learnt more about the genetic make-up of *Homo sapiens* in the last ten years than in the whole of the preceding thousands of years of human existence.

By comparing DNA samples, it is possible to identify the degree of physical relatedness between any two individuals. And by taking samples from different geographical and racial groups, geneticists have a new and powerful tool to investigate our human history and the racial migrations which have taken place since we first appeared on the planet. This is because our DNA has been passed down to us from our ancestors, accumulating mutations on the way. Modern techniques for DNA analysis have led to an upsurge of scientific interest in human diversity and evolution.

Terrible, disabling conditions such as thalassaemia, sickle-cell disease and Huntington's disease all stem from 'point mutations', minute changes in our genetic code – a single misprint in an encyclopedia of millions of words. Many more common diseases, such as insulin-dependent diabetes and many forms of cancer, result from an interaction between genetic variants (polymorphisms) and environmental factors. Disturbingly, serious abnormalities are surprisingly common in our genetic code. In fact, all of us harbour within our DNA abnormal genes which carry the possibility of serious diseases for ourselves and for our children. 'For his birthday Daddy gave him a time bomb' reads the slogan of a poster campaign about hereditary heart disease. By detailed analysis of an individual's DNA, it is increasingly possible to calculate the risk of future diseases, and before long it may be possible to give increasingly accurate risk estimates for any one of hundreds of conditions, from coronary artery blockage to Alzheimer's disease.

Of course, it is not only human genetics that has seen an explosive rate of scientific advance. In virtually all areas of human biology – embryology, neuroscience, cancer medicine – the reductionist scientific methodology has been spectacularly successful, leading to an explosive growth in the basic medical sciences. The importance of this development for the future of medicine is hard to overestimate.

What is our reaction to this explosion of scientific information about our bodies, about the stuff of our humanity, the microscopic mechanisms of which our physical being is constructed? How have these scientific advances affected our view of ourselves and our place on the planet? What does it mean to be a human being in the light of modern biology?

As a number of Christian writers have pointed out, a successful scientific approach, splitting down complex systems into more basic constituents, tends to transform unnoticed into a philosophical view which assumes that any system can be explained wholly by the properties of its component parts. To put it more technically, a reductionist methodology tends to merge imperceptibly into a reductionist ontology. Professor Donald MacKay, a distinguished Christian neuroscientist, christened this attitude 'nothing buttery'. Nothing buttery is the belief that because we are composed of chemicals, we are 'nothing but' chemicals.[1]

Certainly 'nothing buttery' seems to be alive and well in modern biology. The well-known zoologist Professor Richard Dawkins, of Oxford University, writes in his influential book, *The Selfish Gene*: 'We are survival machines – robot vehicles blindly programmed to preserve the selfish molecules known as genes. This is a truth which still fills me with astonishment.'[2]

Dawkins describes his striking vision of the process of Darwinian evolution which proceeds inexorably from the first living, replicating cell all the way to human beings:

Replicators began not merely to exist, but to construct for themselves containers, vehicles for their continued existence. The replicators which survived were the ones which built survival machines for themselves to live in . . . Survival machines got bigger and more elaborate, and the process was cumulative and progressive . . . Four thousand million years on, what was to be the fate of the ancient replicators? They did not die out, for they are past masters of the survival arts. But do not look for them floating loose in the sea; they gave up that cavalier freedom long ago. Now they swarm in huge colonies, safe inside gigantic lumbering robots, sealed off from the outside world, communicating with it by tortuous indirect routes, manipulating it by remote control. They are in you and in me; they created us, body and mind; and their preservation is the ultimate rationale for our existence. They have come a long way, those replicators. Now they go by the name of genes, and we are their survival machines.[3]

Dawkins once asked a little girl what she thought flowers were for. She thought for a moment and said: 'Two things; to make the world pretty and to help bees make honey for us.'

'Well, I thought that was a very nice answer,' said Dawkins, 'and I was very sorry to tell her it wasn't true.'

What then is Dawkins's answer? What are flowers and human beings and everything else for?

He says: 'We are all machines built by DNA whose purpose is to make more copies of the same DNA. Flowers are for the same thing as everything else in the living kingdoms, for spreading "copy me" programs about. That is exactly what we are for. We are machines for propagating DNA . . . It is every living object's sole reason for living.'[4]

To the consistent reductionist, our bodies are ultimately just survival machines; our brains are, in reality, computers constructed out of flesh and blood rather than silicon and wires. The sole purpose of the human body is to ensure our ability to survive and replicate. Even our most erudite thoughts or passionate emotions are merely the by-products of our neural-computer circuitry. When challenged about the nature of human love in an interview in *Third Way* magazine, Dawkins replied: 'Brains being what they are, they have a capacity to invent spurious purposes of the universe . . . [love] is an emotion which is a manifestation of brain stuff.'[5]

Of course, there are serious problems with thorough-going reductionism as an all-encompassing philosophy. If all our thoughts and beliefs are mere by-products of neural-computer circuitry, there are serious reasons to doubt whether our beliefs actually match with reality, with the way the world is. It could be that some of my thoughts and beliefs merely have survival value but are ultimately faulty, including my beliefs about reductionism. If the structure of my brain has evolved solely to ensure my survival, there are serious questions as to whether its beliefs can be reliable. Dawkins has claimed that religious belief represents an aberrant way of thinking which replicates from mind to mind (a malignant meme or God-virus).[6] But the argument is two-edged. A belief in reductionism may also be aberrant and faulty. Thorough-going reductionism raises the question of whether it is possible to generate rational beliefs through a process of discovery and discussion. If our beliefs and convictions are simply an artefact created by the firing of brain cells, then there is no reason to think that they should have any connection with reality. In fact, the very possibility of rational thought is called into question. Yet Dawkins clearly believes most passionately, not only that his view of the world has survival value for his own genes, but also that it is true – that it matches with the way the universe is.

It's interesting that Charles Darwin himself was aware of this implication of evolutionary thinking:

> But then with me the horrid doubt always arises whether the convictions of man's mind, which has been developed from the mind of the lower animals, are of any value or at all trustworthy. Would any one trust in the convictions of a monkey's mind, if there are any convictions in such a mind?[7]

Despite its philosophical problems, biological reductionism is part of popular culture today. It has penetrated into the foundations of modern people's thought-forms. It is the unchallenged perspective of the scientific and educated elite. How has this perspective affected our view of ourselves as human beings? I want to spell out four consequences.

Scientific reductionism leads to a 'machine' view of humanity

In the history of biology, human beings have always tried to understand the human body by comparison with the most potent forces we observe in the world around us. The ancient physicians conceived of the body as operating according to the four basic elements that philosophers had identified: fire, water, air and earth. The Victorians, in an age when the power of hydraulics was omnipresent, conceived of the body as composed of incompressible fluids which generated powerful pressures and forced their way through microscopic tubes. Even the Freudian conception of psychodynamics can be seen in this way. The libido is an incompressible fluid which is channelled through the structures of the unconscious, but has a tendency to burst out in uncontrollable energy. At heart it's a hydraulic view of the mind!

Now, as modern society has been transformed by machines of all types, it is perhaps not surprising that the commonest perception of our bodies is as merely another sort of machine, especially an information-processing machine. We understand machines; we operate and control them. We are surrounded by them. So the idea that the human being is merely another form of machine makes sense to modern people. It is a frequent theme in scientific documentaries and high-school and undergraduate courses in biology. We explain the working of the human body by analogy with machines.

An undergraduate textbook of cell biology shows a <u>photomicrograph</u> of a <u>neuron</u> growing on top of a computer microprocessor. The text states: 'The neuron is the fundamental information-processing unit of the brain, which might be compared to the transistor as the fundamental processing unit in the computer. However, the brain has 15 billion <u>neurons</u>, whereas microprocessors have only millions of transistors.'

In the words of theologian Helmut Thielicke: 'Instead of man being the measure of things, the things he has made . . . come to determine the lines along which man himself is to be structured.'[8]

There is a paradox here. All the machines we know were designed by humans in order to achieve a particular purpose. That is what a machine is – a way for a human designer to achieve a human purpose. Every microprocessor was laboriously created by teams of human designers in order to accomplish a series of complex design objectives set by other humans. Yet in the human body we have a machine which is apparently designed by no-one for no purpose! From a reductionist perspective we can call the human body an extraordinary coincidence, a cosmic accident, but we cannot call it a *machine*. The analogy begs more questions than it answers.

This 'machine thinking' leads inexorably to a sense of alienation from our own bodies. In some sense, the real me is trapped in a frighteningly complex and ultimately alien machine which has its own agenda, its own programme, its own laws, and its own capacity for breakdown. Each person's future is deter-mined by the mysterious and ultimately incomprehensible laws of science which are controlling the machinery.

The sense of alienation from our own physical structure, and from the lives of other people, strikes deeply in our modern society. It contributes to the modern philosophical concept of the isolated autonomous individual, to which we will return later in this chapter.

Scientific reductionism offers a way to self-mastery or self-transcendence

It may not be very comfortable to discover that we are only survival machines, but it has an advantage for modern people. By understanding how the machine works, we can satisfy a deep drive we all have to understand and hence control ourselves. I think this explains the particular fascination of modern neuro-science: the observation of the living, functioning, thinking, feeling human brain. By observing our own brain function, we can learn to conquer it. By making ourselves an object of study, we assert our own self-mastery; in philosophical terms, we attempt to transcend ourselves.

The managing director of a high-technology Japanese company which devoted large amounts of research money to the development of a new form of brain scanning told me that his ultimate aim was the prevention of war: 'What causes wars and conflicts between people is the malfunctioning of the human brain. By understanding how the brain works we can bring world peace.'

Take all the forms of human behaviour which threaten our future: violence, drug addiction, inter-racial conflict, religious fanaticism, paedophilia, selfish squandering of the world's resources. At heart these can all be seen as due to a malfunctioning of the human brain. If we can only understand how to prevent brain malfunctioning, we will be able to usher in a new dawn of social harmony and global peace. By making our own human functioning an object of scientific study – by objectifying ourselves – we hope to control ourselves, to achieve self-mastery.

Since the attacks on New York on 9/11, politicians and policy makers have been particularly concerned about violence linked with so-called 'religious fundamentalism'. It is not surprising that there is an active area of scientific research into the brain mechanisms that underlie religious beliefs and experiences. MRI and PET brain scans have identified brain regions which are activated during meditation and 'out of body' experiences, and neuroscientists like V. S. Ramachandran have performed studies indicating that the brain has specialized circuits which mediate belief and which are central to religious behaviour.[9]

Of course, brain scans can never conclusively prove whether a belief is founded in reality or is delusional. We may observe the brain regions which are activated when a young man thinks of his girlfriend, but this will never tell us what she is really like, or indeed whether she exists or is just a figment of his fevered imagination!

A United States 'consumer consultancy' company has promoted the idea that the 'next important evolution in marketing' will be based on brain imaging. The consultancy performs brain scans on subjects while they are observing advertisements, to investigate 'what drives consumer behaviour at a conscious and subconscious level', with the aim of helping clients establish 'loyal, long-lasting' relationships with those who buy their products.[10]

A research group at Dartmouth College in New Hampshire investigated brain activity while subjects looked at photographs of people from different racial groups. The scientists found that when white volunteers looked at faces of Afro-Caribbean people, there was a strong link between activity in the right dorsolateral prefrontal cortex and scores on a previously performed word association test of racial attitudes. Professor Richeson, the leader of the group, concluded that the brain activity arose because the volunteers were concentrating on not doing or saying anything offensive.[11] Not surprisingly, the research provoked controversy, with some experts arguing the conclusions were misplaced. At its most far-reaching, the study raised the possibility that the minds of people, including police recruits, could be screened for racist attitudes. It is clear that neuroscience is providing new insights into the way our brains work, but our desire for self-mastery will lead to troubling and profound dilemmas in the future.

Scientific reductionism leads to a belief in pure chance – the lottery of life

Ever since the triumph of neo-Darwinism as the dominant theory of modern biology, the ruling intellectual orthodoxy is that all organisms, including the human organism, are products of blind chance. Any hint that organisms have an underlying purpose or design, apart from replication, is derided by most biological scientists. Jacques Monod, the eminent biologist, summed it up in this eulogy to chance: 'Chance alone is at the source of every innovation, of all creation in the biosphere. Pure chance, absolutely free but blind, is at the very root of the stupendous edifice of evolution. The universe was not pregnant with life . . . Our number came up in the Monte Carlo game.'[12]

The eighteenth-century clergyman William Paley used the analogy of a watch to defend the divine creation of human beings. If, when you were crossing the heath, you stumbled upon a watch on the ground, you might not know where the watch came from, but you would have to conclude that somewhere there was a watchmaker, someone who planned, designed and constructed the mechanism. Richard Dawkins demolishes Paley's argument:

> The analogy . . . between watch and living organism is false. All appearances to the contrary, the only watchmakers in nature are the blind forces of physics . . . A true watchmaker has foresight: he designs his cogs and springs, and plans their interconnections, with a future purpose in his mind's eye. Natural selection, the blind, unconscious, automatic process which Darwin discovered . . . has no purpose in mind. It has no mind and no mind's eye. It does not plan for the future. It has no vision, no foresight, no sight at all. If it can be said to play the role of the watchmaker in nature, it is the blind watchmaker.[13]

Each individual evolutionary step that led to the production of *Homo sapiens* was pure accident, 'chance caught on the wing' in the evocative words of Jacques Monod. Any appearance of design is purely illusory – the effect of billions of random genetic mutations and varying environmental pressures.

Reductionism leads to pessimistic fatalism

The Enlightenment philosophers of the eighteenth century placed great emphasis on the evidence of divine design inherent in biological organisms. But in 1857, as Charles Darwin worked towards the publication of his theory of natural selection, he wrote a bitter aside on the implications of his scientific discoveries: 'What a book a devil's chaplain might write on the clumsy, wasteful, blundering, low and horridly cruel works of nature.' The challenge was taken up by Richard Dawkins who in 2003 published a collection of essays under the title, *A Devil's Chaplain*.[14]

As reductionism penetrates the modern worldview, it goes hand-in-hand with a resurgence of pessimistic fatalism. Our future is determined by the chance alignment of genes which occurred at our conception, and random events which have moulded our development. Our belief that we can alter the future by our choices is purely a comforting illusion generated by our evolved brains to enhance our survival. In reality we are trapped by the hidden but inexorable blind forces of genetics and biology. As medical knowledge advances, it reveals more of the stupefying complexity of the machine, and more about its understandable tendency to malfunction.

With increasing knowledge, we can predict when malfunction will strike, but what are the psychological effects of living with this godlike knowledge? How can we live, knowing which diseases will strike us in the future, and the likely date and manner of our death? Clinical geneticists thought that most people, when offered genetic testing for an incurable condition like Huntington's disease, would want testing so that they could plan their lives. In fact, when given the choice, most people would rather not know their future fate or that of their children. A study of pregnant women at risk of Huntington's disease found that only 30% requested prenatal testing, some of those withdrew before performing the test, and only 18% actually underwent testing.[15] The truth is that, in a fallen world, the ability to foretell our biological future can be a curse as well as a blessing. One of the paradoxical effects of modern biology is that it tends to lead to a fatalistic worldview similar to that of the ancient Greeks: human beings are seen as the playthings of inexorable and possibly malevolent forces – the Fates.

If blind chance is our ultimate creator, this has profound implications for the ethics of medical interventions. If our human structure is the product of random forces, then it is hard to understand why it should have any intrinsic value, any more than the apparent 'design' produced by the random etchings of waves and wind on a shoreline. It is nonsensical to believe that our bodily design is in any way sacrosanct. Therefore, it is argued, we do not have to surrender to a pessimistic fatalism. We can do better than the blind watchmaker, for, thanks to the workings of blind chance, we have eyes and minds. Medical technology can be used to improve and enhance the fundamental structures and capacities of our bodies. For the first time in human history, we can improve on the physical structure of our humanity. At last we can wrest our humanity from the forces of blind chance and become our own creators. If the biological structure of our bodies, with all their quaint idiosyncrasies, is a product of blind chance, there is absolutely no reason why we should not attempt to improve on our own design. Dawkins ends his book, *The Selfish Gene*, with this triumphant flourish: 'We are built as gene machines . . . but we have the power to turn against our creators. We, alone on earth, can rebel against the tyranny of the selfish replicators.'[16] This is where technology, our second theme, comes in.

Theme 2: Advances in biotechnology – unparalleled technological inventiveness

Along with growing scientific knowledge goes the technical ability to manipulate our bodies and the potential to alter the stuff of our humanity. As Gareth Jones, Professor of Anatomy and Structural Biology at Otago University, New Zealand, put it, 'Science aims not merely to describe the world, but also to control it.'[17] Richard Dawkins describes the bleak sermon of the Devil's Chaplain as a 'call to arms'. We alone on the planet can use our big brains to combat the blundering waste of evolution: 'We are the only potential island of refuge from the implications of the Devil's Chaplain; from the cruelty and the clumsy, blundering waste'.[18]

The idea of using technology to improve and enhance the capacities of the human body is a potent dream for many biological scientists. Here are the words of Lee Silver, a molecular biologist from Princeton University:

> The mechanisms for implanting modified or completely artificial genes
> into mammalian cells are advancing rapidly in laboratories across the world.
> Genetically modified animals are being produced in large numbers. If we are
> prepared to accept genetic enhancement of plants and animals, on what rational
> basis can we possibly forbid parents to seek to enhance the capabilities of their
> own children? While selfish genes control all other forms of life, master and slave
> have switched positions in human beings, who now have the power not only to
> control but to create new genes for themselves. Why not seize this power? Why
> not control what has been left to chance in the past? Indeed we control all other
> aspects of our children's lives and identities through powerful social and
> environmental influences . . . On what basis can we reject positive genetic

influences on a person's essence when we accept the right of parents to benefit their children in every other way?[19]

Silver is one of a group of scientists and philosophers who have adopted a creed described variously as transhumanism or posthumanism. Their dream is to use a range of 'converging technologies' to enhance and improve every aspect of human existence. Why should we passively accept the painful realities of the 'human condition' – frailty, weakness, limited mental ability, ageing and death? Instead, we should grasp the new opportunities which technology gives us to transform the nature of humanity itself. We will return to this theme in the last chapter of the book.

Biotechnology changes our view of what is 'natural'
In the past, the world was divided into things which were natural (given in nature) and things which were artificial (made by human craft). But technology changes this understanding. As Professor Oliver O'Donovan of Edinburgh University expressed it: 'When every activity is understood as making, then every situation is seen as a raw material, waiting to have something made out of it.'[20] In his 1983 London Lectures in Contemporary Christianity, published under the title *Begotten or Made?* Professor O'Donovan argued that the relation of human beings to their own bodies is in some ways the last frontier of nature.

However much we modify the natural environment in our modern cities and our homes, and surround ourselves with the products of our invention, we cannot get away from the 'givenness' of our own bodies: 'When we take off our clothes to have a bath, we confront something as natural, as given, as completely non-artefactual, as anything in this universe; we confront our own bodily existence.'[21] But now this last frontier of the natural is being broken. We do not have to accept our bodies as they have been given to us. The original Mark I human model is not the only one in town. We can improve things; we have the technology. I shall call this the 'Lego kit' view of the human body. There is nothing 'natural' about a Lego kit. There is no right or wrong way to put the pieces together. There is no masterplan from the designers. There is no ethical basis of Lego construction. You can do what you like. In fact, as it says in the adverts, 'the only limitation is in your own imagination.'

In chapter 3 we will look at some of the new and mind-boggling choices which reproductive technology raises. Technology is changing the very nature of parenthood, and the boundary between what is natural and what is unnatural becomes blurred. Is a frozen embryo in a tank of liquid nitrogen a being of nature, or is it a product of human planning, ingenuity and forethought, an *artefact* of human creation? Does reproductive technology mean that the process of making babies has changed from being a 'natural' activity to being an 'artificial' activity? Or is the distinction no longer meaningful?

Biotechnology allows us to conquer our fears

The growth in health technology demonstrates how greatly modern people and societies value health and long life. It shows the extreme measures we are prepared to undergo in order to improve the chances of survival for ourselves or for our children – to buy an extra year or two of life. These are the words of Stanley Hauerwas, a distinguished theologian from Duke University, North Carolina:

> I sometimes point out to my students that people now go to Europe to see the great cathedrals, wondering what kind of people would build such things . . . Some day I think that people may well come to see major medical centres like the one we have at Duke University, and ask what kind of people would build such things. If they are astute they will think the builders certainly must have been afraid of death.[22]

In medieval society it was the church building which dominated the local community, as an illustration of the social and economic power of religion in that society. Now the billions of pounds spent every year on health care and on medical research tell their own story. Why do the public pour money into medical research? Is it an altruistic desire to help humankind, or is the public support for research at least partly motivated by fear – fear of death, fear of disease, fear of disability? The way we spend our money is very revealing. In the words of Jesus, 'where your treasure is, there your heart will be also' (Matthew 6:21; Luke 12:34).

Biotechnology gives us new responsibilities for 'quality control'

Technology always brings new responsibilities. When we make choices, we must carry responsibility for the consequences. This process can be seen especially in the area of reproductive technology. When we change the nature of parenthood, imperceptibly our attitude to our children changes. Most people in our society still see their newborn baby as a gift: a mysterious present from a higher power, a gift from God, or, if they do not believe in a God, then from Nature with a capital N. But when a child is created by the technology of embryo donation and *in vitro* fertilization, the child may be seen no longer as a mysterious and wonderful gift, but more as the product of human ingenuity and meticulous planning. Unfortunately, no form of human construction is perfect, and an essential part of all technology is 'quality control'. If technology has gone wrong, if the product of our planning is less than perfect, then we must take responsibility to prevent the consequences. It is standard practice for detailed prenatal testing to be undertaken on all fetuses conceived through reproductive technology. The unwritten implication is that if an abnormality is detected, it is morally responsible to carry out an abortion. If we make a baby by technology, we must use technology to make sure that the baby is all right. That is the essence of quality control.

The concept of a 'wrongful life' stems directly from the drive for quality control in a medical approach to pregnancy. If technology provides the knowledge that a fetus is abnormal, many feel that we have a responsibility, even a duty, to end that life and prevent the birth of a disabled child. So, godlike knowledge has given rise to godlike responsibility.

Theme 3: Rising consumer expectations

Medical technology has led to new expectations. To many people it seems that doctors really can perform miracles. They can allow us to fulfil our dreams and overcome our limitations. Every problem, every malfunction, can be overcome by a technological fix. After all, that is what doctors are there for.

The implication is that medical technology is there to allow people to fulfil their deepest desires. And it seems that many of our deepest desires are centred on having children. For some people, embarking on a pregnancy with medical supervision is akin to entering a contractual arrangement. My part of the deal is to be a compliant, well-informed and responsible patient. But the professional's part of the deal is to provide me with a perfect baby. Having a baby is a lifestyle choice. I want the perfect baby to match my perfect lifestyle. If the baby is less than perfect, the response may not only be grief but also a degree of outrage. Some would argue that since abortion is a possibility, disabled children should no longer be born in the twenty-first century. Technology should make sure that fetuses with congenital abnormalities are identified and aborted.

But if I can use technology to abort an imperfect child, why can I not use technology to determine the sex of my child? If I can choose where to live, what my work is, how to spend my money, whom to marry, and when to have a child, then why can I not choose whether I have a boy or a girl? In a book called *The Perfect Baby: A Pragmatic Approach to Genetics*, Glen McGee argues that there is no difference between spending money on education and spending it on the genetic enhancement of our children.[23] Both are ways of improving our children's chances in the lottery of life. Although we should proceed cautiously and gradually, McGee argues, there is no reason why we should not use genetics to improve human nature a little at a time. In fact, some biologists are claiming that the improvement of the genetic make-up of each individual is an essential goal of the human community. Biologist Bentley Glass said: 'The right of individuals to procreate must give place to a new paramount right: the right of every child to enter life with an adequate physical and mental endowment.'[24]

It is now possible to test embryos for susceptibility to a range of inherited diseases, including breast cancer and Alzheimer's disease. In the future it may be possible to test for a wide range of characteristics, including aspects of intelligence, physical strength and size. For the first time in history, couples may be genuinely able to select the child of their choice. Perhaps, before too long, selecting the best embryo will be seen as an essential part of responsible parenthood: 'I owe it to myself and to my future child to give him or her the best possible genetic start in life.' Under the guise of middle-class responsibility, the stranglehold of the god of consumerism will have finally extended to parenthood. (We shall explore further the difficult issues of genetic screening of the embryo in chapter 4.)

Just as we have rising expectations at the beginning of life, so also at the other end of life. Modern people expect to maintain health, mobility and independence right through to their eighties and beyond. Why should we accept a gradual decline into senescence and disability? Along with the rest of society, the elderly are becoming better informed about the range of available treatments, and more assertive about their needs and demands. And when we reach the stage where curative medicine has no more to offer, we are no longer prepared to be passive observers as we approach death. We want the right to be in control at the end of life. We want to decide when it is time to die and how it should happen. We want to procure the death that will fit with our lifestyle choices. (We shall look in more detail at dying, euthanasia and physician-assisted suicide (PAS) in chapter 9.)

The consumerist trend has affected every aspect of modern health care. Health managers have adopted the attitudes and practices of the modern service industry. Offering choices and meeting the needs and aspirations of consumers becomes a central goal of health care. Customer satisfaction is the yardstick by which we are assessed. But how realistic are consumer aspirations when health resources are finite and limited?

Theme 4: Health economics and resource limitations

At the inception of the UK National Health Service in 1948, it was widely predicted that the provision of free nationwide medical care would lead to a fall in the total amount of money spent on health care by the country. It seemed obvious to the early health planners that improved medical care would lead to a healthier population and that this in turn would lead to less demand for medical care. The subsequent experience of the NHS and of every other developed nation has demonstrated the naivety of this prediction. The combination of new technology and new consumer expectations has had an inevitable consequence – a dramatic and steady rise year on year in the cost of providing health care. This has been exacerbated by demographic changes in developed countries. Rising numbers of elderly people in the population are now major and expensive consumers of health-care resources. When death approaches, health expenditure frequently rockets as the patient is admitted to hospital, and expensive surgery or intensive care is undertaken in a desperate attempt to ward off the inevitable.

In a liberal society in which the right of individuals to choose is a primary value, basic health is seen as one of the indispensable conditions for the exercise of personal choice or autonomy. The 1976 declaration of the World Health Organisation stated: 'The enjoyment of the highest attainable standard of health is one of the fundamental rights of every human being without distinction of race, religion, political belief, economic or social condition.' The high view of health in a modern society means that the ever-increasing resource requirements of health care have the potential to trump all other economic demands in the modern state. In Britain, the total annual health expenditure rose from £17 per head in 1960 to approximately £1,800 in 2007. Even when inflation is taken into account, this represents a dramatic increase. In the USA the total health bill in 1960 was £9.8 billion, rising to £617 billion in 1994. As a percentage of total economic wealth, health spending in the USA rose from 5.2% in 1960 to 15.4% in 2004, a total sum of $1.8 trillion![25] The demand within modern societies for expensive health care seems inexhaustible.

Faced with the spectacle of inexorably rising costs, the aim of central-government health planners has been to attempt to maximize the economic efficiency of the provision of health care. If costs are to be controlled, it is essential to maximize the benefits of health care while minimizing the expenditure. In the crude language of big business, planners want to buy 'the maximum number of bangs for each buck spent'. This has led to a strong drive to assess in quantitative terms both the exact costs and the 'benefits' of each intervention. The aim is to provide a ranking system to guide spending priorities. The UK government has established the National Institute of Health and Clinical Excellence to provide explicit guidance on which treatments should be centrally funded.[26] What has happened is that the old paternalism, in which the medical profession controlled the allocation and distribution of health-care resources, has been replaced by a new paternalism, where health economists, policy planners and bureaucrats are increasingly controlling health care in the name of 'rational' cost-effective planning.

Some of the findings from this economic analysis are hardly surprising. One of the main ones is what I have christened the 'first law of health economics'. It states that 'the cheapest patient is a dead patient'. In financial terms, death is always a 'cost-effective' solution. The patients planners need to worry about are the living ones, especially the long-term sick or the chronically disabled. One of the arguments put forward for making antenatal screening universally available is the cost saving to the country that follows abortion of affected fetuses. For example, a 1995 paper concluded that the cost of antenatal screening for cystic fibrosis ranged from £40,000 to £100,000 per case detected. Since the annual costs of treatment for people with cystic fibrosis were estimated at £8,000, and there were many additional unquantified economic costs of the disease, screening for cystic fibrosis provided a net economic benefit.[27]

Similarly, an argument frequently used in cases of persistent vegetative state is the economic cost of keeping severely brain-damaged patients alive. In 1994 the estimated cost of long-term nursing care for patients with PVS in the United States was up to $180,000 per year and the total annual costs in the United States for the care of adults and children in a persistent vegetative state was between $1 billion to $7 billion.[28] Think how much money we can save if we accept that these lives should be brought to an end.

Finally, we turn to the fifth and possibly the most important theme of all.

Theme 5: Bioethics – an adventure playground for philosophers

The academic discipline of **bioethics** has been one of the most remarkable growth industries since the late 1970s. Ethical reflection on medical practice has become a major branch of academic moral philosophy, and seems increasingly divorced from the experience of practising clinicians and their patients. Contemporary bioethicists start from the recognition that modern Western societies are unique in the history of civilization in the breadth and depth of their diversity. They are multicultural, multi-religious and ethically pluralist. There is wide disparity between individuals in religious and moral beliefs and practices. The traditional sources of moral teaching, the religious and political authorities, no longer receive universal, or even majority, support in our society. How then can we resolve the intractable ethical problems raised by biological and medical advances? Where can modern people find the 'core values' for morality on which we can base our bioethical discussion and debate?

The 'four principles' approach to medical ethics: Beauchamp and Childress

One of the most influential approaches has been that of two American ethicists, Tom Beauchamp and James Childress. Their textbook, *Principles of Biomedical Ethics* (now in its sixth edition), has had a remarkable influence in the field, being regarded by many as the Bible of modern bioethics.[29] Beauchamp and Childress have based their ethical system on the assumption that the only hope for consensus in modern societies is to find the lowest common denominator values or 'common morality' on which we can all agree. They claim that there is a set of moral rules or norms which is shared by all the members of a society and which is therefore a source (and possibly the only source) of consensus in a pluralistic society. Beauchamp and Childress have reduced this common morality to four fundamental principles or rules of medical ethics:

1. Respect every person's desire for autonomy, for self-determination, for a 'personal rule of the self that is free from both controlling interferences by others and from personal limitations that prevent meaningful choice'.
2. Inflict no harm or evil on others (the principle of non-maleficence).
3. Act in the best interests of others (the principle of beneficence).
4. Ensure that health care is distributed in society in a way which is fair and equitable (the principle of justice).

The 'four principles' approach has been widely adopted and popularized by clinicians. It has the great merit of being simple to remember, providing an aide-memoire, even a modern-day ethical mantra, which can be chanted by medical students and busy doctors. Yet anyone who has tried to use these four principles as a means of finding a practical solution to the problems of medical ethics is immediately made aware of their limitations. Take the case of a mother who is carrying a fetus with a genetic abnormality, such as Down's syndrome. Should she be offered an abortion? First, we have the principle of respect for autonomy. But whose autonomy should we respect? The mother's, the father's, the doctor's or the fetus'? Does the idea of respect for the autonomy of a fetus have any meaning? Conversely, can we simply ignore the fetus' future right to self-determination? Secondly, we should do no harm to others. This principle immediately seems to rule out abortion, which clearly harms the fetus. But some ethicists argue that, in reality, the life of a severely disabled child can be a greater evil than no life at all. To 'inflict' life on a disabled fetus is to inflict harm on it. Thus, to end a disabled life is not to cause harm; in fact, an abortion may be carried out in order to respect the third principle, that of beneficence. We may be acting in the fetus' best interests by ending its life cleanly and painlessly. Of course, others would violently disagree with this interpretation, claiming that

life is always a 'good' in itself. Although we may be able to agree on the principles
of beneficence and non-maleficence as abstract moral concepts, it seems that
we cannot agree on what they actually mean – on the substantive content of
the principles – when applied to particular cases. Finally, how does the principle
of justice apply to the case of a fetus with Down's syndrome? If we must respect
fairness, does this mean we must offer abortions to all mothers carrying Down's
syndrome fetuses? But what about the thousands of people in our society who
already have Down's syndrome? Is it unjust to them to discriminate against
fetuses with the same syndrome? What is justice? Who says?[30]

Liberal individualism: Ronald Dworkin

The difficulty of finding a moral consensus in modern societies has led some
philosophers in a more radical direction. Rather than pretending that there is
a mysterious common morality, a common ethical denominator, they believe
that we should recognize the truth, which is that we shall never agree on these
fundamental issues. The only way that we will live together in peace is to agree
to disagree. This is the concept of radical liberal individualism which has been
expounded by the legal philosopher Professor Ronald Dworkin in his book
Life's Dominion. 'The most important feature of [Western political culture] is a
belief in individual human dignity: that people have the moral right and the
moral responsibility to confront the most fundamental questions about
the meaning and value of their own lives for themselves.'[31] 'At the heart of
liberty is the right to define one's own concept of existence, of meaning, of the
universe, and of the mystery of human life.' Only if we are free can we respect
ourselves. 'Freedom is the cardinal, absolute requirement of self-respect: no-one
treats his life as having any intrinsic objective importance unless he insists on
leading that life himself, not being ushered along it by others.'[32]

As a constitutional lawyer, Dworkin appeals to two fundamental constitutional principles of liberal societies. First is the right to religious toleration. He
states that, even for atheists, ethical decisions about life and death are, at heart,
religious questions. He quotes a US Supreme Court judgment which concluded
that an atheist's system of beliefs may have 'a place in the life of its possessor
parallel to that filled by the orthodox belief in God'.[33]

As such, these beliefs are matters of individual conscience, not public
legislation. Therefore, we must tolerate our religious differences: 'We must
insist on religious tolerance in this area as in all others . . . Tolerance is a cost
we must pay for our adventure in liberty. We are committed by our love of
liberty and dignity to live in communities in which no group is thought clever
or spiritual or numerous enough to decide essentially religious matters for
everyone else.'[34]

Secondly, Dworkin appeals to the constitutional right of privacy. Like many other liberal philosophers, he draws a strong distinction between the public and the private arena. The public arena is the place in which laws must govern human behaviour. But in the private arena of personal morality, the law must withdraw. In the words of the US Supreme Court: 'If the right of privacy means anything it is the right of the individual . . . to be free from governmental intrusion into matters so fundamentally affecting a person as the decision whether to bear or beget a child.'[35] In other words, the state must withdraw to allow individuals to exercise their own individual autonomy. In the field of reproduction, Dworkin calls this 'the right of procreative autonomy'.

Dworkin accepts that the state has an interest in protecting the sanctity or inviolability of life, but says there are two ways in which this can be achieved. The state may have the goal of conformity (to enforce people to obey moral rules), or the goal of responsibility (to encourage people to act from individual moral responsibility): 'If we aim at responsibility we must leave citizens free, in the end, to decide as they think right, because that is what moral responsibility entails.'[36] We shall see how Dworkin applies these principles to issues at the beginning and end of life in later chapters, but his overall thrust is clear. We must agree to disagree: 'Whatever view we take about abortion or euthanasia, we want the right to decide for ourselves'[37]

The modern emphasis on autonomy can be traced to the Enlightenment philosopher John Stuart Mill. 'The only purpose for which power can be right-fully exercised over any member of a civilized community against his will, is to prevent harm to others . . . Over himself, over his body and mind, the individual is sovereign.'[38] The wording is significant. There are other sovereigns in the public or political realm, but in private life and morality, the individual is sovereign; there is no-one who can exercise authority over him or her. At the time of the Enlightenment the political concept of the sovereign nation-state was being developed. Mill extends this understanding to individual behaviour. Each individual becomes their own nation-state with their own sovereign in absolute control. In traditional Western moral philosophy, autonomy was seen as an essential precondition for people to choose what is good. But in a liberal society, autonomy is a good in itself – in fact, it is the supreme good. Each person within a liberal society has his or her own moral style of life or vocation. Each person is engaged on an individual 'experiment in living'.[39]

In effect, Dworkin, and other liberal philosophers such as Max Charlesworth, have reduced the four 'common morality' principles of Beauchamp and Childress to one overriding principle: respect for autonomy, with all its implica-tions: 'No life is a good one if lived against the grain of conviction.' But I think this contributes to the deep sense of aching loneliness, isolation, alienation and estrangement which is the experience of so many in our society. The concept of a liberal society can be a bleak vision in which a collection of ultimately egocentric individuals are making autonomous choices, continually reconstructing themselves and striving for their own goals. Dependence is seen as threatening and dehumanizing precisely because it threatens one's sense of identity, one's sense of personal worth.

Many liberal thinkers have argued that, if we are to survive in a multicultural society, religious groups must give up the right to any claims to absolute truth. These are the words of Max Charlesworth: 'Multiculturalism requires that the constitutive subgroups recognize some form of the liberal ideal and subscribe to the liberal "act of faith" that it is possible to have a society without moral, religious and social values, save for consensus upon the values of personal autonomy and liberty.'[40]

So, belief in the possibility of a liberal society is an act of faith. But faith in whom or what? Presumably in the liberal philosophers who are our benevolent mentors. Charlesworth argues that in a multicultural society the mainstream or majority culture must not abuse its position: 'The mainstream culture must tolerate and be sensitive to a minority culture's views as well as recognizing that its own views are embedded within a complex network of cultural beliefs and attitudes, and that they have a certain degree of cultural relativity. *This does not however involve any kind of culturalism which would see the values of liberalism as being culturally determined.*'[41] As has often been pointed out, modern liberalism is remarkably illiberal when it encounters a challenge to its own 'core values', and here is a classic example. Charlesworth argues that we must realize that all our moral beliefs are culturally determined, embedded within our own belief systems, and therefore relative, except for the 'values of liberalism' themselves, which are apparently culture-free and objectively true for everyone. Yet, as a number of commentators have observed, the 'values of liberalism' are very clearly a product of a particular culture and historical period – the European Enlightenment of the eighteenth century. To claim that those liberal values are unique among all other beliefs by being culture-free and objective is the most blatant form of special pleading.

The five new commandments of bioethics: Peter Singer
As we have seen, the new discipline of bioethics offers the opportunity for radical voices to challenge the medical and religious establishment and its prevailing orthodoxy. One such voice is that of Professor Peter Singer of Princeton University in the USA. In his book *Rethinking Life and Death*, he proclaims (not without a certain glee) the end of the era in which Christian views of the sanctity of human life have dominated: 'After ruling our thoughts and our decisions

about life and death for two thousand years, the traditional Western ethic of the sanctity of human life has collapsed.'[42] 'The traditional religious view that all human life is sacrosanct is simply not able to cope with the array of modern medical dilemmas.'[43] Singer cannot be accused of excessive modesty. To replace the old worn-out Judaeo-Christian ethic based on the biblical revelation, he puts forward five new commandments from his own Mount Sinai.

First, in place of the command to treat all human life as of equal worth, he offers: *Recognize that the worth of human life varies.* For Singer, it is self-evident that the lives of people with <u>dementia</u> or in a permanent coma, are of no value to themselves or to anyone else. We should cease our 'pious pretence' that their lives have any special significance. He points to the Law Lords' judgment in the case of Tony Bland, the young man in a persistent vegetative state, saying that they 'have taken the brave step of recognizing that, at a minimum, consciousness is essential if life is to be worth having'.[44] If you are permanently unconscious, therefore, the value of your life is reduced to nil. Similarly, he argues that the widespread acceptance of prenatal diagnosis, and abortion for fetal abnormality, implies that we accept that the life of a handicapped child is not as worthwhile as that of a healthy child. Hence 'we should treat human beings in accordance with their ethically relevant characteristics'. These include consciousness, the capacity for physical, social and mental interaction with other beings, having conscious preferences for continued life, and having enjoyable experiences. Other relevant characteristics depend on relationship to others – having relatives, for instance, who will grieve over your death. These characteristics are the proof of a worthwhile life, and the ultimate value of a life varies according to how much they are present. Singer concludes, in effect, that a worthwhile life depends upon the adequate functioning of the cerebral cortex, the part of the brain which governs the highest cerebral functions such as consciousness. Human beings who do not have a fully functioning cortex, including fetuses and even newborn infants, as well as brain-damaged individuals or those with conditions such as Alzheimer's disease, cannot be regarded as having a right to life. They are human beings, but they are not 'persons' in the full sense of the word. We should cease our hypocritical pretence that their lives are as valuable as that of a healthy and normally functioning adult, a real 'person'. Instead, we should recognize the obvious truth that some lives are more valuable than others; some human beings are 'persons' (or, as it is sometimes expressed, they have 'personhood'), and some are not.[45]

The inevitable conclusion from this argument is that society consists of a hierarchy: at the top are the prize specimens of humanity – the Olympic athlete, the Nobel Prize winner – then ordinary, healthy, adult human beings; then the less healthy, with enough brain activity to recognize their own existence; and then the non-persons – babies, the brain-damaged, the mentally disabled, the sufferers with Alzheimer's disease, those whose lives are of little value. All of us fit somewhere in the pecking order, and the value of our life goes up or down according to the passage of events.

Secondly, Singer argues that the traditional prohibition of the taking of innocent life should be replaced by an acceptance of mercy killing: *Take responsibility for the consequences of your decisions.* This means in practice that if we have decided that a life is not worth living, on the grounds of 'ethically relevant characteristics', then we as a society should take the responsibility to end that life in a humane way. It is immoral to allow a human individual to linger on in a condition that is 'not worth living'. Singer recognizes that this new approach to worthless life may lead to 'a colder, less cohesive society', but he thinks this is a small price to pay.[46]

Thirdly, the traditional prohibition of suicide should be replaced by the new commandment: *Respect a person's desire to live or die.* If autonomous individuals want to carry on living, then we should respect their wishes. Of course, only a 'person' can want to go on living. Hence killing a 'person' against his or her will is a much more serious wrong than killing a human being who is not a 'person'. In other words, only a 'person' has a right to life. Conversely, if an autonomous individual, a 'person', concludes after due reflection that his or her own life is valueless, it is a medical duty to end that life cleanly and painlessly.[47]

The old biblical command to be fruitful and multiply should be replaced by a fourth new commandment: *Bring children into the world only if wanted.* There are already as many people on this planet as it can reasonably be expected to support. This, together with the fact that the human embryo and fetus are not 'persons' and hence have no intrinsic value or rights, means that there can be no harm in killing an embryo or fetus. Hence contraception and abortion on demand are matters of individual choice. But Singer goes further. He argues that, in addition, we should be prepared to accept the medical infanticide of unwanted or deformed newborns. 'Human babies are not born self-aware or capable of grasping that they exist over time. They are not persons. Hence their lives seem to be no more worthy of protection than the life of a fetus.'[48] Why on earth should we use expensive technology and scarce medical resources to ensure the survival of a handicapped or unwanted baby, when the world already has too many mouths to feed?[49]

In his earlier book *Should the Baby Live?*, Singer and his colleague, Helga Kuhse, suggested that a period of twenty-eight days after birth might be allowed before an infant is accepted as having the same right to life as others. This would give time for a couple to decide whether it is better 'not to continue with a life that has begun very badly'.[50]

Finally, in place of the old commandment, 'Treat all human life as more precious than non-human life', Singer offers his modern replacement: *Do not discriminate on the basis of species.* Modern Western liberalism recognizes that we should not discriminate on the basis of attributes that lack moral significance. Racism, sexism and ageism are wrong because these attributes lack moral significance. But why, the argument goes, should an individual's species be of any greater ethical importance than his or her race, gender or age? To value a human life as of more importance than that of another sentient being is to be guilty of speciesism: 'If we compare a severely defective human infant with a non-human animal, a dog or pig for example, we will often find the non-human to have superior capacities, both actual and potential, for rationality, self-consciousness, communication, and anything else that might be morally significant.'[51] Even rats and fish 'are indisputably more aware of their surroundings and more able to respond in purposeful and complex ways to things they like or dislike, than a human fetus'. With unimpeachable logic but questionable wisdom, Singer follows the train of his argument: 'There is no reason to think that a fish suffers less when dying in a net than a fetus suffers during an abortion, hence the argument for not eating fish is much stronger than the argument against abortion . . . '[52]

In summary, on the basis of 'ethically relevant characteristics', not all members of the species *Homo sapiens* are persons, and not all persons are members of the species *Homo sapiens*. Singer suggests that we are on the brink of a new Copernican revolution in human self-understanding. Four hundred years ago Copernicus braved the wrath of the religious establishment by showing that human beings were not at the centre of the physical universe. Now we are coming to realize that we are not at the centre of the moral universe either. We must abandon the old religious prejudices about human superiority. *Homo sapiens* is just one among many sentient species on this planet, each with its own moral rights and privileges.

Of course, one could point out, in passing, that Singer has merely replaced one kind of discrimination with another. He wants to discriminate between individuals, not on whether they are members of the human race or not, but on whether their <u>cortex</u> is working properly. One could call him a 'corticalist'. Is there any logical basis to the assertion that corticalism is morally preferable to speciesism?

Making better humans – the argument for enhancement

The final trend in bioethics in this brief survey is that of increasing support for human enhancement. In his 2008 book *Enhancing Evolution* John Harris, Professor of Bioethics at the University of Manchester, provides a sustained moral argument in favour of using biotechnology to improve all aspects of human functioning. The current form of our humanity is just an accident of evolutionary history. We should not make a 'fetish of a particular evolutionary stage'.[53] Instead, we have a moral duty to intervene in the lottery of life. It is morally desirable to use technology to change and enhance our capacities in whatever direction we choose. This includes all aspects of the transhumanist's agenda referred to above. The only argument for restraining human enhancement is if there is evidence that it is seriously harmful to others and that these harms are real and present, not future and speculative.[54]

Harris argues that if there are rational reasons to believe that technical enhancement of our children will bring greater happiness into their lives (for instance by using genetic or stem cell therapies at the embryonic or fetal stage to enhance brain development), then not only is this morally acceptable, but there is a moral duty on us to enhance our children. Harris argues from a consistent utilitarian moral perspective. To choose not to enhance our children is morally equivalent to choosing an intervention to make them disabled. In both cases the total happiness in the world is reduced.

Many people are tempted to dismiss this kind of ethical argument as the sort of ivory-castle nonsense that academics are paid to produce. I have a certain amount of sympathy with the cynic who remarked that 'medical ethics has become an adventure playground for philosophers'. But Singer, Harris and other radical bioethicists are not other-worldly eggheads. They are highly sought-after and popular speakers at conferences and public debates on ethical issues. Their writings, elegant and popular in style, have become basic reading material for high school and undergraduate courses in philosophy and ethics. But these men are also courted by technologists and legislators. They provide the moral justification for the removal of constraints on biotechnological innovation. It seems they regard themselves as the storm troopers of the 'big push', a major assault on traditional medical ethics, designed, according to its proponents, to rid medicine of its roots in 'religious prejudice', and usher in a new dawn of rational, benevolent and enlightened ethical practice.

These, then, are five influences on the development of bioethical thinking today: biological reductionism, technology, consumerism, limited resources and ethical diversity. Of course, many more issues could be brought out, but I believe these are five of the most important influences in the public debates about medicine and biology in which we are currently engaged, and we shall return to them repeatedly.

In the next chapter I attempt a brief panoramic view of the historic biblical worldview as it relates to humanness and health. As we shall see, this biblical perspective reveals an understanding of the nature of persons that is very much at odds with the presuppositions of the philosophers discussed above. Later, in chapter 3, I will highlight two fundamental and contradictory ways of looking at human beings.

2. BIBLICAL PERSPECTIVES ON HUMANNESS

When we turn from recent advances in biology and medical technology to the Bible, we are immediately struck by the gulf between the biblical world and our own. The world of the Bible is pre-scientific, technologically primitive, predominantly rural, and dominated by the realities of an agricultural existence. It reflects a society in which knowledge about the universe scarcely changed from one generation to the next. It is a world in which no-one questioned that unseen and powerful spiritual forces controlled all aspects of human life, from the weather to the mysteries of human reproduction and infertility. How can the Bible possibly have anything relevant to say to the complexities of bioethics in our radically different society?

But historic, trinitarian Christianity can retain its authenticity only if it remains faithful to the biblical revelation. We are not at liberty to conclude that the Bible has little or nothing to say of relevance to contemporary ethical debates. Nor are we free to manipulate or distort the biblical message to make it more acceptable to modern ears and prejudices. If Christians are to be faithful to our calling to live in the modern world as disciples of the historic Christ revealed in Scripture, we must learn to apply with integrity the unchanging principles of the Bible to the world in which we live. My profound conviction is that if we are prepared to enter into the historic biblical worldview, we can find insights and principles which connect directly with the debate about medical ethics. There are no simplistic or slick answers, but I believe there is a way forward, a way of thinking about these issues which is at the same time authentically Christian, relevant and practical.

We cannot minimize the difficulty of the task that we face. There is no hope of finding simplistic proof-texts which will genuinely apply to the dilemmas of embryo research, technological enhancement or the persistent vegetative state. God has not given us a selection of isolated epigrams, like a dictionary of quotations. Instead, he has given a comprehensive revelation which covers the sweep of world history. It is our task to try to saturate ourselves in the fullness of the scriptural revelation in order to discern its relevance to the modern world.

I have found it extraordinarily helpful to use the four-fold scheme of biblical history developed by a number of theologians over the centuries and used by John Stott in his book *Issues Facing Christians Today*.[1] The Bible divides human history into four epochs: creation, fall, redemption and future consummation. As we view any issue from each of these four perspectives, we appreciate a different aspect, so that as we integrate the four perspectives into one whole we develop a full-orbed and detailed image.

I have become convinced that we frequently obtain distorted and partial ideas of Christian truth because we fail to use this four-fold perspective. In particular, modern evangelical Christians frequently concentrate on the middle two perspectives to the exclusion of the first and the last. To caricature this view: 'All human beings are fallen, but Jesus can save us through the cross.' But we cannot understand what it means to be fallen unless we grasp the full meaning of the creation, what we have fallen *from*. Similarly, we cannot understand what it means to be 'saved' unless we understand the end in store, the purpose, the goal that God has saved us *for*.

As we attempt to develop a biblical understanding of bioethics, we need to work at a full-orbed understanding of creation, and in particular of creation design and creation order: the moral principles that God has embedded into the structure of the universe. This is a theme to which we shall return on several occasions as we approach different ethical dilemmas. So it is to creation that we must turn first.

Creation

Biblical teaching about creation is present in many places in Scripture (see, for example, Psalms 8, 104 and 139), but the majestic first two chapters of Genesis are where we must start. Henri Blocher, in his book *In the Beginning*, provides a helpful overview of these chapters and I am indebted to him for much of what follows.[2]

The seven days of creation

The first chapter of Genesis is not just a list of God's creative activities, but a skilful literary composition, an artistic construction. In days one to three we have the creation of the sky, the waters and the land, and in days four to six we have the creation of their corresponding inhabitants: heavenly bodies, sea creatures and birds, and land dwellers. The careful, symmetrical structure of Genesis 1 allows the author to express his theological purpose. As Blocher puts it, the narrative has two peaks: humankind and the Sabbath. The creation of human beings crowns the work, but the Sabbath is its supreme goal. The existence of the Sabbath keeps human beings from total absorption in the task of subduing the earth. It reminds them that they will fulfil their humanity, not finally in their work of transforming the earth, but in the delight and recreation of relationship with God himself.

Throughout the creation narrative of Genesis runs the important concept that God imbues his creation with order. His creative work brings order into the world of living creatures. Everything is assigned a place and a function. In biblical imagery, the sea is often used as an image of disorder, of chaos. In creation, however, God imposes limits on the sea itself. As he said rhetorically to Job:

> 'Who shut up the sea behind doors
>   when it burst forth from the womb . . .
> when I fixed limits for it
>   and set its doors and bars in place,
> when I said, "This far you may come and no farther . . . "?'
> (Job 38:8–11)

God creates the limits beyond which his creation cannot transgress. There is no part of creation, however chaotic, however autonomous, which is not subject to intrinsic limits set by the Creator. Within the order of creation, although each element has its own dignity, and receives the commendation of its Creator, human beings are pictured as the crowning work of God. 'What is the work of the six days,' asked Gregory of Nyssa, 'other than the building of the palace, until the entry into the place prepared of the prince beloved by the Father?'[3]

At the centre of the biblical worldview is the concept of God as designer. God is the one who imposes order, meaning and purpose on the whole creation. In the biblical narrative both the origin of the human species (Genesis 1 and 2) and the development of the individual fetus within the womb (Psalm 139:13–16) are pictured in terms of meticulous, loving and personal design. This is the creation order, conceived by the Creator's mind and imposed by the

Creator's will. If we lose the concept that human beings are in some sense designed by God, we strike at the heart of the biblical understanding of what it means to be human.

Of course, the question of *how* God's creative activity was expressed in the development of humans is a matter of continuing controversy and debate among Christians. Some see God's creative design in terms of the providential ordering of environmental contingencies in Darwinian evolution from <u>hominid</u> life forms,[4] whereas others have doubted whether neo-Darwinian thinking can be compatible with Christian thought.[5] This is not the place to enter into that debate. But whichever view we take of the origin of human beings, we cannot escape the biblical teaching that God's loving and meticulous design, enshrining the Creator's purpose for each of our lives, lies at the heart of that origin.

The image of God

Then God said, 'Let us make man in our image, in our likeness, and let them rule over the fish of the sea and the birds of the air, over the livestock, over all the earth, and over all the creatures that move along the ground.'

> So God created man
>   in his own image,
>   in the image of God
>   he created him;
> male and female
>   he created them.
> (Genesis 1:26–27)

Human beings are unique in all the vast array of creation because they alone of all creatures are made in God's image, or, as an alternative translation puts it, they are made *as* God's image. Human beings are God-like beings. We reflect God's reality back to himself in worship and communion, and we reflect God's reality to the rest of creation in stewardship. God has chosen no other image-bearer, animate or inanimate, on planet Earth. In the ancient world, it was apparently common for a king to set up a stone or metal image of himself as a physical symbol of his sovereignty over a particular territory. It represented him to his subject peoples. A recently discovered statue of an ancient Assyrian governor carried this inscription written in Aramaic, a language closely related to biblical Hebrew: 'This statue is the image and likeness of Hadad-yis'i the Governor of Gosan.' The words used for 'image and likeness' are virtually identical to those of Genesis 1:26.[6]

It is human beings, then, who are called to rule over the rest of creation in the place of God, as his authorized representatives. Adam and Eve are instructed to subdue the earth and to rule over the rest of the biological kingdom in God's name. We bear God's image so that we can truly be God's representatives, so that we can reveal God's character to the rest of creation. Sadly, this concept has frequently been abused and distorted to imply that humans have the right to dominate and misuse the rest of creation as we wish. The biblical narrative reveals God's rule as one of ordering, life-generating, life-preserving servant-hood and as a celebration of his kingdom. These, then, should be the characteristics of human rule over the physical creation. It should not be abusive or exploitative, but enabling, so that each part of the created order is able to express its full potential. O'Donovan says, '[Man's] rule is the rule which liberates other beings to be, to be in themselves, to be for others, and to be for God.'[7] In the words of theologian Vinoth Ramachandra, 'We are neither owners of the planet – to do with it as we please, nor mere guests – to observe its develop-ment passively. We are stewards.'[8]

But what does it mean to be made 'in God's image'? Since the writings of the Early Church Fathers, theologians have laboured to explore the significance of this tantalizing phrase. It has frequently been suggested that its meaning lies in the capacities or attributes that human beings possess which are Godlike – their rationality, creativity and spirituality, for instance. The rationality of human beings, in distinction from animals, has been particularly emphasized by theologians from Augustine onwards. In ancient Greek philosophical thought, humanity was defined by individuation (separateness from others) and by rationality. Boethius defined a human being as 'an individual sub-stance of a rational nature', and this definition has been hugely influential in the philosophy of Thomas Aquinas and in the development of modern liberalism.

But although rationality is part of the biblical understanding of humanity, as distinct from the animal kingdom, Greek influences led to an overemphasis on it. As we face the challenges of advances in biology and biotechnology, it is vital for Christians to rediscover an authentically biblical view of what it means to be a human being – a biblical anthropology. As we shall see, the Bible tends to emphasize the fact that God's image is seen not only in our capacities or attributes, in what we can do, and in the duties which God gives us, but also in what we are by creation, in the stuff of our humanity.

God's image implies dependence
Human beings are not self-explanatory. We derive our meaning from outside ourselves, from God, in whose image we are made. We are not autonomous

individuals, constantly creating ourselves by the decisions and choices we make. No: we are images, we are reflections of another reality.

Imagine a super-intelligent alien population on a distant planet receiving a distorted image transmitted from planet Earth. The alien beings pore over the image, analysing a curious pattern of colours and lines. The yellow lines are six pixels in width and tend towards circular symmetry; the black lines are of similar width but more vertical. The colours reflect varying absorption in the limited wavelength range 400–700 nm, and so on. However much the image is dissected and analysed, the alien intelligences will never understand what they are looking at until they recognize that the collection of colours and patterns is a *map*, in fact it is an image of the London Underground map. The strange coloured lines reflect another form of reality, a series of tubular metal structures in the ground of a particular planet in a particular location in the universe.

In something of the same way you will never understand what a human being is by detailed examination of the human genome or analysis of the billions of neural connections within the human brain. Human beings reflect another form of reality, the character and being of God himself. We are not self-explanatory.

Another way of expressing this is that the dignity of our humanity is derivative: it comes from him whose image we bear. As Blocher says, 'being made in God's image stresses the radical nature of [our] dependence'.[9] The ethicist Paul Ramsey, speaking of the unborn child, put it in these words: 'The dignity of a human being is an overflow from God's dealing with him or her and not primarily an anticipation of anything they will ever be by themselves. The Lord did not put his love upon you because you were intrinsically more than a blob of tissue in the uterus.' The theologian Helmut Thielicke expressed it like this: 'The divine likeness rests on the fact that God remembers us . . . ' The divine image is like a mirror reflecting God's glory. Like a mirror, it goes dark if the source of light is withdrawn. In Thielicke's words, 'It possesses only borrowed light.'[10]

As we saw in the previous chapter, Ronald Dworkin said that 'Value cannot be poured into a life from the outside, it must be generated by the person whose life it is.' I beg to differ: the biblical worldview claims that the dignity of our humanity comes precisely from outside ourselves: it comes from God whose image we bear. The 'radical nature of our dependence' has inescapable consequences for bioethics. Within the story of my life, I have a degree of independence, the dignity of genuine choice, the relative freedom of a creature. But it is not simply my life to do with as I please. The ultimate meaning of my life can be found only within the Godhead.

For a society penetrated by liberal individualism as ours is, this concept is peculiar, nonsensical, even outrageous. Yet the biblical revelation stresses our creaturely dependence. Job expresses this poetically:

> Your hands shaped me and made me.
>   . . . you moulded me like clay . . .
> Did you not pour me out like milk
>   and curdle me like cheese,
> clothe me with skin and flesh
>   and knit me together with bones and sinews?
> You gave me life and showed me kindness,
>   and in your providence watched over my spirit.
> (Job 10:8–12)

Similarly, Elihu in the book of Job reflects on the dependence of the entire human race on God's continual sustenance:

> If it were his intention
>   and he withdrew his spirit and breath,
> all mankind would perish together
>   and man would return to the dust.
> (Job 34:14–15)

The same concept is found in the words of Jeremiah: 'a man's life is not his own; it is not for man to direct his steps' (Jeremiah 10:23).

We have to recognize that current secular views of autonomy are a modern fantasy. They are out of touch with reality, with the way we and the rest of the universe are made. The Christian revelation reminds us, as Meilaender says, that 'we are most ourselves not when we seek to direct and control our destiny, but when we recognize and admit that our life is grounded in and sustained by God'.[11]

God's image implies communion

In the mystery of the Trinity, historic Christianity teaches that the persons of the Godhead are in communion from eternity to eternity. God the Father loves God the Son, God the Son loves God the Father, God the Father loves God the Spirit, and so on. This is the ultimate meaning behind the biblical statement, 'God is love', a continual self-giving of the persons of the Trinity to each other. The persons of the Trinity are conssstituted by their self-giving love to the other. The Father cannot be the person he is unless the Son exists. The

Son cannot exist without the Father. Yet the Father and the Son are different and unique.

The original Greek word for person (*prosōpon*) means literally 'the face', but in ancient Greek it also referred to the mask that actors used to represent the character they were playing in the theatre. In Greek and Roman thinking, what mattered about an individual was the face they showed to the world, the role they played in society. We have retained this meaning when we refer to someone's 'persona'. It is the public face they show to the world. It is interesting that this is how the word is used in the Greek New Testament. At several points God is described as one who shows no favouritism. The literal Greek says that he is not a respecter of persons, meaning that he is not influenced by our external and social role.[12]

However, in Hebrews 1:3, the Son is described as the exact representation of God's person and a different Greek word is used, *hypostasis*, which literally means 'what lies under'. The Church Fathers, as they reflected on the nature of the Godhead and the meaning of the Trinity, fastened on this word 'hypostasis' to describe the three persons of the Trinity. God's ultimate being (what 'lay under' his activity) was in the form of persons – persons giving themselves to one another in love.

The meaning of personhood is derived from the Godhead. In philosophical language, it is ontologically foundational. You can't define what it means to be a person using other more foundational concepts such as rationality or individuality. To be a person is both to be a unique 'other' and to be in communion, in relation with other persons.[13]

Thus, when the text of Genesis says, 'Let us make man in our image', the 'us' is the Godhead-in-community. And because the Godhead consists of persons-in-community, to be made in God's image is to be made a person-in-community, in relationship. We reflect God's nature in our personhood; we are constituted by our relationships, created to give ourselves to God and to others in love.

An isolated person, an 'autonomous individual' in the language of Dworkin or Singer, is a contradiction in terms. The concept is incoherent. It is in relationship, in self-giving, in communion that we find our meaning. Hence, in biblical thought, humanity is defined not so much by rationality as by relationality.

Descartes made the famous statement, 'I think, therefore I am'. In other words at the heart of the individual person is an individual consciousness. It's a definition that led ultimately to the modern concepts of Singer and Harris. By contrast we might suggest an alternative Christian version, 'You love me, therefore I am'. My being comes, not from my rational abilities, but from the fact that I am known and loved – first of all by God himself, and secondly by other human beings. This is why the experience of rejection and isolation can be so psychologically devastating, and why children who have never experienced love and acceptance fail to develop into normal healthy adults.

But even if I am rejected by other humans, I am still a person. Ultimately my personhood rests on the fact that God called me into existence and that he continues to know and love me. In chapter 7 we will discuss the implications of this at the beginning of life.

The apostle John states: 'No-one has ever seen God; but if we love one another, God lives in us and his love is made complete in us' (1 John 4:12). John implies that the invisible God is made visible and tangible when human beings are in loving relationship. We reflect God's character and being to the world by being persons in love. Of course, rationality is an extremely important part of our created nature as human beings. But it seems to me that, biblically speaking, the defining characteristic of humanity is not so much our ability to think, as the web of relationships into which we are created, as persons-in-community.

God's creation of humans in his image is also a call to relationship with him. God creates us as relational beings and calls us to enter into communion with him. To speak of God's image is to speak of God's love for us. God creates each one of us out of love, calls us out of love and redeems us out of love. Even though the image is distorted by sin, God 'remembers' us and calls us back to himself. And his plan for each one of us is that through his grace we will become increasingly accurate reflections of his reality, we will become increasingly God-like. In fact we will increasingly become what we already are – the image of God. So, our creation in God's image is both a reflection of what we already are, in the stuff of our beings, and also a promise of what by God's grace we are to become.

Finally, the Genesis text seems to suggest that the creation of human beings as sexual beings, male and female, reflects the nature of the Godhead. The image of God is seen in our sexuality. Because we are made as male and female, we image God fully only when we are together, in a face-to-face relationship, as God himself exists in face-to-face relationship. But the relationship of male and female implied in the Genesis narrative cannot refer only to the marriage relationship, but rather to all male-female partnerships. It is when man and woman are united in a partnership of co-operation that we are at our most Godlike.

God's image implies that we are his children
In the thought-forms of the Ancient Middle East, the image of the father was passed on to the next generation when a child was begotten. In the fifth chapter of Genesis, we read the same statement as previously – that God created human

beings in his own likeness – and then: 'When Adam had lived 130 years, he had a son in his own likeness, in his own image; and he named him Seth' (Genesis 5:3). Adam's image is passed to his own child in procreation. In the genealogy of Jesus found in Luke's Gospel, the line is tracked back to Adam, 'the son of God' (Luke 3:37). The divine image is passed on as we beget children.

We must not, however, fall into the pagan belief that human beings are intrinsically divine. Although all of us carry God's image, it is only in a limited and incomplete sense. According to the New Testament, there is only one human being who rightfully bears the title of God's perfect image and God's Son: Jesus, the Second Adam, the perfect human being, who is both the Son and the supreme and unique image of the invisible God (Colossians 1:15). As the apostle Paul puts it, we who are called by God are called 'to be conformed to the likeness of his Son, that he might be the firstborn among many brothers' (Romans 8:29). To look ahead to the future for a moment, this is what God has in store for us, what he has called us for – to be re-formed in Christ's image, to rediscover our status as God's children, to enter into a face-to-face relationship with our Maker and Father.

God's image implies the dignity of each human life

In biblical thought, as each human life has a unique dignity because of the divine image, therefore each life has an incalculable and incommensurable value. In other words, it is not possible to calculate the value of a human life in material terms, and it is not possible to compare the ultimate value of one human life with another. Each human being is a unique masterpiece of God's creation. Each individual is, in the literal words of the eighth Psalm, 'lacking a very little of God' (Psalm 8:5). It is as though an economist asked, 'How much is the *Mona Lisa* worth, and is it worth more or less than the roof of the Sistine Chapel?' There can be no answer, because the value of a supreme masterpiece is incalculable and incommensurable. In place of the Lego-kit view of humanity, then, we have what I will call the flawed masterpiece view of humanity. Yes, the masterpiece may get defaced, it may decay from old age, the varnish may be cracked and yellowed, the frame may be riddled with woodworm. But through the imperfections we can still perceive a masterpiece – and therefore, as we shall see, medicine is more akin to art preservation and restoration than it is to Lego-kit construction.

To Peter Singer and Ronald Dworkin, the dignity of personhood depends on your function: on what you can do, on how well your cortex functions, on whether you can choose, and exercise autonomy. If your level of cortical functioning is critically reduced, because of Alzheimer's disease, say, or just because you happen to be a fetus, then you have less worth. But in Christian thought, the dignity of a human being resides, not in what you can do, but in what you are, by creation. Human beings do not need to earn the right to be treated as Godlike beings. Our dignity is intrinsic, in the way we have been made, in how God remembers us and calls us. So biblical ethics, the way we are called to treat one another, is derived from biblical anthropology, the way we are made.

God's image implies the equality of human beings

Our creation in God's image implies, not only a radical dependence, but also a radical equality. Each one of us bears the family likeness, yet each one is a unique masterpiece. We are all equal because we all bear the family likeness. The need for justice, equality and fairness in human society comes from our radical equality by creation. Whereas Peter Singer's view of human society tends towards a hierarchy, the Christian view of humanity is fundamentally egalitarian. Males are equal to females, adults are equal to children, the powerful are equal to the weak, the disabled are equal to the healthy, the so-called non-person is equal to the person. Why? Because we are equal in the stuff of our being. As the book of Proverbs says: 'Rich and poor have this in common: the Lord [Yahweh] is the Maker of them all' (Proverbs 22:2).

In the human community, we are surrounded by other reflections of God who are different but fundamentally equal in dignity to ourselves. The making of representative images of God is prohibited by the law of Moses (Exodus 20:4), at least partly because there is no need for another representation of God on the planet. God himself has placed his image here, and he wishes us to respect and care for his image in the way we treat one another. This is why Jesus joins the two great commands, 'Love the Lord your God . . . Love your neighbour as yourself' (Mark 12:29–31). The two commands are interrelated, because in loving and respecting our neighbour we are in fact showing honour to God. Similarly, the apostle John shows the organic connection between love of God and love for human beings: ' . . . anyone who does not love his brother, whom he has seen, cannot love God, whom he has not seen' (1 John 4:20).

Responding to God's image in others

How then should we treat human beings – these amazing Godlike beings? I would like to draw out four responses.

Wonder

The first response to another human being should be one of wonder at the miracle of our creaturely existence. Of all the marvels of the creation, it is the existence of human beings which should evoke the greatest awe. Hard as it may be at times, we must try never to lose a sense of wonder at the mystery and the existence of another human being. It is the wonder which a parent feels at the moment of birth. Before, there were only two people in the room – but now there are three. How did that happen?

I am afraid that a loss of the sense of wonder is especially common among health professionals and carers. We become blasé and cynical. We've seen it all before. We are just doing our job, just going through the motions. But Christian thinking calls us to retain a sense of wonder at the mystery of each human being.

Respect

Along with a sense of wonder goes respect – respect for the mysterious, immutable dignity of the image of God. I am increasingly convinced that respect for others is one of the hallmarks of authentic Christian compassion. We are called to treat one another with the same respect and dignity with which God himself treats us. There is a tendency for secular philosophers to view the weak, the demented, the disabled, with a degree of contempt: they are non-persons, they have no autonomy, they don't count, their biology is substandard, their cortex is malfunctioning. But the mark of genuine Christian love for the disabled, the sick and the dying is not pity but respect – 'respect-love', as Mother Teresa called it.

To abuse, manipulate or ill-treat a fellow human being is to show contempt for God. In the words of the biblical proverb, 'He who oppresses the poor shows contempt for their Maker, but whoever is kind to the needy honours God' (Proverbs 14:31). To abuse or manipulate another human being is in fact a form of blasphemy against God. It is to spit in the face of the Creator, to treat the divine image with contempt. This is why biblical ethics does not draw a distinction between religious behaviour (what we do in a church or a temple) and secular behaviour (what we do in the marketplace or, for that matter, in the hospital). God's moral order, the order of creation, permeates the whole of life.

Empathy

Empathy means to enter into the experience of the other, to share the pain and the joy. Because we are all the same in the stuff of our humanity, we are able to enter into the other's experience. Interestingly, the neural circuits and processing abilities to empathize, to imagine what it is like to be another human being, are much more highly developed in the human brain than in other mammals. We seem to have a unique ability to see the world through someone else's eyes. This is part of our created human nature. We are designed not to function as isolated, autonomous individuals locked in our own separate universes. We are able to share one another's joys and pains.

Secular philosophers tend to emphasize the gulf between the healthy and normally functioning, and the severely disabled or the critically unwell: I am a person, you are a non-person; I am the doctor, you are the patient. But Christianity says, 'We are both human beings; we are the same, you and I. We are in this together; we will share the pain.'

Protection

Finally, because each human life carries God's image, each life is sacrosanct. In the ninth chapter of Genesis is found the *lex talionis*, one of the oldest legal formulae in world literature, which prescribes the death penalty for the crime of shedding human blood:

> Whoever sheds the blood of man,
>   by man shall his blood be shed;
> for in the image of God
>   has God made man.
> (Genesis 9:6)

This passage expresses the idea that, because of the awesome dignity of human life, paradoxically, only capital punishment is sufficient retribution for murder. To destroy innocent human life is uniquely scandalous because it desecrates God's image, God's masterpiece. In John Harris' view of society, stronger persons can use brain-damaged non-persons for their own ends. For instance, we can take the organs from PVS sufferers or malformed babies and transplant them into somebody who is worth more. The strong can make use of the weak. But Christian thinking turns this on its head. The weak are worthy of special protection precisely because they are vulnerable, and the strong have a duty to protect the weak from manipulation and abuse.

Wonder, respect, empathy, protection: these are the responses which we owe to one another, because of the way we are made, because we are image-bearers, because each one of us is a mysterious reflection of the Godhead.

Made from the dust of the earth

Although the creation accounts stress the lofty dignity of humankind, they also draw attention to our physical nature and to our solidarity with the animal kingdom. Human beings are made on the sixth day, like all the other living creatures on land. In case we forget our lowly origins, the name that is given by God, 'Adam', is derived from the Hebrew for 'ground', *'ădāmâ*. Adam is the 'groundling'. In English also, the word 'human' is derived from the Latin *humus*, the soil. Like all the other living creatures, human beings are formed out of the dust of the ground

(Genesis 2:7), and, as with the animals, the breath of life is breathed into our nostrils. Although, as image-bearers, we are different from the rest of the animal kingdom, we are created in such a way as to share their physical structure. Like them, we are dust, we are the groundlings. Genetic analysis demonstrates that there is a remarkable homology (identity) between our DNA and that of other living organisms. It is said that about 50% of our genetic material is virtually identical to that of an oak tree. Over 98% of our DNA is identical to that of a chimpanzee. Even fruit flies and intestinal worms share a remarkable amount of genetic material with us. That is why molecular biology and basic science research have been so successful for human medicine. The gene cluster which instructs the fruit fly embryo which is the head end and which is the tail (the homeobox genes) is almost exactly the same as those which tell the human embryo which is the head end and which is the bottom. By researching fruit flies we can understand more about the way we are made. This should not surprise us. We are made out of the same stuff as the rest of the biological world.

Psalm 104, the 'ecological' psalm, in particular, emphasizes the common dependence of all living beings on God, the provider and sustainer: 'These all look to you to give them their food at the proper time' (Psalm 104:27). Or, in Job's words, 'In his hand is the life of every creature and the breath of all mankind' (Job 12:10). One of the Christian heresies that has recurred over the history of the church is that of 'superspirituality' (sometimes called the Gnostic heresy), the attempt to deny the significance, value and dignity of the body and the material world. But the biblical faith affirms the physical stuff of our nature. This is the way we have been made.

Because we are made out of the same stuff as everything else, we also share the frailty, the vulnerability, the contingency, of the rest of the living world. If I am deprived of liquid, I will die of dehydration; if a rock falls on my head I will suffer brain damage; if the neurotransmitters in my brain are disturbed, I will become psychotic. My life and health hang by a thread. Yet our heavenly father is not heedless of our fragility. In the wonderful words of Psalm 103, the compassion and gentleness of the Creator are seen:

> As a father has compassion on his children,
>   so the LORD has compassion on those who fear him;
> for he knows how we are formed,
>   he remembers that we are dust.
> (Psalm 103:13–14)

If God, our Creator, remembers the physical stuff from which we are formed, so should we. The awareness of our dust-like origins should give us a gentleness, a compassion – dare one say a humanity – in the way we interact with one another. We are not angels, a form of spiritual life unencumbered by physical constraints; neither are we merely animals, limited to a physical existence. We are a unique creation, 'a disgusting hybrid', in the words of C. S. Lewis's whimsical devil, Screwtape. The human person is the place where freedom and physical dependence are united. Because of the created, multifaceted, yet integrated nature of human beings – physical, emotional, spiritual, social – when we express care for our fellow human beings, we must respect each aspect of human nature. In the buzz words beloved by some professionals, caring must be integrated and holistic.

Made into one human family

God has not made us as independent individuals sprouting up like mushrooms in a field. He has put us in families, locked together in mutual dependence. Not only are we designed to depend on God; we are also designed to depend on one another.

We come into the world as helpless infants, totally dependent on another's love and care. You would not be here reading these words, if it was not for the fact that somebody cared for you, fed you, protected you, and wiped your bottom when you were a newborn baby. Then we go through a phase of our lives when other people depend on us. We protect them, feed them, pay for them. And then most of us will end our physical lives totally dependent on the love and care of others. We will need other people to feed us, protect us, and wipe our bottoms. And this is not a terrible, degrading inhuman reality. It's part of the design. It is an integral part of the narrative of a person's life.

This was brought home to me forcefully a few years ago when my mother was tragically struck down by a rapidly progressive, dementing illness. She was transformed over a space of months from a lively, vivacious, articulate person to someone who became totally dependent on 24-hour nursing care. I was visiting her towards the end and one of the carers put a yoghurt pot and teaspoon into my hand. It was supper time. So with the teaspoon I tried to put the food into her mouth. 'Open wide, here it comes . . . ' And suddenly the thought struck me that this was exactly what she used to do with me, all those years ago. But now the tables were turned. And though this was a painful and strange experience, in some mysterious way it felt right. This was the way it was meant to be. I was learning more of what it meant to be a son, and she was learning more of what it meant to be a mother.

In the words of theologian Gilbert Meilaender, 'We are dependent beings, and to think otherwise – to make independence our project, however sincerely – is to live a lie, to fly in the face of reality.'[14]

One of the greatest fears expressed by elderly or disabled people is that they will become a burden to others. But, in God's creation order we are meant to be a burden to one another! This is an essential part of what it means to belong to a family or to a community. Paul commanded the Galatians, as members of the Christian family, to 'carry each other's burdens, and in this way you will fulfil the law of Christ' (Galatians 6:2). To be called into a family is to be called to share the burdens of the life which God has given us, the burdens which come from our creation out of dust. The life of a family, including the Christian church family, should be one of 'mutual burdensomeness', to use Gilbert Meilaender's phrase.

'The family of man' used to be a common phrase of left-wing activists, although now it has an outdated ring. But the basic sentiment is biblical. We are a human family because in biblical thought, we are physically descended from one couple. Each of us can trace, in theory, a direct lineage to Adam and Eve.

When I was a medical student, the concept that all of the several billion humans on the planet were descended from single progenitors was greeted with cries of derision by scientists. It seemed obvious to students of evolution that the human race must have evolved at multiple times and in multiple places from a range of hominid ancestors. But the recent advent of detailed population DNA analysis has allowed the genetic relationship between different human beings on the earth to be investigated much more precisely. As Professor Steve Jones puts it, 'To a geneticist, everyone is a living fossil . . . Genes recreate history, not just since humans appeared on earth, but since the origin of life itself.'[15] By making assumptions about the rate of spontaneous mutations in DNA, geneticists have estimated that modern humans, *Homo sapiens*, are a relatively recent innovation, probably appearing on the planet fewer than 150,000 years ago.

The evidence is incontrovertible that genetic variation is much greater in African populations than elsewhere, strongly suggesting that *Homo sapiens* has been present longer in Africa than anywhere else. Most population geneticists now support the 'out of Africa' hypothesis, which holds that there was a single origin for modern humans in Africa less than 200,000 years ago. Current evidence suggests that modern humans migrated out of Africa some 60–70 thousand years ago and dispersed all over the globe. In fact, although still the subject of scientific controversy, the current evidence from population genetics is arguably consistent with the biblical view that all human beings currently alive have single male and female ancestors.[16] Interestingly, there is no definite genetic evidence that modern humans interbred with pre-existing hominid populations such as the Neanderthals, although the fossil record strongly suggests that they must have coexisted in certain regions.

There are obvious difficulties in relating the modern genetic and anthropo-logical evidence to the biblical account of the creation of Adam and Eve, and many unsolved questions remain. How does molecular genetic dating fit with biblical chronology? I am not able to address these issues here. But if our common human ancestors did exist less than 200,000 years ago, they would have looked virtually identical to modern humans. If we could meet them, we would recognize the family likeness. We must treat the biblical narrative with due seriousness. Human beings are both theologically and, it seems, in genetic reality, a single extended family. Not only do we carry the mysterious image of God, we also carry the image of our distant grandparents, Adam and Eve. This is the meaning of the biblical phrase to be 'in Adam': 'As in Adam all die, so in Christ all will be made alive' (1 Corinthians 15:22). Adam is the representative of the human race because he is our great-great-great-grandfather. We have an organic solidarity with him.

Not only that, but when I meet another human being, whether down the street or in the distant jungles of Borneo or the Amazon rainforest, I am meeting a distant relation. That is why I can recognize the family likeness. The rules that should govern human relationships, then, are family rules. We must treat even the stranger, the alien, the malformed, with care, with respect, with affection and with generosity. Why? Because we are family.

Creation mandates and creation order

In the Genesis creation narrative, having created human beings to be his representatives, God blesses them and then gives them their instructions, like a king providing a mandate for his governor (Genesis 1:28–30). First comes blessing, the wonderful, liberal giving of our Creator. In the old cliché, 'The best things in life are free.' But why is this? Because the best things in life have been bountifully given, extravagantly poured out on us by our Creator. In the created order, Adam and Eve are given an astonishing degree of freedom and liberty to enjoy the gifts of the creation. But after being blessed, they are given creation mandates: 'Be fruitful and increase in number; fill the earth and subdue it. Rule over the fish of the sea and the birds of the air and over every living creature that moves on the ground' (Genesis 1:28). In the parallel creation account in Genesis 2, Adam is placed in the Garden of Eden 'to work it and take care of it' (2:15). Although the basic creation order has been established by God, then, the work of creation is not completed. It is up to God's author-ized representatives to continue and fulfil what God has initiated.

Notice that the creation mandates are given jointly to male and female, as an illustration of the partnership for which they were created. There is no clear evidence of division of labour prior to the fall and the terrible curses of

Genesis 3. Human beings are jointly instructed, first to procreate, to fill the vast emptiness of the earth; secondly to subdue the earth, to impose order on its chaotic elements; and thirdly to cultivate, to bring out the potential that God has placed within the creation. God is the Creator; humans are the cultivators.

The creation narrative goes on to give a beautiful poetic description of the search for Adam's partner, because 'It is not good for the man to be alone' (Genesis 2:18). There is only one thing that is not good in the whole of the good creation. It is the aloneness of the man. In all the animal kingdom no suitable partner is found, and so the woman is created out of the body of the man. (One of the ancient commentators wrote that Eve was taken, not out of Adam's head to rule over him, or out of his feet to be dominated, but out of his side to be his companion.) Then comes Adam's joyful cry of recognition: 'This is now bone of my bones and flesh of my flesh' (2:23). Immediately after this comes the most-quoted biblical text on marriage: 'For this reason a man will leave his father and mother and be united [cleave] to his wife, and they will become one flesh' (2:24).

This passage implies that the union of man and woman in marriage is in some poetic sense a *reunion*, the re-creation of a mysterious unity that was severed at the beginning of time. In other words, man and woman were created or designed for each other; we are complementary; we fit together, not just in the obvious physical sense but in the very nature of our beings. When we come together in marriage and in any form of male-female partnership, there is therefore a sense of naturalness. This is how it was meant to be. In the Genesis account, the literal Hebrew for the act of sexual intercourse is the verb 'to know'. 'Adam knew Eve his wife' (Genesis 4:1, Authorized Version). Part of the creation order is that in the intimate knowing and self-giving of sexual intercourse lies our ability to pass on our created image to our children. In God's plan, making love and making babies are inextricably linked.

Finally, God respects the moral integrity of human beings by giving them freedom to enjoy the rich diversity of his creation. 'You are free to eat from any tree in the garden . . . ' (Genesis 2:16). But there are limits to freedom: of all the riches of the garden, there is one fruit which is forbidden: ' . . . but you must not eat from the tree of the knowledge of good and evil, for when you eat of it you will surely die' (2:17). Human freedom can operate only within the limits set by God. This is the difference between human freedom (freedom within the limits set by our physical design and by the moral order) and Godlike freedom (freedom without limits, except those set by God's faithfulness to his own character and purposes).

The biblical concept that God has placed a hidden moral order within the design of the creation is of central importance for a Christian view of morality.

God has not only created the physical structures of creation, including the physical structure of our bodies. He has also created a hidden moral order which directs how those structures should be used; in other words, how we should behave. It is as though there is a hidden 'grain' within all creation. If we live our lives 'along the grain', behaving in a way which is consonant with the created moral order, then our lives will work and we shall flourish. This is what the Bible calls the 'way of wisdom' (as in Proverbs 4:10–13: 'Listen, my son, accept what I say, and the years of your life will be many. I guide you in the way of wisdom and lead you along straight paths. When you walk, your steps will not be hampered; when you run, you will not stumble'). So wisdom, wise living, is living in accordance with the hidden moral order of the universe.

God imprints his moral order in the design of the creation and makes his image-bearers rational and morally responsible, capable both of understanding and responding freely to God's commands. The concept of a created moral order is central to an authentically biblical worldview. To most secular philosophers, morality is imposed on reality by the human mind. Ethical values are a human invention, part of human storytelling. But in biblical thought, the moral order is a part of objective reality. It is an aspect of the way that the world is made. This is why what philosophers call the fact/value distinction (see chapter 11) does not fit with a biblical worldview. God created the physical universe – the facts – and God created the hidden moral structure of the universe – the values. And since both come from the mind and intention of God, the physical structure and the hidden moral order are coherent. They match. The two are intimately related within the mysterious design of the cosmos. If human beings live their lives in a way that is inconsistent with the created moral order, against the hidden grain of creation, their lives will not 'work'; they will find disaster instead of blessing. And of course this is exactly what happened.

Fall

At the heart of the account of the fall in Genesis 3 is a rejection by human beings of the creation order that God has instituted for their enjoyment and well-being. Adam and Eve strike a blow for moral autonomy independent of God and his rules. By eating the fruit which had been forbidden, they discover the catastrophic consequences of disobedience. The stark words of Proverbs 14:12 summarize the consequences of human autonomy detached from creation order: 'There is a way that seems right to a man, but in the end it leads to death.'

Although God's image is defaced, the biblical revelation makes it plain that it is not destroyed (Genesis 9:6; James 3:9). Human beings are still Godlike beings, but our humanity is fatally contaminated and distorted by evil. In Pascal's words, 'Man is the glory and the shame of the universe.' C. S. Lewis said through Aslan: 'You come of the Lord Adam and the Lady Eve, and that is both honour enough to erect the head of the poorest beggar and shame enough to bow the shoulders of the greatest emperor on earth.'[17]

Although the universe is fractured and broken, a crucial part of biblical understanding is that the universe still displays the moral order, the hidden grain. Its brokenness is the brokenness of order, and not chaos. The terrible three-fold curse which God pronounces after the fall (Genesis 3:14–19) brings home the reality of the human condition contaminated by evil.

Death and decay

As God had warned them, the disobedience of Adam and Eve led directly to the entrance of death into the world: ' . . . for when you eat of it you will surely die'. In the poetic imagery of the creation narratives, within the Garden of Eden, Adam and Eve had access, not only to almost all the other fruit within the garden, but also to the tree of life. It seems they could have chosen to eat the fruit of that tree and live for ever. Instead, they chose to disobey God and eat the fruit of the one tree that was forbidden. By giving access to the fruit of the tree of life, God showed that his original intention for human beings was everlasting life. In biblical thought, the death of human beings, in all its horror and mystery, is not 'natural', it is not the way it was meant to be. In fact, death is seen as a punishment which is inflicted on humankind because of our moral disobedience.[18] The deep intuition which most of us share, that physical death (especially the death of a child or young person) is an outrage, an alien interruption in the nature of being, reflects the original creation order. Similarly the inexpressible longing we have for eternity, for stability, for freedom from decay, reflects our created nature. We were not intended to die: we were made to live for ever. That is why death is the 'last enemy' (1 Corinthians 15:26).

It seems futile to speculate on what would have happened if human beings had not disobeyed. What is clear is that, in biblical thought, human death is not an original part of God's creation order; it is a mysterious and terrible interruption in the nature of being. And because human beings are 'in Adam', we have an organic physical solidarity with him. Like the first humans, we too are subject to death and decay. C. S. Lewis once pointed out how strange it is that human beings are constantly surprised by the passage of time, despite the fact that we spend the whole of our lives within time: 'It is as strange as if a fish were repeatedly surprised by the wetness of water. And that would be strange indeed; unless of course the fish was destined to become, one day, a land animal.'[19]

We may detect an echo of this in the biological understanding of human ageing and death. It is interesting that death is not a biological necessity. Every organism is equipped with the essential cellular machinery to ensure repair and renewal so that life can continue indefinitely. Surprising as it may seem, eternal life is not a biological impossibility! In one sense, although individual cells are destined to die, organisms seem to be designed to live for ever. The ageing process involves active biological mechanisms such as telomere shortening, as yet very poorly understood, which cause the repair and renewal processes to progressively malfunction, leading ultimately to a point at which death is inevitable. Perhaps this is a physical counterpart of the biblical truth that, through human evil, the creation is in 'bondage to decay' (Romans 8:21).

The inevitable accompaniment of death is fear. The blessing of human life is transformed into a slavery of fear, especially fear of death. The terrible, all-pervading fear of death drives human beings to extraordinary and frequently pathetic lengths. As we shall discuss in a later chapter, the last decade has seen the rapid development of scientific research dedicated to the extension of human life to 150 years and more, and the ancient quest for the elixir of eternal life has resurfaced in a surprising new guise. But in less spectacular ways, the fear of death drives both medical research and our desperate attempts to use technology to prolong life. There is a better answer to the fear of death. As the writer to the Hebrews states, Christ came to 'free those who all their lives were held in slavery by their fear of death' (Hebrews 2:15).

For all its terror and mystery, in the biblical worldview, death is not an entirely negative concept. It may be, in C. S. Lewis's wonderful phrase, 'a severe mercy'. At the end of the account of the fall, human beings are banished from the Garden of Eden, precisely to prevent their eating the fruit of the tree of life and living for ever. And to prevent their return and capture of the fruit by force of arms, cherubim and a flaming sword are set to guard the way to the tree of life (Genesis 3:21–24). In God's providential care of his creation, then, human beings are not meant to live for ever in their degraded fallen state. The human lifespan is limited, not just as a curse, but out of God's grace. The flaming sword reminds us that human ingenuity and power cannot force a route to the tree of life.

Later on in the book of Genesis, because of the escalating wickedness of the human race, human longevity is limited to 120 years (Genesis 6:3); and Psalm 90, attributed traditionally to Moses, teaches that because of human sinfulness, 'the length of our days is seventy years – or eighty, if we have the strength; yet their span is but trouble and sorrow, for they quickly pass, and we fly away' (verse 10). The psalmist expresses grief and regret at the evanescence of human existence. 'Teach us to number our days aright, that we may gain a heart of wisdom' (verse 12).

In God's providence, death may be a merciful release from an existence trapped in a fallen and decaying body. Christian attitudes to death should reflect a curious ambivalence. We need to retain, first, a sense of outrage at its alien, destructive character; and secondly, an acceptance that the end of physical life may be evidence of God's grace, a 'severe mercy'; and finally a sense of future hope in the knowledge that ultimately death will be destroyed (as we shall see below). Christian health-care professionals are called to struggle against death whilst recognizing the ultimate futility of their struggle and seeking to discern when active life-sustaining treatment may become inappropriate, when the dying process becomes a severe mercy, even a strange form of healing.

Futility

The entrance of death into human life condemns our physical existence to an awful futility. Humans are condemned to return to the ground from which they are taken: 'Dust you are and to dust you will return' (Genesis 3:19). In the poetic, yet bleak, words of the Anglican funeral service, the futile cycle of human existence is exposed: 'Ashes to ashes, dust to dust'. So the dust of the ground, which is both the origin of our human bodies and the source of their food, becomes a symbol of their eventual decay and death. The futility of human existence is expressed most powerfully by the Preacher, the writer of the book of Ecclesiastes, whose bleak perspective on life is limited to the natural world – 'life under the sun', as he puts it. 'I have seen all the things that are done under the sun; all of them are meaningless, a chasing after the wind' (Ecclesiastes 1:14). 'This is the evil in everything that happens under the sun: The same destiny overtakes all. The hearts of men, moreover, are full of evil and there is madness in their hearts while they live, and afterwards they join the dead' (Ecclesiastes 9:3).

The reality of death traps human beings in the same cycle of futility as the rest of the animal world. 'As for men, God tests them so that they may see that they are like the animals. Man's fate is like that of the animals; the same fate awaits them both: As one dies, so dies the other. All have the same breath; man has no advantage over the animal. Everything is meaningless. All go to the same place; all come from the dust, and to dust all return' (Ecclesiastes 3:18–20). The futility and grief of physical ageing, its progressive decay and biological malfunction, are also graphically illustrated by the Preacher at the end of Ecclesiastes (12:1–8). They are 'days of trouble . . . when you will say "I find no pleasure in them."' To the Preacher ageing brings darkness, physical weakness, fear, disability, apathy and loss of libido ('desire no longer is stirred'), before death brings its inevitable release. The biblical revelation is unsparing in its bleak depiction of the cycle of human life from an earthly perspective. We have come a long way from the creation blessings of Genesis 1 – 2.

This perspective helps us to retain a sense of the limitations of medicine and health care. For all our wonderful knowledge and technology, we are unable to redeem our physical bodies from the cycle of death and decay. There can be no technological or biological fix for the ultimate mysteries of the human condition. We cannot, by medical technology, finally overcome ageing and eventual death. In God's providential mercy, that route to the tree of life remains blocked by a flashing sword.

Suffering

'I will greatly increase your pains in childbearing; with pain you will give birth to children' (Genesis 3:16). In the past, some biblical commentators took this verse to imply that the pain of childbirth should not be combated. As a result, it is said that the introduction of obstetric anaesthesia was vigorously opposed by some. (The widely circulated assertion that Christians opposed the use of chloroform for childbirth has been recently challenged as having no historical basis.)[20] It seems clear that the pains of childbirth described in this verse are merely illustrative of the physical and mental anguish which has invaded not only the experience of human procreation, but also every other aspect of our created human experience.

Yet, like death, in biblical thought, suffering is not an entirely negative phenomenon. To the secular mind, suffering is a futile, bewildering and purposeless reality. It is the negation of all that is good in life. It is the destroyer of autonomy – an evil to be feared and avoided at all cost. In utilitarian philosophy, the aim of all moral decision-making is to avoid or minimize suffering. But in the biblical worldview, suffering can never be meaningless, even if it seems so. We must cling by faith to the belief that suffering comes from the hand of a loving God, even despite appearances. In the experience of Job, physical suffering was revealed both as the destructive activity of Satan the accuser, and as a divinely authorized plan, to test the reality of Job's commitment to God. The book of Job has a great deal to teach us about human suffering. I believe it is particularly relevant in an age which has lost a belief in any positive aspect of suffering. Christians too have been affected by this secular disease. One of the greatest needs of the church today is to rediscover a biblical theology of suffering, and the book of Job is of special significance in this regard.

If Genesis 3 represents the entry of death into the creation, the book of Job represents the entry of suffering. As psychologists have frequently pointed out, at the heart of suffering is loss. Job loses his family, his wealth, his security, his social status. And the final blow is the loss of his own bodily integrity. He is

covered in 'painful sores from the soles of his feet to the top of his head' (Job
2:7). For thirty long chapters of theological argument Job protests his outrage
at God's apparently capricious dealings, while his so-called friends try to persuade
him that the root of his suffering is some hidden sin in his life. To Job's friends
there is a clear explanation for his experience. Their simplistic theology relates
suffering to guilt. But Job begins not with theological principles but with his
own experience – suffering apparently bequeathed capriciously by a silent and
unaccountable God, an experience of chaos and meaninglessness. Job calls
upon God for the opportunity to question him face to face.

Eventually God's prolonged silence is ended. He answers Job 'out of the
whirlwind' (38:1, Revised Standard Version). As commentators have pointed
out, for the first time since the prologue, the author uses the covenant name,
Yahweh (the Lord). God reveals himself not as a capricious and unaccountable
deity, but as the gracious and faithful Lord of the covenant. He does not rebuke
Job for his temerity; rather, he rebukes his friends for their trite and blasphemous
theology: ' . . . you have not spoken of me what is right, as my servant Job has'
(42:7). God, however, provides no explanation for Job's suffering. Instead, he
points to his own creative freedom and concern for all creation. The world
expresses the freedom and delight of God. In place of the human-centred
perspective of Job and his comforters, God gives glimpses of a radically different
viewpoint. The cosmos does not exist merely for human beings, and the meaning
of human suffering cannot be fathomed within a limited, anthropocentric
worldview. There are hints within the book that Job's inexplicable suffering has
a redemptive aspect. In the final chapter, Job as Yahweh's suffering servant,
prays for his friends and his prayer is accepted (Job 42:7–9). But the mystery
of God's purposes is never fully revealed.

When confronted by suffering, like Job's friends we frequently have an overwhelming and very human desire to provide neat explanations. 'This happened
because of that . . . God is teaching you to . . . ' Instead, we should learn from
the book of Job. There can be no human explanations for the mystery of
suffering – only the presence of a loving, suffering and redeeming God.

The corruption of technology: the Tower of Babel

As the Genesis narrative unfolds, we see the gradual escalation of human
folly and wickedness. Cain's jealous hatred of his brother erupts into murder.
Wickedness spreads across the earth and is destroyed in the flood. And then
comes the tragicomedy of the Tower of Babel (Genesis 11:1–9). As Vinoth
Ramachandra points out, 'The story of Babel is the story of Eden all over again,
but the difference is between the individual deed and the collective act.'[21] Prior
to Babel, several characters in the Adamic family had initiated different aspects

of human work. Jabal was the father of all those who live in tents and raise livestock. Jubal was the father of all who play the harp and flute. Tubal-Cain forged all kinds of tools out of bronze and iron (Genesis 4:19–22). To the author of the narrative, it is likely that these characters are living out the creation mandates, subduing the earth and bringing out the wonderfully diverse potential locked in the raw material of the earth. In pictorial form, this is the earliest reference to human artifice, to primitive technology.

At Babel we see a darker side to technology. The builders are driven by a two-fold desire: to 'make a name for ourselves' and to avoid being 'scattered over the face of the whole earth' (Genesis 11:4). Ramachandra suggests that Babel is the marriage of three human dreams: the technological (to build a city that would be the envy of gods and nations), the religious (to divinize humankind by reaching up into the heavens) and the political (to build a totalitarian society based on technology). Babel symbolizes the use of human artefacts, technology, to celebrate human autonomy. The words, 'Come, let us build . . . ' (11:4) echo the very words of God in making human beings: 'Let us make man in our image . . . ' (1:26).

Babel symbolizes the myth of technology which recognizes no limits to human technical possibilities – technology that is used to seize God's rightful place as Creator, and to overturn creation order. It is a story of human collective action, a unity which ends in confusion and dispersion. But the confusion created by God is both an act of judgment and, again, an act of mercy. The unfinished tower stands as a monument to the folly of human arrogance, and a sign of the mercy of a God who intervenes to prevent a technological dream (or nightmare) coming to fruition.

Redemption

Even as God pronounces the terrible curses in the Garden, the first glimmering of the gospel hope of redemption is seen. God promises that the offspring of the woman will come to crush the serpent's head (Genesis 3:15). Later, God enters into a solemn covenant with Abraham, promising to bless him and, through his children, ultimately bless all the nations of the earth (Genesis 12:2–3; 17:3–8). The giving of the law at Mount Sinai symbolizes the justice and mercy which lie at the heart of God's gracious covenant with his people. The Old Testament laws are not the arbitrary commands of a primitive desert god. They are the Maker's instructions, endorsing and protecting the hidden moral order of the creation. They reinforce the equality of all human beings before God, and uphold the sanctity or inviolability of all human life.

Defending the defenceless

A beautiful expression of God's grace and mercy is found in the Deuteronomic law. In Deuteronomy 10, the mighty Yahweh is revealed as the defender of the defenceless. 'For the LORD [Yahweh] your God is God of gods and Lord of lords, the great God, mighty and awesome, who shows no partiality and accepts no bribes. He defends the cause of the fatherless and the widow, and loves the alien, giving him food and clothing. And you are to love those who are aliens, for you yourselves were aliens in Egypt' (Deuteronomy 10:17–19). There is a striking contrast in this passage between the person of Yahweh in his absolute power, and his gracious concern to defend the nobodies of society. The significant triad of widows, orphans and aliens recurs many times throughout the Scriptures. They symbolize those who were most vulnerable in the social structures of ancient Israel. The widow had no husband to defend her from abuse and manipulation; the orphan had no parent; the alien or immigrant had no community, no religious or family structures to fall back on. All three were uniquely open to all kinds of abuse within society: physical violence, psychological manipulation, economic sharp practice and the effects of corruption. To the triad of the widows, orphans and aliens, the Old Testament later added the poor (as in Proverbs 22:22), because of their economic vulnerability. Yahweh, then, declares himself the defender of the socially defenceless, and calls on his people to defend them in his name. A particular responsibility was laid on rulers to create social structures that protected the weak. Jeremiah referred to the righteous reign of King Josiah: '"He defended the cause of the poor and the needy, and so all went well. Is that not what it means to know me?" declares the LORD' (Jeremiah 22:16). Strikingly, the personal knowledge of God, the heart and goal of the biblical covenant, is defined, not as a mystical religious experience, but rather in practical concern for the defenceless in society. If we are genuinely in covenant with the living God, then our actions will reflect his heart concerns.

In the New Testament, James carries on the same theme: 'Religion that God our Father accepts as pure and faultless is this: to look after orphans and widows in their distress . . . ' (James 1:27). As we debate the appropriate use of new and powerful medical technologies, a special responsibility rests on us, the strong, to defend the vulnerable in our midst. Who are the modern counterparts of the widow, orphan and alien? The God revealed in Scripture is committed to be their defender, and calls on us to protect them from abuse in his name. The fetus, the newborn infant, the disabled child, the brain-damaged adult, the elderly sufferer with Alzheimer's disease, and the psychiatric patient – we do not have to look far to find them. Will we receive the commendation that Josiah received: 'This is what it means to know me . . . '?

Christ, the Word made flesh

In Christ, God affirms and fulfils the original creation. When God breaks into human history to bring redemption to his fallen people, does he overturn the created order he has previously established to introduce a completely new kind of reality, a radically new way of being? No. God reveals himself as a human being, a Mark I, original human model. Christians treat the human body with special respect. Why? Because this strange and idiosyncratic collection of 35,000 genes, 10 billion nerve cells, several miles of wiring, eight metres of intestinal plumbing, five litres of blood, and assorted biochemical engineering – this is the form in which God became flesh! In the incarnation, death and resurrection of Christ, the created order is both re-established and fulfilled. Before the resurrection it might have been possible for someone to wonder whether creation itself was a lost cause: perhaps the only possible ending for the tragic story of a fallen creation is God's final judgment and destruction of the created order. But when Christ is born and raised as a physical human being, God proclaims his vote of confidence in the created order.[22] Jesus shares in the stuff of creation. His body, like ours, is made from dust, from physical atoms. The Gospel writers go to great lengths to stress Christ's full humanity. He is tired, angry, hungry, distressed, in agony . . . And in the resurrection of Christ, the physical creation is not overturned but subsumed, or caught up, into a greater and richer reality. In Jesus, the Second Adam, we see both a perfect human being (what the original Adam was meant to be) and the pioneer, the blueprint for a new type of human being, the one in whose likeness a new creation will spring, the firstfruits of those who are to come (1 Corinthians 15:20).

Our humanity is not something which comes between us and God. No, it is the means by which God is made known. '"Destroy this temple [said Jesus], and I will raise it again in three days." . . . But the temple he had spoken of was his body' (John 2:19, 21). Here is a new and exalted view of the human body – a temple. If Christ's body was a temple, then I must treat all bodies with a new reverence. Furthermore, Jesus comes, not as a sovereign king, as Caesar or Herod, the symbol of human power and authority. He does not come as the imperial Caesar, the world president, the Olympic athelete. He comes as a pathetic, vulnerable and totally defenceless newborn baby. We are so familiar with the doctrine of the incarnation that it loses its force. God makes himself a baby who can do absolutely nothing for himself, a being who depends on human breasts for milk, and human hands to wipe his bottom. No wonder this was the aspect of Christian theology which the sophisticated Greek philosophers of the day found most scandalous and frankly laughable.

Jesus starts his life totally dependent on the love and care of others. And how does his earthly life come to a close? With arms and legs stretched out and from his parched lips comes the words, 'I am thirsty . . . '.

So if we take this scandalous teaching seriously, then it has radical implications. We can no longer view the state of dependence as being dehumanizing. If it's good enough for Jesus then it's good enough for us. Jesus shares the created stuff of our humanity, and the narrative of a human life. As Gilbert Meilaender puts it, 'Jesus has been with us in the darkness of the womb as he will be with us in the darkness of the tomb.'[23] Because Jesus was a baby, all babies are special. Because Jesus was a dying man, all dying people are special.

In Christ, God reveals a deeper and richer reality

Jesus both shows us the importance of our current physical bodies, and also points to something that is even more important: the future resurrection life which is invading the present. He shows us that our present limited physical existence is not the only, or even the most important, part of reality. As Jesus interacted with hurting people, he not only made blind eyes see and lame legs walk. He healed them internally – on the cross he healed their spiritual alienation from God himself. So Christians affirm the importance of physical healing, while recognizing that behind our current physical experience lies a deeper, richer, even more wonderful reality.

This means that we cannot make the extension of physical life by technology the ultimate goal of medicine. Sometimes we have to say no to medical progress. Sometimes we shall need the trust and the courage that enable us to decline what medical technology makes possible. This physical existence is not all there is: we need a deeper healing.

In Christ, we see a new way to love, the way of self-giving

Jesus was not just a preacher, a talker, a teller of parables. He did not just sit on the Mount of Olives and instruct people how to live. He entered into the experience of pain, suffering, loneliness, emptiness and despair. Together the incarnation and the cross are the ultimate expression of empathy. God himself entered fully into the experience of being a human being. He experienced humanity from the inside. As John Stott writes, 'Christ laid aside his immunity to pain.'[24] And in doing so, he showed the paradoxical nature of God's love. God's love is love that gives; it is self-sacrificial, costly love. It is a practical love, down-to-earth, washing feet. As Jesus entered into the mystery of human suffering, he gave us a model of how we can care for others who are suffering – not by providing neat answers to the questions raised by human pain, but by being there. In the words of an anonymous writer, 'Suffering is not a question that demands an answer; it is not a problem that demands a solution; it is a mystery which demands a presence.'

If we want to care for people as Jesus cared for people, we have to give ourselves, we have to pay a price. We have to show genuine empathy, to enter into and experience the pain of the other. There is an old Christian proverb: 'He who would be Christ must expect a cross.'

Consummation

Christian caring does not stop at the agony of the cross. It is shot through with hope, expectation and longing for the future. The resurrection of Christ points towards the future of humanity. And the future is not in some disembodied, immaterial and purely 'spiritual' existence. The Gospel writers go to great lengths to emphasize the physical reality of Christ's restored body and its continuity with his old physical body. The Gospel narratives are all adamant that *the tomb was empty*. The risen Jesus eats and drinks. He breaks bread. He talks. He is touched. He is recognized by his friends. His body even bears physical scars. There is no room to doubt the physical continuity between Jesus' original body and the resurrection body. It is the same, but different.

So, in one sense, the resurrection looks back to Jesus' life on earth. But in the same resurrection we also see that the physical man has been subsumed, transformed by God's power. His body is now part of a new reality – a future reality which has somehow penetrated backwards into our space-time. O'Donovan says, 'The resurrection appearances are encounters with divine power and authority. Humanity is elevated to that which it has never enjoyed before: the seat at God's right hand which belongs to his Son.'[25] Christ's resurrection, then, points backward to the creation of human beings and forward to the future transformation of human beings.

Our humanity is both vindicated and transformed. In God's mysterious purpose, this is what human beings were always intended to become. This is the ultimate goal of the created order. As Paul writes: 'Just as we have borne the image of the earthly man, so we shall bear the likeness of the man from heaven' (1 Corinthians 15:49). The image of God inherited from Adam will be fulfilled and transformed into a new and much more glorious image. Yes, we shall still be reflections. We shall not lose our creaturely dependence. But we shall discover the true likeness that we were always intended to bear.

Not only that, but, it seems that the transformation of our physical bodies is a central element in the transformation of the entire physical universe. The second person of the Trinity enters into our space-time universe and takes on physical form. His body is composed of dust – carbon, phosphorus, trace elements, cells, mitochondria, DNA – the ashes from a burnt-out supernova billions of years old. And then, by the working of God's resurrection power, those particular carbon atoms are somehow transformed into a new kind of physical reality, the resurrection body of Christ. Those same atoms are removed from the space-time universe at the Ascension. But God's intention is that Christ's risen body should be the first-fruits, the foretaste, of what he has in store for the cosmos. Because, in God's grace and resurrection power, at the end of the age our physical bodies, composed of carbon, phosphorus, mitochondria and the rest, will also be transformed in the same way that Christ's body was transformed. And then as those physical atoms are transformed into the new reality, it seems that the entire physical universe will be transformed into the new creation. It's as though God stoops down, incorporates a few atoms into his body and then draws them out of the old space-time into a new reality. Christ's risen body draws the human bodies of the redeemed community out of the old space-time into a new reality, and behind our bodies comes the whole of creation: trees, animals, planets and galaxies.[26] That's why Paul says:

> The creation waits in eager expectation for the sons of God to be revealed. For the creation was subjected to frustration, not by its own choice, but by the will of the one who subjected it, in hope that the creation itself will be liberated from its bondage to decay and brought into the glorious freedom of the children of God.
> (Romans 8:19–21)

Only by the transformation of our physical bodies can the physical creation, of which we are part, be transformed. For 'the created order . . . cannot be itself while it lacks the authoritative and beneficent rule that man was to give it.'[27]

Perhaps this seems like abstruse and speculative theology. What possible relevance can it have to the practical medical dilemmas that we face? Let me suggest just two practical outworkings.

We can make sense of the present only in the light of the future

When the apostle Paul talks about the resurrection of the body, he uses the dramatic image of the seed and the flower. 'The body that is sown is perishable, it is raised imperishable; it is sown in dishonour, it is raised in glory; it is sown in weakness, it is raised in power; it is sown a natural body, it is raised a spiritual body' (1 Corinthians 15:42–44). The image is familiar and we easily lose its power. But if we had never seen a tiny brown seed transform into a spectacular flower, we would never believe it was possible. Yet the transformation is a commonplace of the natural creation. And modern molecular biology has revealed the power of that image. In the tiny and pathetic brown husk is packed all the DNA, all the information, that is required to make the miraculous flower. The two entities which seem so utterly dissimilar share a hidden identity. The seed is becoming what it already is. And that, says Paul, is a picture of what will happen to our human bodies.

In my job as a paediatrician, I have had the privilege of caring for many babies who are dying. It has been part of my job; it is what I was there for. I have held the body of a dead baby in my arms and wept together with the parents at an overwhelming sense of helplessness, of emptiness, of outrage, at this cruel, untimely death. And nearly every time I have had this experience, I have taken comfort from Isaiah's wonderful description of the new heaven and the new earth:

> . . . be glad and rejoice for ever
>   in what I will create,
> for I will create Jerusalem to be a delight . . .
> I will rejoice over Jerusalem
>   and take delight in my people;
> the sound of weeping and of crying
>   will be heard in it no more.
> Never again will there be in it
>   an infant who lives but a few days,
>   or an old man who does not live out his years.
> (Isaiah 65:18–20)

God himself recognizes the peculiar outrage of an infant death. It's the Christian hope; and it is what this particular paediatrician longs for. That day is coming: the day when never again will there be an infant who lives but a few days. Some years ago, I shared the loss of another baby's death, and as I sat in a rather weepy silence with the family (who shared a strong Christian faith), the passage in Revelation came into my mind: 'Now the dwelling of God is with men [humans] and he will live with them . . . He will wipe every tear from their eyes. There will be no more death or mourning or crying or pain, for the old order of things has passed away' (Revelation 21:3–4). God will wipe away every tear from their eyes. It suddenly struck me what a remarkable image this is. It is not a picture of the majestic, all-powerful, glorious God. No, this is a picture of a weeping child, of a mother's lap, and the gentle stroking of a loving hand across a tear-stained face. This is our God, the one we will meet; this is our hope. Only this future makes sense of the present.

We can dare to act only in the light of the future

A fellow paediatrician, with whom I worked closely over many years, once said to me: 'You know, it's easier for you than it is for me, John. When I'm looking after a dying baby I'm sending them into the ground, into oblivion. When you're looking after a dying baby, you're sending them to heaven.' It was meant as a joke, but we both knew it was true. Maybe it is easier for the Christian doctor who can act in the light of the future. I can dare to act, to take the really hard and painful clinical decisions – about withdrawing intensive treatment in a dying baby, for example, or decisions concerned with recognizing the point at which medical treatment becomes futile and meddlesome, and when death may be a strange kind of healing. We can dare to act because of the Christian hope, because of the new day which is dawning – because death has been ultimately defeated.

I have tried to give a brief panoramic overview of the biblical teaching about humanness. These are the principles which must guide us as we attempt to tackle the complex and ever-changing dilemmas of modern health care. In the next chapter we will look at advances in reproductive technology, and ask how biblical principles can be applied to the creation of new human lives.

3. REPRODUCTIVE TECHNOLOGY AND THE START OF LIFE

The ethical dilemmas that both doctors and parents face at the start of life are particularly complex and troubling. They have led to ferocious controversy and even violence. This is especially obvious when we look at the painful subject of legalized abortion. In the USA, doctors working at abortion clinics have been assaulted and even murdered, rival demonstrators have fought one another, and hospitals and clinics have been fire-bombed. Although there has not been the same level of violence in the UK, the debate has at times been unpleasant, polarized and even vitriolic. Even the language has become a battleground. Do we talk about the fetus or the unborn child? About terminating a pregnancy or murdering unborn babies? Sometimes, in the attempt to win the public-relations battle, Christians have resorted to harsh rhetoric, negative campaigning and questionable publicity tactics. I strongly believe there is a better way to tackle these issues. If we are aiming to put forward a Christian perspective on these disturbing questions, we have not only to explain Christian ideas, we have to present them in a Christian way. That means speaking the truth in an honest but also a gentle and respectful manner. If we are to act with Christian integrity, the way in which we speak on these issues is just as important as what we actually say.

Above everything else, the dilemmas at the beginning of life are matters of extreme personal pain. Whenever we discuss infertility, abortion or disabled babies, we are treading on other people's secret sorrows. Here are three terrible and sad problems: first, the lack of a baby who is desperately wanted; second, the baby who is developing but is desperately unwanted; and finally the baby who is severely disabled, and will never live a normal life. They are tragedies which go back to the dawn of time; they are recorded in the biblical narrative and in other ancient literature. They are part of the human condition. And these are not just issues 'out there', that affect other people. They affect us all, including those reading this book.

In the UK it is estimated that approximately four out of ten women will have an abortion in their lifetime, about one couple in seven is unable to have children without medical help, and about one child in twenty-five has a significant disability or congenital malformation. Many of us are carrying secret and painful sorrows from our past which we cannot share with others. Indeed, every one of us is carrying genetic variants, 'misprints', which may well affect any children we have. None of us is immune from tragedy. So before all else, our responsibility is to try to empathize, to enter into the experience of people in our midst who are hurting.

Infertility and reproductive technology

The pain of infertility
The development of reproductive technology has brought to light the depth and extent of the pain felt by infertile couples within our society. A 1997 report from the National Infertility Awareness Campaign gave the results from a survey of one thousand infertile people. One in five said they had contemplated suicide while waiting for fertility treatment. Depression, isolation and frustration were reported by more than nine out of ten of those surveyed. One in three said that the relationship with their partner had been adversely affected by the result of their failure to conceive. Adding to the pressure of trying to have a baby were the financial and psychological consequences of undergoing fertility treatments. The sense of despair and isolation felt by couples is revealed by their willingness to spend large amounts of money, and undergo the prolonged stress of repeated and sometimes increasingly desperate attempts to have a child. Infertility is a silent suffering, largely ignored by the rest of society and by the Christian community. Yet unless we understand the experience of infertility, at least in part, we cannot make sense of the extraordinary pressure on doctors and biological scientists to employ increasingly technological methods to make babies.

So why does infertility cause such suffering? There is the family-orientated nature of modern society, including family-orientated churches, and the isolation from peer groups which infertility brings; the subtle pressure from well-meaning friends and relatives; the desire to give love to a child, and the sense of loss when that love is thwarted; a feeling of 'genetic death' as a result of making no contribution to the next generation; the tension between partners which spills over into needless arguments and disputes; the loss of self-esteem and a feeling of biological failure.[1]

One woman described her menstrual periods as her body's way of mocking her hopes of pregnancy. It is not being over-dramatic to say that infertility can be a form of bereavement, a loss that is ongoing and repetitive. A South African woman with long-standing infertility expressed her sense of suicidal despair: 'If I kill myself I die once, if I live I die every day.' It is ironic that while the very existence of reproductive technology offers a possible solution to those experiencing this bereavement, it also prevents acceptance and healing. The desperate but thwarted desire for a pregnancy may be kept alive for years by the hope that maybe, just maybe, the next cycle of treatment will work.

Human reproductive technology has developed, not because doctors and scientists have been consumed by an overwhelming desire to 'play God', but because of pressure from ordinary people with a desperate wish for a child. Although the problem of childlessness is an intricate web of biological, psychological, human and social factors and pressures, technology, as so often, offers an apparent 'quick fix' for complex human issues. It is a theme which recurs constantly in modern bioethics. Technology offers apparently neat solutions to the fundamental problems of the human condition. Unfortunately, the last hundred years have taught us that the solutions which technology offers may come with a higher price tag than we had imagined. Even the technical word 'reproduction' has hidden implications, as Leon Kass demonstrates:

> Ancient Israel, impressed with the phenomenon of transmission of life from
> father to son used a word we translate as 'begetting' ... The Greeks impressed
> with the springing forth of new life in the cyclical processes of generation
> and decay called it 'genesis', from a root meaning 'to come into being' ... The
> pre-modern English-speaking Christian world, impressed with the world as given
> by a Creator, used the word 'pro-creation'. We, impressed with the machine and
> the gross national product, (our own work of creation) employ a metaphor of the
> factory, 're-production'.[2]

The development of in vitro fertilization
When I was a medical student in the 1970s, virtually the only form of technological assistance for infertile couples was the use of artificial insemination, either by husband (AIH) or by anonymous donor (AID, now usually called

donor insemination, DI). But the work of embryologist Dr Robert Edwards showed that it was possible to fertilize mouse eggs in the laboratory and reimplant them into a mouse uterus. A few years later he showed that it was possible to fertilize human eggs with human sperm and grow the embryos in a laboratory dish for several days – *in vitro* fertilization. Edwards struck up a collaboration with Patrick Steptoe, a gynaecologist from Oldham in the north of England, who was looking for ways to help his infertile patients. Steptoe reimplanted the embryos created by Edwards into the wombs of a number of his patients. After numerous failures, their perseverance was met with spectacular success. On 25 July 1978, Louise Brown, the world's first 'test-tube baby', was born in Oldham District General Hospital. One commentator described this birth as 'a singular moment in human evolution'.[3] Steptoe and Edwards were the founding fathers of a new science of reproductive technology. Louise Brown has been a figure of international interest ever since, and in December 2006 there were newspaper reports that she had given birth to her own child, apparently conceived naturally.

From a single birth in a British hospital, the use of IVF has rapidly expanded worldwide. In addition to Western nations, there are well-established programmes in Eastern Europe, Middle East, Asia and Latin America. In 2006 it was estimated that more than three million babies had been born worldwide using IVF and related technologies.[4] In Denmark, children born by IVF make up as much as 4–5% of the population. However, the success rate for IVF is still relatively low with 15–30% of treatment cycles resulting in a live baby. There are also substantial commercial profits to be made. A typical IVF cycle costs up to $15,000 in the USA, and many times this sum may be required to achieve a single pregnancy. Surveys have shown that reproductive specialists are among the highest-earning doctors in the US.

IVF changes our view of ourselves
Not only has IVF provided a means of providing children for infertile couples, it has given laboratory access to the human egg and the human embryo, enabling embryo testing, research and manipulation to be carried out. Robert Edwards has recently stated that IVF was always seen as an experimental research method with enormous potential for providing new insights into human development and developing new therapies. It is no exaggeration to say that the development of IVF has changed for ever our understanding of human reproduction and parenthood. It is a classic example of a disruptive technology – changing attitudes and practices, even changing the way we think of our own humanity.

In the light of IVF, each child can now be regarded as the product of four components: (1) an egg source, (2) a sperm source, (3) a womb and (4) one or more caregivers after birth. Another way of looking at this is that any child may have three mothers: a *genetic* mother, the source of the egg; a *carrying* mother, the provider of the uterus; and a *social* mother, the one providing care after birth. The possible permutations and combinations are remarkable.

Sperm or egg donation means that one element of the genetic make-up of the embryo is provided by a donor; alternatively, there is embryo donation, where the genetic parents donate the embryo to a carrying mother who goes on to care for the child. Then there is surrogate pregnancy, where the genetic parents donate an embryo to a carrying mother with the intention that the child should be handed back to them after birth. Finally there is embryo 'adoption', in which an 'abandoned' embryo is donated to a carrying mother who then passes the child to adoptive parents for care after birth.

How is IVF performed?

In the most common form of the procedure, hormones are given to a woman to induce superovulation. Instead of producing one egg at each monthly cycle, the ovaries are stimulated to produce between five and twenty eggs. This process carries a degree of risk from inadvertent overstimulation, and tragically a small number of deaths have occurred from the complications of this process. The eggs are 'harvested' using a laparoscope, a fine telescope which is inserted through the abdominal wall. They are then incubated in the laboratory and mixed with sperm obtained from the donor. Fertilization occurs in a few hours, and embryos can be assessed and 'graded' by microscope. Over the next three to five days, the embryos develop from a single cell to a bundle of fifty cells or more, called a blastocyst. (Some clinics now provide photographs, even streaming video pictures via the internet, and daily progress reports for couples on how their embryos are developing.)

Between the third and fifth day, one or more embryos are selected for insertion into the carrying mother's womb. By increasing the numbers implanted at each attempt, the chances of a successful pregnancy are increased to some degree. But for every additional embryo implanted, there is an increasing chance of multiple pregnancies (twins, triplets or more), with all the associated risks of prematurity, severe handicap and death. Approximately a quarter of all pregnancies resulting from IVF are twins or triplets. Two decades ago, I and my colleagues at University College Hospital were responsible for caring for a group of tiny quintuplets, born three months premature, after six embryos were implanted by IVF. The headlines the next day proclaimed, 'World's first test-tube quins!'. Remarkably, all five babies survived, following several months of intensive care.

As a result of growing concern in the UK about the rise in the number of multiple pregnancies, national guidelines now recommend that only two embryos should be inserted in most circumstances, and single embryo transfer is increasingly common. This avoids the deeply disturbing option, euphemistically known as 'fetal reduction', in which selective abortion is used in a multiple pregnancy to ensure that only the desired number of fetuses survive.

The immediate problem however is the fate of the remaining or 'spare' embryos. In essence there are only four possibilities: (1) freeze them for reinsertion into the genetic mother's uterus at a later date; (2) allow them to be inserted into the womb of another carrying woman (embryo donation); (3) use them for research, with their ultimate fate being destruction; or (4) discard them immediately. Embryos can be frozen in liquid nitrogen and stored under laboratory conditions for many years. Different techniques have been employed, and chemicals, called cryoprotectants, are used in the freezing process. But what are the implications of the prolonged storage of embryos? Who 'owns' the embryos? How long should they be allowed to be stored? What happens if there is a disagreement about what should happen to them? Should embryo research and manipulation be permitted?

The UK Human Fertilisation and Embryology Act

In the early 1980s there was growing public concern in the UK about the implications of these advances in reproductive technology. At the same time, many responsible scientists and clinicians were calling for the creation of official guidelines so that the legal and ethical position could be clarified. In response, the British Government set up a Committee of Inquiry into Human Fertilisation and Embryology under the chairmanship of Oxford philosopher Dame Mary Warnock. The committee was known universally as the Warnock Committee. It received over 250 oral and written submissions from interested bodies and individuals, including many from churches and Christian organizations. It rapidly became apparent that there were wide and seemingly irreconcilable differences between different groups on the moral status of the embryo.

It is very significant that the primary question which Mary Warnock's committee chose to address was a sociological rather than a philosophical one. 'What kind of society can we praise or admire? In what kind of society can we live with our conscience clear?' In her report Mary Warnock stated, 'People generally want some principles or other to govern the development and use of the new techniques. There must be some barriers that are not to be crossed, some fixed limits, beyond which people must not be allowed to go ... The very existence of morality depends on it. A society which had no inhibiting limits ... would be a society without scruples and this nobody wants.'[5]

In 2003, Mary Warnock wrote:

> An absolutely central consideration in the work of the committee . . . was the
> difference between what one might personally think was sensible, or even morally
> right, and what was most likely to be acceptable as a matter of public policy. Time
> and again we found ourselves distinguishing, not between what would be right or
> wrong, but between what would be acceptable or unacceptable.[6]

Mary Warnock defended her approach as the realization that 'the language
of right and wrong was inflammatory'; it was antisocial and 'it sounded arrogant
and provoked conflict'.[7] The 'Warnock strategy' has been described as
substituting an apparently robust regulatory infrastructure for clear moral
principles. It established a precedent, which has continued in Britain, of a very
liberal but highly *regulated* practice of biomedicine and research. This charac-
teristically British approach has been influential internationally, and several
other countries are now adopting the same pragmatic strategy (although the
openness of reproductive policies in the UK has also received trenchant criticism
in some European countries). It reflects a striking trend in modern societies to
convert questions of morality into questions of law. For many modern people
and for modern institutions the really important question is not 'Is this right
or wrong?' but rather 'Is it allowed or not?'

The 1990 Human Fertilisation and Embryology Act set up the Human
Fertilisation and Embryology Authority (HFEA), which reports to Parliament.
It created a complex, bureaucratic procedure for regulating and supervising all
fertility clinics and procedures and embryology laboratories in the UK.
Counselling must be provided prior to treatment and, although single women
could receive fertility treatment, the 1990 Act stated that 'account must be
taken of the welfare of any resulting child' and this should include 'the child's
need of a father'. Surrogate pregnancy arrangements were allowed, but they
were not enforceable in law. Thus the law provided protection for a carrying
mother who entered into a surrogacy arrangement, but then wished to change
her mind during the pregnancy or at the birth of the child. Research on human
embryos was allowed in licensed centres with the consent of the egg and sperm
donors. Research was allowed up to a fourteen-day limit and at that point the
Act stipulated that the embryo must be destroyed. (It was recognized that
the fourteen-day limit was arbitrary, but as the Committee stated in their report
'some precise decision must be taken, in order to allay public anxiety'.)[8]

The legalization of embryo research, including the creation of embryos
especially for the purpose, caused considerable controversy at the time. In the
parliamentary debate, Baroness Warnock spoke strongly in its favour, arguing

that the rejection of research would put the clock back to the seventeenth century, when scientific progress was regulated by religion: ' . . . we must be allowed to take risks when we pursue knowledge, and regulate our lives in accordance with the knowledge we have. We cannot undo the Enlightenment and it would be morally wrong to place obstacles, derived from beliefs that are not widely shared, in the path of science and the practice of medicine.'[9]

Behind the regulation of IVF as a treatment for infertile couples, the Warnock Committee was considering a more wide-reaching possibility. The distinguished embryologist Ann McLaren at University College London, herself a member of the Committee, had published a paper in 1985 discussing the development of embryo biopsy in order to undertake diagnostic tests on the embryo. This technique had been successfully achieved in animal experiments – could it be used in humans for preimplantation genetic diagnosis (PGD)? In 1989, PGD was first successfully carried out at the Hammersmith Hospital in London by Alan Handeyside and Robert Winston. The technique was used to identify female embryos in families with rare X-linked recessive genetic disorders, in order to prevent the birth of a male child who would be severely affected. There is little doubt that the Warnock Committee was concerned to allow embryo research to continue because they were aware of the potential that PGD represented. (We shall look further at the issues which PGD raises in the following chapter.)

The UK legislation represents the most detailed form of governmental supervision of reproductive technology, but many other developed countries have struggled with the ethical and legal implications of IVF and embryo research. Very different stances have resulted. Some European countries such as Austria, Germany and Ireland ban all embryo research. In most developed countries, unlike the UK, the creation of embryos specifically for research is outlawed. In the USA, no formal regulatory authority exists, but there are some restrictions on federal funding for embryo research and some individual states have laws that restrict the creation of human embryos for research purposes.

Since the creation of the HFEA, the range of procedures which are allowed in the UK has steadily extended. PGD has been licensed for the detection of a wide range of conditions, including late-onset adult conditions such as Alzheimer's disease. The screening of embryos to provide matched donors (so-called 'saviour siblings'), and the creation of embryos by nuclear transfer (so-called 'therapeutic cloning'), have been approved. At each stage the HFEA has maintained the Warnock strategy of progressive liberalization in order to maximize opportunities for scientific and medical innovation and medical advance, while allaying social concerns through creating strong regulatory frameworks.

In 2008 the Human Fertilisation and Embryology Bill was passed by Parliament. It enshrined the current practice of the HFEA in primary legislation, and represented a further liberalization of the law. Human-animal hybrid embryos could be created for a range of scientific purposes, the requirement to take account of the child's need for a father was removed, the conditions for which PGD could be employed were extended and the creation of tissue-matched donor children was legalized. In keeping with the need to demonstrate a strict regulatory framework, the Bill is immensely detailed and complex, running to more than 110 pages of text, ranging from the conditions under which licensed premises will be inspected and approved, through to the precise procedures to be adopted if children conceived through the use of donor gametes wish to contact their genetic parents.

One of the most far-reaching features of the 2008 Bill was the implicit redefinition of the legal concept of parenthood. The Bill removed the requirement that clinicians in IVF clinics should take into account 'the need of the child for a father' in making the decision whether or not to give treatment to a woman on her own, or to a woman in a lesbian partnership. Where two women are in a civil partnership, the second woman will automatically become the child's other legal parent on the birth certificate, provided that they have not withheld their consent. The Bill introduced a system of notices (called the 'agreed female parenthood conditions') that should be exchanged between the woman carrying the child and any woman she wishes to be the child's 'second parent' in order to establish the agreement of both parties. There is even provision for the implanted woman to change her mind about who will become the 'parent' before registration of the child's birth.

Where two women have become 'parents', the Bill states that 'no man will be the father of the child'. In other words a child conceived in this way has no possibility of having a legal father. Further complicated procedures have been created to deal with the situation in which an intended female 'parent' dies after the creation of a suitable embryo but before the embryo is implanted into the body of the first woman. The Bill also states that any reference to the 'father' of a child created in this way is to be treated in law as a reference to the female 'second parent'. The Bill creates parallel procedures for single men or those in a male civil partnership where a child is created using a surrogate pregnancy. In such circumstances a nominated male, who need not be the sperm donor, is treated as the legal 'father' of the child.

It has been argued that the Bill represents a remarkable change in the legal understanding of parenthood. It moves away from the traditional view that parenthood is defined primarily by biological relationships, and accepts as normative the view that family structures are a social and legal construct, the consequence of autonomous choice. Within the HFE Bill the 'mother', 'father' or 'parent' of my child is the person I have *chosen* to play that role.

The growing demand for fertility treatments has meant that there is a marked shortage of suitable eggs for the creation of embryos. Many women are infertile because they are unable to produce eggs at all. Some fail to respond to the hormone treatment used in IVF. And other women may be carriers of inherited disorders, such as haemophilia, which are passed on through their eggs.

Several clinics have launched public campaigns to encourage women to become egg donors. As the HFEA has restricted the payments that can be made to individual donors to the sum of £15 plus 'reasonable expenses', the emphasis has been placed on altruistic reasons to become a donor: the primary reason should be to help a childless couple have a baby. Understandably, not many women appear to wish to undergo the invasive, complex and potentially dangerous process of donating eggs. Another approach has been 'egg-sharing' schemes which have become commonplace at many IVF clinics. In return for IVF treatment at a greatly reduced price, women agree to share their eggs with other infertile women who have none of their own. The donor gets IVF treatment at reduced cost or even free. The practice of egg-sharing remains controversial, with accusations that clinics are exploiting couples who cannot afford expensive private IVF treatment. But those who offer the schemes say that without egg-sharing, these women would have no chance of having a baby through IVF.

Recent data from the HFEA indicate that about 2% of all treatment cycles involve egg donation or egg-sharing. With improvements in technology which allow the partner's sperm to be employed, the use of donor sperm in IVF is steadily declining. In 2006 about 4% of all treatment cycles used donor sperm.[10]

In the UK it is prohibited to sell human eggs for commercial gain, but in the USA and some other countries there is a flourishing industry in all aspects of reproductive technology, including egg donation. A brief internet search reveals hundreds of commercial sources for eggs. Egg Donation Inc ('Where dreams come true') is a Californian egg-donation agency. Their website gives extensive details of potential egg donors, including medical history, racial and physical characteristics, personality and leisure interests.[11] At the time of writing the stated total costs of an egg-donation cycle, including psychological screening of the donor, legal representation for both donor and recipient, donor fee and expenses and medical costs of the transfer procedure amount to $40–50,000. The fee the egg donor received was said to range between $6,000 and 15,000. The commercial value of eggs seems to depend on the character-istics of the donor. Apparently, the most highly sought donors are intelligent, tall, slim, blonde and musical! The director of Cryobank, a commercial sperm bank, has also reported that their ideal sperm donor has a college degree, is six feet tall, has brown eyes, blond hair and dimples. This is simply a reflection of market pressure. The director states, 'If our customers wanted high-school dropouts, we would give them high-school dropouts.'[12]

Advances in reproductive technology

When IVF was first conceived by Steptoe and Edwards, it was intended for the use of mothers who had blocked Fallopian tubes, enabling an embryo to bypass the blockage and enter the womb so that implantation and development to maturity might occur. Today, IVF, combined with other forms of reproductive technology, can be used to treat a wide range of fertility problems. If the sperm and egg do not fuse spontaneously, a single live sperm can be picked up using a micromanipulator, and injected directly into the egg cytoplasm under direct vision. This process, called ICSI (intra-cytoplasmic sperm injection), has expanded rapidly following its development in 1992. With ICSI it is possible to overcome infertility due to abnormalities in the concentration and quality of sperm. And by removing primitive developing cells from the testes of infertile men, and injecting their nuclear material into an egg, it is even possible to create a baby using genetic material from men who produce no sperm at all.

The 1990 Act which created the HFEA came into force in 1991. In order to minimize the complications which might result from indefinite storage of embryos, the Act stated that frozen embryos should be stored only for an arbitrary period of five years before they must be discarded. As the five-year deadline approached, on 31 July 1996, there was growing concern at the prospect of deliberately discarding a large number of viable embryos. In response, Parliament amended the Act to allow an extension of fetal storage to ten years, provided that couples gave specific consent. At the time, it was estimated that there were a total of 52,000 frozen embryos in the UK, of which about 9,000 had been created before the Act came into effect and were therefore scheduled for destruction in July 1996 unless the parents could be contacted. The impending destruction of embryos was opposed by a number of groups, and some women volunteered to 'adopt' the embryos, becoming their legal guardians. Despite frantic attempts by fertility clinics to contact couples before the deadline expired, about 650 couples were uncontactable and their embryos were therefore destroyed.

The whole bizarre episode highlighted the confusion and ambiguity in the public response to the existence of thousands of embryos stored in flasks of liquid nitrogen around the country. How can we think of these beings? Are they merely bundles of cells, similar to tissue biopsies from cancerous growths stored in culture medium in a laboratory, or are they people, to whom we owe a duty of care and protection? It is estimated that more than 250,000 embryos have been frozen in the UK since 1990. The number of embryos currently kept in the frozen state increased from 51,000 in 1999 to about 116,000 in 2003. In 2009 the UK regulations were changed to allow frozen embryos to be kept if necessary for up to fifty-five years![13] Are they merely bundles of cells, similar to tissue biopsies from cancerous growths stored in culture medium in a laboratory, or are they embryonic people, beings to whom we owe a duty of care and protection? (See more material on the website.)

Oliver O'Donovan points out that the processes of embryo creation and destruction should not be regarded as the old-fashioned crime of killing babies, but the new and subtle crime of making babies to be ambiguously human, 'of presenting to us members of our own species who are doubtfully proper objects of compassion and love'.[14] (We shall return to the controversial question of how Christians should view the embryo in chapter 7.)

Applications of IVF

Not only does reproductive technology itself cause concern. Equally problematical is the question of who should have access to it. At present the vast majority of IVF treatment cycles are performed for infertile couples who are either married or in a stable relationship. However, liberal Western governments have concluded that they cannot legislate for, or attempt to control, the reproductive liberty of adult individuals. It is not necessary to complete a questionnaire, fill out a registration form or pass a simple examination before embarking on the process of conceiving a child! Even donor insemination is remarkably easy. Lesbian groups, for instance, have circulated self-help information on how to conceive, using a sperm sample donated by an acquaintance and nothing more technologically elaborate than a syringe used for basting turkeys. If human beings are capable of conceiving children naturally for any reason at all or none, on what logical grounds can we restrict the use of modern reproductive technology to those of whom we approve?

One of the most remarkable features of modern reproductive technology is how globalization has encouraged its spread across the world. IVF clinics are found in virtually all countries in the world, including some of the poorest. And in many countries there is little or no regulatory control. In January 2008, the world's media reported the birth of twins to seventy-year-old Omkari Panwar in India. Although Mrs Panwar had adult children, they were all female, and she and her husband were desperate to have a male heir. To pay for the IVF treatment, Omkari's husband sold his buffalos, mortgaged his land, spent his life savings and took out a credit card loan. And it all paid off when Mrs Panwar gave birth to twins – a boy and girl – in hospital in Muzaffarnagar, north of the

Indian capital New Delhi. The Panwars already had two adult daughters, and five grandchildren, but the latest arrivals were what they were waiting for – not least because the son will benefit from a dowry when he marries and will be able to work their land.[15]

Professor Robert Edwards, the pioneer of IVF, has frequently supported the use of IVF in older mothers: 'In the last twenty years attitudes have changed so rapidly. Women are much younger in their later years and the biological evidence suggests the womb is capable of coping with pregnancy in the 50s. It is a cruel evolutionary trick that the ovaries stop producing eggs.'[16]

Reproductive tourism

In 2004 a study of reproductive tourism in Europe was published:[17] 'A country like Belgium, which has no law on assisted reproduction and an abundance of high quality infertility centres, attracts people from all its neighbouring countries and beyond. Patients in need of egg donation or donor sperm are coming over from Germany. Other substantial groups are lesbian couples and single women from France. From the Netherlands come women over 40, donor sperm recipients and couples who want to use surgically obtained sperm for ICSI. In Belgium 30% of women receiving IVF and 60% of recipients for egg donation had travelled from another country. Similar flows of patients exist between other countries.' With the opening of the former Soviet Union the options for reproductive treatments have been extended and several countries such as Ukraine offer egg and sperm donation, surrogacy and embryo adoption with the minimum of legal or regulatory restriction.[18] (See website.)

Parenthood by choice

Reproductive technology allows single women to have children without the need to find a partner. In the USA, the support group Single Mothers by Choice provides information and runs workshops addressing issues such as finding a suitable sperm donor. In the UK, an internet-based organization called *Mannotincluded.com* provided a service until recently, enabling women from around the world to obtain sperm for insemination. The London Women's Clinic website[19] states that it has been treating lesbian couples and single women (using donated sperm) for more than ten years. Over that period the clinic claimed to have helped more than 2,000 single women and lesbian couples to have babies.

Most studies of children born following assisted conception have suggested that they are reassuringly healthy.[20] However, it is estimated that as many as 85% are never informed about their genetic origins and accept the false information perpetrated by their birth certificates. There is increasing awareness that those born following sperm or egg donation may have long-standing psychological distress, and some first-hand accounts have recently been published.[21] Those who discover that they were conceived by anonymous donation may experience a sense of having been deceived, together with 'genetic bewilderment'.

One adult conceived by donor gametes wrote, 'I now live with the absence of knowledge relating to half my medical history, ethnicity and genetic kin. This is preferable and less dangerous than false knowledge, but by no means something that should have been deliberately construed by medical professionals bound by the Hippocratic principle of "do no harm" . . . The contradictions inherent in an industry that seeks to provide maximum genetic continuity for its customers, yet routinely treats the genetic kinship of the offspring and donors as expendable, are blinding.'

'Many people love to talk about their ancestry . . . Yet society is encouraged to turn a blind eye to the inherent discrimination involved in kinship construction and destruction via use of donor gametes. It is a type of empathetic blindness, encouraged and appealed for by the infertile, the fertility industry and its advocates. It is fuelled, not just by the personal convictions of those in the industry, but by that industry's undeniable profits. The donor offspring are made to order, to fit a design; they are the next best thing to having one's own genetic child, and they are presented and objectified as something to which someone else has a right.'[22]

'Just as infertility is grieved, because people grieve the loss of having and raising their own genetic children, so too can that loss be mirrored by not knowing or being raised by one's own genetic parents. Indeed for many, this loss is exacerbated when it is intentionally and institutionally created, unlike infertility.'[23]

'Ninety per cent of couples choose to discard their spare embryos. Surveys show that one reason that so few embryos are donated is that couples attach great significance to genetic parenthood. Why assume that those commissioned into existence would not also attach great significance to genetic parenthood? . . . I know personally what it is like to be experimented on and those who were involved got it wrong . . . To intentionally create life carries with it a grave responsibility. Admittedly there are many who are naturally conceived, and who are also deceived and denied knowledge of their genetic kinship. However, to use the worst-case scenario as a benchmark for setting standards of professional practice, which are then seen as "good enough", is ethically bankrupt. We would not accept standards such as these with other forms of professional practice . . . certainly they would be rejected in the case of adoption, where children's kinship and best interests are paramount.'[24]

In April 2005, following a challenge under human rights legislation, the UK law was changed so that anyone conceived with donated gametes had the right, once they reached the age of eighteen, to request from the HFEA information about the identity of the donor.[25] Understandably, this has led to a reduction in the willingness of some men to act as sperm donors, and in 2006 a survey of fertility clinics in the UK said that almost 70% had difficulty in obtaining suitable donor sperm.

Natural fertility treatments

Although the advance of complex and expensive reproductive technology seems unstoppable, there have been recent developments in the use of so-called 'natural' fertility treatments which can be applied in a primary care setting. These involve teaching women to monitor biomarkers of their own ovulatory cycles, and providing medication with the goal of optimizing the physiological conditions for normal conception to occur. A recent published study of this approach in an Irish general practice found that the rate of live births for those completing a two-year period of treatment was comparable to that obtained with more invasive treatments, including artificial reproductive technology.[26] Although this form of treatment is controversial and currently it is not supported by 'mainstream' fertility clinics, it seems to offer an alternative approach for those troubled by the artificiality and invasiveness of conventional treatments. (See website.)

Having reviewed some of the issues raised by these developments in reproductive technology, in the remainder of this chapter I shall try to develop a Christian response.

Christian perspectives on reproductive technology

Lego kits

As we saw in chapter 1, our bodies used to be the last frontier of the natural world. But the development of reproductive technology seems to have broken for ever this last barrier. We do not have to accept the limitations of our bodies as they have been given to us. By understanding the molecular and biological mechanisms of which our bodies are constructed, we can learn how to manipulate them; we can improve on the Mark I original design. The old technological dream of controlling, mastering and improving on nature, a dream which stems from the period of the Enlightenment, has been extended to the design of the human body itself. This is what I have called the 'Lego kit' view of the human body. To recap: the essence of Lego construction is, first, that there is no internal or 'natural' order to a Lego kit, and secondly, there is no single purpose for which the kit is intended by its designers. From the point of view of the philosophical facts/values distinction, the Lego kit can be viewed as all facts and no values. It is delightfully value-free.

In the same way, because many modern scientists regard the human body as a complex mechanism generated by millions of years of random forces, they regard the structure of the body as essentially value-free. We are liberated from ancient taboos concerned with the dangers of tampering with the natural order. The difference between the 'natural' and the 'artefactual' has been obliterated: we are free to become our own designers.

Even in this technological Utopia, however, some regulation of scientific activities must be applied. There are some fundamental questions which responsible Lego users must ask of any new construction they produce. First, *does it work?* Does it satisfy the purpose which the constructor has imposed? Secondly, *is it safe?* Will the presence of this wonderful new construction adversely affect the constructor or others? Do the advantages and benefits of our construction outweigh its possible risks? As the 'Lego kit' way of thinking has penetrated modern reproductive technology, it is not surprising that these are the dominant questions which are asked, as each advance becomes technically feasible. Already many ethicists have concluded that the only substantial objection to human cloning and asexual reproduction is the potential of physical harm to any children born as a result. In other words, it now seems fairly clear that it will work, but is it safe? Within the mentality of the Lego constructor, there are no other substantive questions to ask.

God's masterpieces

By contrast, as we saw in chapter 2, the Christian worldview takes seriously the concept of the natural order which penetrates both the physical structure of our bodies and the hidden ethical grain of our universe. Our bodies do not come to us as value-free. They are instead wonderful, original artistic masterpieces which reflect the meticulous design and order imposed by a Creator's will and purpose. This concept is amplified and reinforced by the biblical doctrines of the incarnation and resurrection. The original design of human beings is not abandoned, despised or marginalized by God's intervention in the person of the Son: it is affirmed and fulfilled. In the incarnation and resurrection of Christ as a physical human being, God proclaims his vote of confidence in the original created order. If we take the biblical doctrines of the incarnation and resurrection seriously, we must conclude that the physical structure of our human bodies is not something we are free to change without very careful thought.

The flawed masterpiece

We must also, however, take seriously the reality of evil in God's world, the all-pervasive distorting and marring effects of the fall. The original masterpiece, created with such love and embodying such artistry, has become flawed, defaced, and contaminated. But through the imperfections, we can still see the outlines of the original masterpiece. It still inspires a sense of wonder at the underlying design.

What is the responsibility that we owe to this flawed masterpiece? What is our duty as a human community? As we have emphasized, biblical ethics derives from biblical anthropology. If a biblical perspective on human beings views them as flawed masterpieces, then our responsibilities are to act as art preservers and restorers. Our duties are to protect masterpieces from harm, and attempt to restore them in line with the original artist's intentions.

The ethics of art restoration

Just like doctors, responsible and professional art restorers must act according to a code of ethical practice. In an article entitled 'The ethics of conservation', Jonathan Ashley-Smith discusses the principles that should guide the professional restorer.[27] He explicitly draws an analogy between his field and the field of medical ethics: 'To deny the practitioner the right to an ethical viewpoint is like denying the right of the doctor to withhold or prescribe dangerous drugs or denying the surgeon the right to refuse to undertake an unnecessary cosmetic operation.' According to the UK Institution of Conservation Guidelines, 'Conservation is the means whereby the original and true nature of an artistic object is maintained.' The true nature of an object is determined by 'evidence of its origins, its original constitution, the materials of which it is composed and information which it may embody as to its maker's intentions and the technology used in its manufacture'.

So, it is the intention of the original creator or artist which is normative. The restorer must use all the information at his or her disposal – X-ray analysis, historical records, sophisticated chemical tests and so on – to determine the object's original 'constitution', to assess what information the object itself embodies regarding the maker's intention. Only when the original creator's intention is revealed can the restorer decide what form of intervention is appropriate. Unethical restoration is the use of technology to alter, improve or enhance the appearance of the artistic piece. The ethical restorer must refuse any request to enhance the object, even if it means that valuable business is lost.

Art restorers are not free to change or improve the masterpiece as they like. They are not at liberty to improve on the original by adding an extra bit here or there. No, the restorer is free only to operate within the parameters fixed by the artist's original intention. Provided they are operating within these constraints, restorers may decide to employ highly artificial and invasive technology. It may be necessary to replace an area of canvas with an artificial plastic substitute carefully modelled to resemble the original material. It may be necessary to remove the yellowed original varnish and replace it with a sophisticated polyurethane covering. The nature and invasiveness of the technology are less important than the *intentions* of the restorer, to protect and maintain the 'original and true nature of the object'.

Of course, art restoration is only an analogy for the role of the doctor, and like all analogies it has limitations and difficulties. Nevertheless, I believe the analogy is helpful as we try to assess the mind-boggling possibilities raised by reproductive technology. The task of health professionals is to protect and restore the masterpieces entrusted to our care, in line with the original creator's intentions. We must use technology in a way which is appropriate to preserve and protect the original design, to maintain and preserve the creation order embodied in the structure of the human body. However tempting it may be, however spectacular the consequences which might result, we must not resort to unethical restoration. We are not free to improve on the fundamental design. With each new advance in technology, we have to ask the basic question: 'Does the use of this technology allow the artist's intention to be fulfilled, or is it changing the design at a fundamental level?'

Creation design in reproduction

In the original human design, making love and making babies belong together. Let me give a personal illustration. A number of years ago there was a junior doctor called John working in a London hospital. One day he met a stranger, a young lady called Celia, who happened to be a hospital administrator. One thing led to another and we fell in love and got married. Because we were two unique beings, our love was a unique entity, a strange mixture, part of me and part of her, invisible, spiritual, hidden in our hearts. Nobody had seen our love; it was private. And then, after five years, the most bizarre and amazing thing happened. Our invisible love took on physical form. It became flesh in front of our eyes: it became a baby whom we called Jonathan James. The unique combination of John and Celia became a physical reality. In fact, this miracle happened no fewer than three times. As we get to know our children, we recognize ourselves: the child is a bit of me and a bit of her, a unique expression of our love. What is more, if our children go on to have children of their own, the unique combination of John and Celia will be represented in their genes, and the human gene pool will have been permanently altered. Even after John and Celia have gone, their unique love, their unique combination, will be enshrined for ever in the physical stuff of humanity.

Because, in God's design, making love and making babies belong together, genetics is important. DNA is the means by which a unique love between a man and a woman can be converted physically into a baby. Your DNA enshrines, embodies, makes physical, the unique loving combination of your father and mother. Not only that, but your DNA enshrines the countless conjunctions of your ancestors, the myriad love-makings of which you are composed. This is why, for adopted children, the task of tracing their physical parents and genetic roots may be so emotionally significant. Whatever our environment, however we are brought up, we can never escape the reality of our physical structure, the recognition that we are each a unique love-child, created by a unique combination of two unique beings. Our genetic structure expresses in a physical form the web of relationships, out of which each of us has been created and into which we are being brought. To the evolutionary biologist, sex remains something of a mystery.[28] It seems to be a mechanism for increasing the random element in reproduction, shaking the dice in order to create novel combinations of genes and reduce the risk of harmful inbreeding. It seems that, by mingling our genes randomly with other genes, we increase the chances that our own genes might make it to the next generation in a self-replicating body. But, in Christian thought, sex is the way of constructing a unique baby to 'incarnate' a unique love. It is part of the creation order, and so, in theological language, the unitive and the procreative aspects of sex belong together.

But not everybody has been given this gift of making love and making babies. I want to be sensitive to the deep pain of those who long for children and find it impossible; those who long for their love to become incarnate and yet it does not happen. As we have seen, the pain of infertility is an overwhelming reality for many in our society. As a Christian community, we need to learn to empathize, to be more sensitive to the deep, but hidden, pain of childless couples and individuals in our midst.

The idea that making love and making babies belongs together is increasingly counter-cultural in modern technological societies. To most young people today, there seems to be little connection between the two activities. Making love is sex, which is a recreational activity: it's about fun, experimentation, ecstasy. And the goal of sexual health professionals is to make this recreational activity as risk free as possible. But making babies is something altogether different. It's a serious business, a project you need to plan for: choose the best time and the best partner, sign up at the hospital, take your vitamins, act responsibly. But this is not the way it was meant to be. In God's mysterious plan every baby should be a unique love-child, the physical incarnation of a unique union.

Begotten or made?

Although I have used the common phrase 'making babies', there is of course a world of difference between making an artefact, such as a house, and making a baby. In biblical thought, we do not make babies, we beget them. As Oliver O'Donovan pointed out in his London Lectures, *Begotten or Made?*, there is a profound thought which goes back to the Nicene Creed, formulated by the Early Church Fathers. The Son of God was 'begotten, not made'. The wording of the Creed was intended to emphasize that the Son was not part of the creation, but was 'of one substance with the Father'. Our offspring are human beings who share with us a common human nature. In God's design, we do not determine what our offspring are: we receive them as a gift, as beings who are equal with us at a fundamental level, in the same way that the Son is equal in being with the Father. By contrast, that which we make is different from us. It is an artefact and is fundamentally at our disposal, a product of our *will* rather than of our *being*.[29] The danger of reproductive technology is that it subtly reflects and contributes to a change in our relationship to our own children. They become a product of our will, an artefact, a commodity at our disposal.

The implications of reproductive technology

The Roman Catholic tradition of theology has argued that each sexual act should combine these unitive and procreative elements. This is expounded in the document *Humanae Vitae* (1968): 'Because God has given marriage as a gift, he alone orders how the gift is to be used.' There is an 'inseparable connection established by God which man on his own initiative may not break, between the unitive significance and the procreative significance, which are both inherent to the marriage Act ... an act of mutual love which impairs the capacity to transmit life which God the Creator, through specific laws, has built into it, frustrates his design which constitutes the norms of marriage, and contradicts the will of the Author of Life. Hence to use this divine gift while depriving it, even if only partially, of its meaning and purpose, is equally repugnant to the nature of man and woman, strikes at the heart of their relationship and is consequently in opposition to the plan of God and his holy will.'[30]

The same rationale that excluded contraception was later applied to any form of reproductive technology that separated conception from sexual union.[31] Both were seen as unacceptable because they divide these two aspects of sex; every act of sexual intercourse must be 'open' to the possibility of procreation, and no child may be conceived without a specific act of intercourse. It seems hard to defend this position on biblical grounds, and many Protestant theologians have argued that the unitive and procreative aspects of sex need to be held together within a marriage relationship viewed as a whole.[32] Even when there is no attempt at contraception, only a small proportion of the individual acts of intercourse actually lead to the formation of a baby. The whole marriage can be viewed as an extended act which combines the unitive and procreative elements of sex. Sexual union forms an important, but not exclusive, part of the way in which a couple express their relational and procreative natures.

As Brendan McCarthy points out, this perspective may have significant implications for our view of reproductive technology.[33] Just as we may argue that contraception is a method by which human beings use their God-given knowledge to help them to reproduce responsibly, so reproductive technology may be a means of allowing an infertile couple to express the procreative aspect of their marriage, even in the absence of a specific sexual act.

Is reproductive technology consistent with Christian beliefs?

Is it, then, appropriate for couples who are infertile to use the new technology, such as *in vitro* fertilization? We have to ask the question, 'Does the use of this technology allow the artist's intention to be fulfilled, or is it changing the design at a fundamental level?' In my view, IVF which is used to assist an infertile couple to have their own genetically related child may be regarded as a form of restorative technology. It is allowing the couple, in a sense, to bring together what the fall had separated – enabling them to express their love physically, in the form of a child which is genetically their own. Even in the case where husband and wife provide the genetic material, however, there are very real anxieties about whether IVF is an appropriate use of technology. There is the intrusive effect of technology, and the implication that the child is an artefact or commodity created by technology – a product of human planning and ingenuity for the parents' use. There are the genuine risks of serious medical harm to the mother and to the child. There is the problem of what to do with spare embryos. Finally, there is the recognition that *in vitro* fertilization techniques have depended on the employment of many years of embryo research in the past. Even if we do not wish that any embryos we create be used for research, we cannot escape the reality of the countless thousands of human embryos that have been intentionally destroyed in the past, in order to bring the technology to its current state of development. My own conclusion is that IVF may be acceptable for a married couple provided that no spare embryos are created, but that the possible negative consequences need to be very carefully considered before embarking on this course.

With embryo or sperm donation and with surrogacy, the unique genetic and biological link between parents and their children is broken. These procedures break the link between making love and making babies. Some have argued that this is already the case in adoption, which has always been regarded as a Christian alternative. Why should we not regard embryo or sperm donation as merely a form of antenatal adoption? There is a very clear difference, however, between a couple who voluntarily receive an already existing child into their family and a couple who consciously decide to bring into being a child who is at most only partly genetically their own. In the first case, an existing child is offered a good which he or she has previously been denied. Adoption is a redemptive act, a sign of God's grace to the unwanted. In the other case, a child is brought into existence in order to provide a good which has previously been denied to a childless couple.

As we saw from the first-hand accounts above, gamete (embryo or sperm) donation may have far-reaching and unforeseen consequences in family dynamics and relationships. We may generate a profound ambiguity about the identity of the baby. Paradoxically, the ambiguity may be greatest when the child is genetically related to one member of a couple but not to another, for instance in a child born by donor insemination. In this case, as the child develops, it becomes apparent that he or she is half of the mother, but also half of a completely anonymous stranger. This child is not the love-child who reflects our relationship, but rather a strange and hidden hybrid. Unbeknown to the child, this man who acts as father is not the 'real' father – or is he?

Some have argued that sperm donation should be regarded as an act of simple altruism like blood donation. We do not regard a child who has received a blood transfusion as changed in any fundamental way by that process, so why should we not regard sperm donation in the same light? But in my view it is naïve to imagine that blood donation and sperm donation are analogous. In the order of creation, sperm, and the DNA of which they are composed, are the means by which a unique love between a man and a woman can be converted physically into a baby. So the donation of sperm cells carries with it a profound significance which is not conveyed in the transfer of blood cells. I would argue that blood donation can be regarded as a form of technology which preserves the creation order, the integral design of humanity. It is an ethically acceptable form of 'art restoration'. By contrast, gamete donation is a form of technology which changes the design at a fundamental level by changing the relationship between a child and its parents.

Part of the ambiguity inherent in gamete donation is seen in the extreme emphasis which many parents place on the confidentiality of the process. Most couples seem desperately keen to hide the fact of gamete donation from other members of their family and very often from the child themselves. Some will go to extraordinary lengths to ensure that no hint of this information could be released, even sometimes insisting that no mention of the genetic origins of the child be contained in medical records, or conveyed to other health professionals. Why do many parents go to such lengths to conceal the genetic origins of their child even if it involves extensive subterfuge? Is it because they sense that this information will somehow alter family and social perceptions of the child, and the child's perceptions of its parents? We should contrast this with the deep Christian instinct for openness and truthfulness in human relationships, especially within the intimacy and security of a family.

Similarly, surrogacy seems to raise profound ambiguities about an individual child's parenthood: 'Who exactly is my mother?' Brendan McCarthy, in his extremely detailed analysis entitled *Fertility and Faith*, argues that surrogacy may be viewed as an acceptable option for Christians, unlike gamete donation. He claims that, although it is normal for the woman who conceived a baby to continue to provide the environment of nurture and protection for the embryo, the connection between conception and nurture is not an essential one in principle:

> Unlike the connection between the unitive and the procreative aspects of sex, the connection between conception and nurture is a biological necessity. Where this connection is physically unsustainable, no principle is sacrificed if the nurturing element in an embryo's development is transferred to another woman as long as the genetic mother remains the mother of the child . . . It is reasonable to see the dual aspects of sex as a matter of principle, but the connection between conception and nurture as a matter of expediency.[34]

I have to say that I find this argument unconvincing. If we take the creation order seriously, then there seem to be strong reasons to preserve the connection between conception and nurture. The very fact that it is a 'biological necessity' should make us ask why God made us this way. Surely the relationship of loving hospitality between the unborn child and its mother is a part of the creation design, the original artist's intention. In God's creation design, when a mother takes her newborn baby into her arms, she is receiving not a stranger, but a being who has intimately shared her life for the preceding nine months. Already the relationship of security and love is established. In my view, therefore, surrogacy is a technology which is at risk of changing the design at a fundamental level. Is it possible that the overwhelming desire to have a child may drive people to use reproductive technology unwisely? Perhaps, as Christian believers, we should be prepared to turn away from technology which is possible but unwise. Our desires to know, to probe the secrets of our human nature, and to combat disease, are expressions of our God-given freedom, yet sometimes we must be prepared to say no to some of the possibilities of human freedom.[35]

What answer is there, then, for the infertile couple, for whom there is no possibility of a child without recourse to gamete donation or surrogacy? I have no easy solution. What I have to say may seem hard, and will be perceived by some as outrageous, an infringement of autonomy. But in a world which has so many sad, abused, abandoned and disabled children, is it possible that an infertile couple may find an alternative way to fulfil their deep, and God-given, desire for parenthood? Is it possible that by adoption or by fostering, by caring for the unwanted and the rejected in our society, there may be a better way than resorting to reproductive technology with all its risks and ambiguities? I am in no position to criticize those who come to other conclusions. I and my wife have been blessed with the gift of parenthood. How can I possibly empathize with the pain of childlessness? It is not for me to judge those who feel emotionally compelled to embark on the technological approach to making babies. And yet it seems that sometimes God calls individuals, in Oliver O'Donovan's words, to 'accept exclusion from the created good as the necessary price of a true and unqualified witness to it'.[36] By refraining from reproductive technology, a childless couple may bear witness to God's creation order while having to pay the price of exclusion from part of the blessings of that order. As a Christian community, we should learn to recognize and honour the painful sacrifice which such couples make.

In the next chapter we move from the pain of infertility to look at some of the problems which arise once a child is conceived: at developments in fetal screening, in which the unborn baby is tested for congenital abnormalities and diseases.

4. FETAL SCREENING AND THE QUEST FOR A HEALTHY BABY

Although reproductive technology allows infertile parents to exercise choices in the process of conceiving a pregnancy, only a small percentage of all pregnancies are initiated in this way. At present the figure is about 1.5% of all pregnancies in the UK. By contrast, the use of medical technology in screening for fetal abnormalities is now widely practised, leading to a major change in the experience of pregnancy for most parents. In the past, the mother's experience of pregnancy was usually fairly positive. Unless they were considering an abortion, most women looked forward to the coming of a new, mysterious being called a baby, about whom nothing was known. No decisions were necessary at this stage. As the baby grew, the parents' commitment to this individual grew. While everybody knew that some babies would be born with a congenital disability, little or nothing could be done about this. But now technology has irreversibly altered the experience of pregnancy for modern parents.

The purpose of antenatal screening

When a woman tells her doctor that she is pregnant, one of the first questions the doctor will ask is, 'How do you feel about your pregnancy?' In other words, 'Do you really want to have a baby or do you want an abortion?' Right from the start the mother is offered choices. If she wishes to continue the pregnancy, she will be offered a series of screening tests for abnormality in the fetus, depending on her age, family history and local practice. Tests are available for a long list of conditions, and, as genetic knowledge advances, the list is growing almost every week. There are about 4,000 known, simply inherited genetic disorders, and in the foreseeable future nearly all of them will be detectable by genetic screening of the fetus or embryo. Most tests used in medicine are intended to guide treatment, leading to a cure or at least alleviation of a medical condition. In general, doctors have agreed that, if no treatment is available, it is unethical to perform screening tests on apparently healthy people. But the ethical principles governing screening tests in pregnancy are rather different. A few treatments are available, but for the majority of abnormalities there is only one option on offer: abortion. Despite a great deal of interest and sensationalism created by the possibility of gene therapy, at present there are few cures for genetic diseases, and such treatments as are currently available owe very little to the new genetics. Instead, most recent developments have been in genetic testing, providing extremely precise information about the presence of genetic mutations, but offering no practical treatment except abortion for the devastating consequences that may follow. And yet fetal genetic screening is being offered to all pregnant women in the UK. To put it in stark and politically incorrect terms, it is the only form of medicine in which doctors offer to treat a condition by eliminating the patient . . .

Although fetal screening for a range of common conditions, such as Down's syndrome and spina bifida, is being offered to all pregnant women in the UK, more detailed screening is employed in families where there is a particularly high risk of an abnormal child. Parents may have watched a previous child suffer because of a terrible congenital disease such as cystic fibrosis or muscular dystrophy. As genetic testing is now available for many of these conditions, some parents feel that they can risk embarking on a further pregnancy only because they know that there is the possibility of abortion if, tragically, the next fetus is found to be affected by the same condition. At present there are only three widely available techniques which enable fetal cells to be obtained for detailed genetic analysis. Chorionic villus sampling, usually performed before the thirteenth week of gestation, involves the collection of a small sample of tissue from the developing placenta. Amniocentesis, usually performed later on, between the fourteenth and twentieth weeks of pregnancy, entails the sampling of amniotic fluid. In cordocentesis, a sample of fetal blood is obtained directly from the umbilical cord under ultrasound guidance. All are performed relatively late in pregnancy, leading to agonizing decisions about the termination of a comparatively mature fetus. The tests also carry small but significant risks (about 1%) of causing a miscarriage leading to the death of the fetus.[1]

Two techniques currently under development are transforming the clinical practice of fetal screening. They are fetal DNA analysis and pre-implantation genetic diagnosis (PGD). The first involves the isolation of 'free' fetal DNA from a blood sample taken from the pregnant mother. This procedure allows detailed genetic analysis of the fetus, simply by taking a maternal blood sample early in the pregnancy. Its apparent simplicity and lack of risk means that the previous technical barriers to detailed antenatal screening are being dismantled. This technique has already been used to detect the presence of Down's syndrome and other chromosomal abnormalities, and to determine the gender of the unborn baby.[2] Within the UK, fetal sex determination is used in families with X-linked genetic disorders, in whom only male children are affected. But in 2007 controversy was generated by the launch of a private service offering fetal gender testing from the sixth week of pregnancy. International company DNA Worldwide offers analysis of free fetal DNA from a finger-prick sample of the mother's blood. A kit that includes materials to take a blood test at home and send to the laboratories costs from about £200, and parents can check for the results of their test online. Ninety-nine per cent accuracy is claimed for the 'Pink and Blue Early Gender Test'.[3] It seems very likely that the trend for home genetic testing, outside a medical context, will increase.

The other technological advance is in the development of PGD. Following IVF a number of embryos are created (usually between five and fifteen), and a single cell is taken from each embryo for genetic analysis. Those embryos which are found to be free of a particular genetic marker can be identified and then transferred to the carrying mother's womb. The same technique has been used to identify the sex chromosomes carried by each embryo in order to select embryos of the desired gender. In the last twenty years, PGD has advanced rapidly and the HFEA has overseen its extension to the screening of embryos to provide matched donors (so called 'saviour siblings'), and the detection of a wide range of single gene disorders including fragile X syndrome, thalassaemia, hypercholesterolaemia.

A 2006 survey of European centres using PGD found that over 32,000 embryos had been tested by PGD, 7,283 embryos had been transferred, and 993 live babies had resulted.[4] Most controversial has been the use of PGD to eliminate embryos at risk of 'late-onset' disorders such as breast and ovarian cancer, and familial forms of Alzheimer's disease. As we will see below, PGD is also being used increasingly in the USA (and elsewhere) for social sex selection.

PGD is invasive, expensive and time-consuming, and appears to be associated with a small but significant increase in the risk of major malformations.

However it is likely to grow significantly over the next few years, encouraging parents to undergo IVF, not because of infertility, but in order to give themselves the best chance of having a child unaffected by genetic disorders.

Difficult choices

Unfortunately, an initial screening test may not provide the precise answer that is required. Instead, it usually leads on inexorably to further testing. For example, the mother may have a screening blood test for Down's syndrome. The result of this test enables the statistical risk of the syndrome to be calculated precisely. But how should she respond if the risk is increased compared to the general population? For instance, she may be told that there is a one in 200 risk of Down's syndrome, compared with an average risk in the population of approximately one in 2,000. If the risk is greater than an arbitrary value of one in 250, she will probably be offered further testing such as amniocentesis or chorionic villus sampling. This will provide a definitive diagnosis of a chromosomal disorder. Unfortunately, these invasive tests carry a significant risk of causing a spontaneous miscarriage and fetal death. Even in skilful hands the risk in amniocentesis may be as much as one in 100. With chorionic villus sampling the risk may be as high as one in 50. The risk of accidentally causing the death of a healthy fetus may thus be somewhat greater than the risk that the fetus is affected by Down's syndrome (see below). So mothers are confronted with a choice between taking a risk with the life of their unborn baby and coping with uncertainty and anxiety for the remaining months of pregnancy.

The ability to detect genetic markers which show an increased risk of diseases in later life creates particular difficulties. One example is the detection of the BRCA1 and 2 genes which lead to a greatly increased risk of breast and ovarian cancer.[5] With BRCA1 the cumulative risk of breast cancer rises to about 50% at age fifty and 85% at age seventy. One mother who underwent PGD for this condition said, 'It is not that we want a perfect child. But having seen my husband's sister die like this, we could never wish that on a child of our own, knowing about that risk. People say that it's a disease that might never develop, and that it won't develop until your thirties, but that ignores the psychological torment that's with you all your life. Besides, when life expectancy is 80-plus, we don't consider it to be "late-onset" if you die in your early thirties.'[6] So what is the humane and socially responsible choice if the BRCA1 gene is identified in your unborn baby? Is it responsible to bring a child into the world, when they carry such a high risk of devastating diseases?

Growth in antenatal screening tests

The rapid growth in genetic knowledge is likely to mean that in the future, very many people will face similar dilemmas during pregnancy. The very existence of tests for fetal abnormality can create pressures to use the technology.[7] From surveys it is apparent that when women book for antenatal care, most have little appreciation of the possible consequences of screening. In fact, when questioned after delivery, many are not aware that they have received blood tests for fetal screening at all. Although all women are supposed to receive non-directive counselling from health staff prior to fetal screening tests, in one study in a London teaching hospital 27% of women did not know they had received blood tests during pregnancy to detect spina bifida.[8] As the number of genetic tests increases, the problems of providing suitable counselling and information are becoming more intractable. Most parents are initially reassured by knowing that the pregnancy is being monitored, and that if there is anything wrong it will be detected and dealt with. They follow procedures presented to them by doctors and midwives because they wish to do the best for their babies. The fact that antenatal tests are routine means that most people assume that they are medically necessary, appropriate and in their babies' best interest. Although staff are instructed to *offer* screening tests and to ensure that parents are informed about the options that are available, in practice, parents often do not feel able to choose freely. They may not be given the appropriate information, or may not have understood the information which has been provided. The screening tests come with an aura of medical authority and respectability. It is as though someone else has already made the decision about their value and suitability for pregnant women. To decline the tests may seem to be acting irresponsibly, to 'go against medical advice'. Yet obstetric and midwifery staff are aware that it will be considered negligent if they fail to inform women of the availability of screening tests.

Effects of screening on the experience of pregnancy

What then have been the consequences of the widespread availability of antenatal screening on women's perception of pregnancy? Not surprisingly, the overwhelming effect has been one of increased anxiety. For many women, pregnancy has changed from a time of expectation to a time of worry. One study found that 79% of pregnant women were made anxious by the screening tests, and 20% described themselves as very worried or upset. The anxiety often persists even after a test has given a reassuring result, and several studies have confirmed this.[9] Once those terrible fears about fetal abnormality have been raised, it is hard to put them to rest. Several studies have found that levels of anxiety in pregnant women who had been tested and received a reassuring result were no lower than levels of anxiety in women who had received no testing at all. The sociologist B. K. Rothman, author of *The Tentative Pregnancy*,[10] argues that antenatal testing encourages women to view their babies as commodities that may be rejected if found to be substandard. The effect of fetal screening is that many mothers hold back from relating to their fetuses until tests have revealed that the baby is healthy. This is mainly to shield themselves from the pain of having to abort a baby they have come to love, and also because of a feeling that the fetus may be less than perfect. The pregnancy is tentative; some women do not tell anyone they are pregnant until the test results show that everything is all right, sometimes twenty weeks or more into the pregnancy.

Technology, then, has had the paradoxical effect of encouraging a mother to distance herself from the child she carries. Instead of pregnancy being an inseparable attachment, which starts early on and grows throughout nine months, antenatal screening means that the relation of the mother and child now begins with separation and distancing, and moves only later to attachment around the time of birth. Until late in pregnancy, some mothers hold themselves back from full commitment: they retain the option of walking away from their child. Interestingly, researchers have commented that there is no evidence that this understandable strategy does in fact reduce the psychological trauma if the test results are abnormal.[11] Many parents look forward to the first ultrasound scan of their baby. It is the first chance to see their child, an event to be shared with the rest of the family. But what was supposed to be a wonderful experience may not be so. As one woman put it, 'Somehow when you go for a routine scan you can't believe that they'll find something so dreadful.'[12]

Several researchers have pointed out a strange paradox of human psychology. Health staff regard the purpose of antenatal screening tests as the detection of serious fetal abnormality. Thus, when the test picks up an abnormality, this is in some sense a triumph. It is what the test is there for. By contrast, many mothers regard the purpose of antenatal tests as to provide *reassurance* that everything is all right. When the test picks up an abnormality they feel shocked and sometimes cheated, especially if they find that the only 'treatment' that the medical staff have to offer is abortion. One woman expressed her ambivalence about the testing process she had entered. 'If they'd handed her to me and said she was Down's, I'd have been upset but I'd have got on with it; but once you've got into the testing trap you have to get to the end.'[13] 'The testing trap' – I am struck by the bitterness that lies behind those words. While health staff feel they are offering a positive service of genuine benefit to pregnant women, not all women respond with gratitude. A number of women say that they feel pressurized by the system. The National Childbirth Trust performed a survey of mothers' experience of antenatal screening: 10% said that they felt pressurized to have tests and 7% said that they did not feel they had a real choice about whether to have the tests or not.[14]

'I don't think that the test for disability in the unborn child is presented as a choice. When I said I didn't want to be tested, the doctor was shocked and she tried to talk me into it because it's an easy test. Everybody gets it done nowadays. It's simple. But I don't think there is a choice. I think that we're pressurized into taking as many of these tests as are available.'[15]

Psychological consequences of abortion for fetal abnormality

One can easily sense the pain and even desperation that lie behind those words. For many people, the experience of abortion may be less traumatic than for those whose words are quoted above, and many even feel a sense of relief as well as sadness. Yet several studies have shown that abortion for fetal abnormality is associated with a high incidence of depression in both parents, with guilt at being responsible for the decision-making, and loss of self-esteem because of the conception of an abnormal fetus. The highest risk of problems occurred when parents were young or immature, or if there was infertility subsequently.[16] Of course, there is terrible pain when a major malformation is discovered after birth. This too can bring depression and feelings of failure. The experience of caring for a handicapped child may be devastating, and can lead to family break-up, but it seems that the feelings of guilt, self-accusation and sense of responsibility for causing the death of an unborn child are often greater and more prolonged.

'We chose to have an abortion because I know Down's syndrome children can be born with physical as well as mental handicaps and that they can suffer greatly. And we had to look at how we would care for a handicapped child when we were sixty. But I didn't want to accept that part of my decision was selfish, that I didn't want a less-than-perfect child. Then when we went to the parents' support group other couples said they blamed themselves for not being strong enough to deal with an abnormal child. When they said this, it was like a dagger through my heart, because I knew it was true for me, too. I cried for two solid days, but I had to face my guilt. Those feelings are there, and if you don't get them out, they eat away at you. I think about it every day, even just for a second. But life has to go on.'[17]

In a two-year follow-up of couples who had undergone terminations of pregnancies affected by fetal abnormalities, 20% of the women interviewed still experienced regular bouts of crying, sadness and irritability.[18] Fathers may be as deeply affected as mothers. 'One father who, having been through years of infertility, had then aborted a baby with Down's syndrome was deeply shaken. He found it difficult to be around children and gave up some friends and favourite recreational activities because he knew children would be present.'[19]

In Britain, the society ARC (Antenatal Results and Choices) was formed to provide emotional support and counselling for parents facing this experience, and provides a range of literature and information.[20] In families with inherited disorders, the decision whether to abort an affected fetus, when parents already have one living child with the same condition, can be particularly agonizing. Undergoing an abortion on an affected fetus may feel as though one is rejecting the existing child. One parent said that she was not able to accept prenatal testing because she wanted to avoid having to say in effect to her six-year-old disabled son, 'We've got another one like you so we're getting rid of it.'[21] Other parents feel that, having witnessed the suffering of a previously affected child, they have no option but to request an abortion, and feel thankful that they were able to take this route, despite their distress. What about those parents who declined screening and then had to face the reality of bringing up a disabled child? How did other people relate to them? A study in the UK found that 'Geneticists, obstetricians and the general public were more blaming towards mothers who gave birth to a child with Down's syndrome, having declined screening, than they were to mothers who had not received screening.'[22] Some have suggested that mothers who have discovered that their fetus carries a lethal abnormality, such as the severe chromosomal disorder Edwards syndrome, have a duty to obtain an abortion. In his book on genetics at the start of life entitled *The Perfect Baby*, Glen McGee states: 'There can be no question that a couple who find out that their infant is sure to suffer and die incurs special responsibilities, and among those responsibilities may be one to abort. From time to time, genetic testing will suggest a duty to abort.'[23]

Notice that ominous phrase 'a duty to abort'. Over the last thirty years we have moved imperceptibly from abortion as an option in extreme circumstances (an argument based on compassion), through abortion as an option on request (an argument based on female liberation), to a duty to abort (an argument based on social responsibility).

Professional views of genetic screening

But what about the health professionals? What do they feel about the programme of fetal screening? Here is one description of the aims of prenatal diagnosis, given by Professor Marcus Pembrey, a distinguished geneticist:

1. to allow the widest range of informed choice to women and their partners at risk of having a child with a genetic disorder
2. to provide reassurance and reduce the level of anxiety associated with reproduction
3. to allow couples at risk of a genetic disorder to embark upon a family, knowing that, if they wish, they may avoid the birth of seriously affected children through termination of an affected pregnancy
4. to prepare a couple who wish to know in advance that their child is affected in order that they can continue the pregnancy prepared, and to ensure early treatment for the child.[24]

Obstetricians and geneticists draw a sharp distinction between giving people information, and letting them make their own decisions on the basis of the information that has been conveyed. In essence this is a version of the distinction between facts and values which is a feature of much modern philosophical thought (see chapter 11). The duty of the clinician or counsellor is to convey the scientific information about screening – the facts, which are objective, neutral and value-free – without making any recommendation. The individual patient is then free to make up her own mind about the values she wishes to follow – to exercise informed choice, individual autonomy free from coercive influences of any kind. This is the philosophical perspective which lies behind the practice of so-called 'non-directive counselling'. Yet when professionals attempt to counsel non-directively, they are aware of grave difficulties. Many, if not most, patients actively seek directive advice. They are uncomfortable with the liberal concept of unfettered individual freedom and autonomous choices. One of the commonest questions asked of professionals is, 'What would you do in my place?', described as the 'terrible question' by an experienced counsellor. Refusing to give advice may impede the counselling relationship of trust and openness, and is often interpreted by the patient as a lack of care. In some cases a strange struggle ensues, with the patient trying to force professionals to say what their own recommendation would be, and the counsellors desperately trying to 'act professionally' and hence not to reveal their own opinions. Faced with this experience, some have concluded that the whole goal of non-directive counselling is flawed. 'It is questionable whether non-prescriptive counselling is really possible . . . no single story, however balanced, can ever be neutral or value free.'[25] 'So-called non-directive genetic counselling . . . is just as dangerous as paternalistic medicine. The physician is unavoidably engaged in the care of parents and patient, and must work toward disclosing all the information available, including his own opinions.'[26] It seems that the fact/value distinction does not work in practice. It fails to fit with reality – with the way the world and human beings are made.

Most obstetricians and geneticists are strongly in favour of fetal screening with the option of abortion, as they see it as a way of preventing suffering for parents and for children. It is unlikely that the considerable resources that have been allocated to antenatal diagnosis would have been given if the main aim was reassurance or psychological preparation for abnormality. Previous surveys of obstetricians have suggested that the majority favoured termination in a number of severe conditions including spina bifida, Down's syndrome, Huntington's disease and muscular dystrophy, and a minority favoured termination in less severe conditions including cystic fibrosis, sickle-cell anaemia, achondroplasia and haemophilia.[27]

Geneticists recognize that the new technology carries with it 'an enormous potential for the avoidance of serious genetic diseases and congenital malformations', in the words of another distinguished scientist, Professor Sir David Weatherall.[28] For the foreseeable future, however, this potential will be realized only if parents are prepared to have abortions when affected fetuses are detected. And with advances in genetics, many more tests are likely to become available. As the number of genetic disorders that can be detected during pregnancy continues to grow, more and more couples will face decisions about terminating affected pregnancies.

Some doctors say that fetal screening enables the 'prevention' of disability. It is claimed that antenatal screening is just another example of preventative medicine. But this is a novel redefinition of the word 'prevention'. To be strictly accurate, prenatal screening and termination do not prevent disability: they eliminate disabled individuals.

Financial implications of antenatal screening

In many countries, large amounts of money and resources have been directed into making fetal screening widely available. Detailed analysis of screening on health economic grounds have concluded that antenatal screening is 'cost-effective'. For example, a review article of screening for Down's syndrome published in 2005 used a lifetime economic cost of $612,000 per individual in the USA with the syndrome. With different screening methods, the cost per case of Down's syndrome 'averted' ranged between $27,000 and $315,000. Hence the methods were all 'cost effective'. The article also calculated the number of healthy fetuses who would die accidentally as a result of the screening programme. These ranged between 0.5 and 4.4 healthy fetuses for each fetus detected with Down's syndrome.[29] It seems that, as a society, we have accepted that it is morally justifiable to end the lives of several healthy fetuses in order to ensure that one fetus with Down's syndrome does not survive.

Of course, the existence of fetal screening programmes can also lead to expenditure, due to the cost of litigation. In one case, Sandra Hurley success-fully sued her doctors because they did not give her accurate information about her baby's risks of Down's syndrome and the possibility of amniocentesis. In the event, her son Matthew did have the syndrome and Mrs Hurley claimed that the burden of bringing him up led to depression and the break-up of her marriage. Her lawyer told the court: 'She is utterly devoted to Matthew but this cannot obscure or dilute the enormous burdens to her.'[30] The financial sums involved in so-called 'wrongful-life' claims can be huge, as parents can claim for the cost of raising and educating a child who would not have been born but for a doctor's negligence. It seems that, as a result of the promotion of antenatal screening tests, it is now relatively common for parents to blame health profes-sionals when a child is born with a genetic disorder. The 'blame game' may well lead to poorer psychological adjustment, and it has been suggested that the availability of prenatal screening may, therefore, be adversely affecting the adjust-ment necessary for parents caring for affected children. Similarly, antenatal screening employs large amounts of scarce resources, sometimes for question-able gains. One programme for the detection of fetuses with blood diseases such as thalassaemia, after screening no fewer than 18,907 people, detected four affected pregnancies, of which just one was terminated.[31]

Attitudes of disabled people to antenatal screening

In general, the voice of disabled people in our society has been marginal-ized and their views have scarcely reached public attention. But things are changing, and over the last decade a number of eloquent voices from the dis-ability rights movement have outlined a penetrating critique of current screening practices. The issues are complex and nuanced and there is no room in this volume to discuss them in any depth, but I believe listening to the voices of disabled people is of central importance in this debate.[32] (More materials and references are available on the website.)

In brief, disabled people argue from the long history of discrimination and unacknowledged prejudice against people with disabilities. As a result, parents and professionals in the 'normal' social group fail to imagine that people who are disabled can lead lives as rich, complex and worthwhile as their own. It is argued that prenatal testing encourages negative social stereotyping and misconceptions about the lives of disabled people. The very existence of screening programmes expresses discriminatory social and professional attitudes, implying that the lives of disabled people are of less value than those of the healthy, and that they constitute a burden to themselves, to their parents and to the community as a whole. Marsha Saxton puts it like this,

> The message at the heart of prenatal diagnosis is the greatest insult: some of us are 'too flawed' in our very DNA to exist. We are unworthy of being born . . .
> Fighting for this issue, for our right and worthiness to be born, is the fundamental challenge to disability oppression; it underpins our most basic claim to justice and equality – we are indeed worthy to be born, worth the help and expense, and we know it![33]

In particular, disabled activists argue that UK abortion legislation which allows termination of a pregnancy in the case of a risk of disability at any stage up to term, is profoundly discriminatory.[34] The effect of the law is that fetuses beyond twenty-four weeks of gestation are protected from intentional killing, unless they are at risk of disability.

Most health-care professionals working in obstetrics have little first-hand experience of the lives of children and adults with disability. Hence, their understanding of the lives of disabled people is mainly drawn from the medical literature, especially standard medical textbooks. There is a strong tendency for health professionals to list and emphasize the precise medical and functional impairments associated with a particular diagnosis, without a counterbalancing emphasis on the abilities and positive features of the lives of people with the condition. Although health professionals generally try to counsel in a non-directive manner, it is inevitable that their attitudes and prejudices concerning the lives of disabled people will colour the way in which information is communicated. There is accumulating evidence that health professionals consistently undervalue the quality of life of disabled, ex-premature adolescents compared with parents and with the individuals themselves.[35]

Instead of promoting antenatal screening, we should be ensuring better provision of welfare services and financial benefits to parents of disabled children, in order to make it easier for parents to decide to continue such a pregnancy. 'To the extent that prenatal interventions implement social prejudices against people with disabilities they do not expand our reproductive choices. They constrict them.'[36]

In 1987, an author called Christy Nolan won the Whitbread Book of the Year prize for his autobiography *Under the Eye of the Clock*. At the prize-giving ceremony, there in a ballroom in London, surrounded by the glitterati of the literary world, was a young, profoundly disabled man in a wheelchair. He had typed the entire book by means of a pointer attached to his forehead. Because he was unable to speak, his mother read his acceptance speech. This is part of what he said:

> You all must realize that history is in the making. Tonight a crippled man is taking his place on the world literary stage. Tonight is my night for laughing, for crying tears of joy. But wait, my brothers hobble after me hinting. What about silent us? Can we too have a voice? Tonight I am speaking for them . . . Tonight is the happiest night of my life. Imagine what I would have missed if the doctors had not revived me on that September day long ago. Can freedom be denied to handicapped man? Can yessing be so difficult that, rather than give a baby a chance of life, man treads upon his brother and silences him before he can draw one breath of this world's fresh air?'[37]

Increasingly, disabled people perceive fetal screening as a form of social discrimination against them. It is a technological means by which the healthy majority implement social prejudices against the minority with disability. Why should we argue that the life of an individual with Down's syndrome is not worth living, and that such a person represents an excessive 'burden'? Instead of discriminating on the basis of skin colour or country of origin, a discrimination called racism, are we are now guilty of discriminating on the basis of chromosomes: 'chromosomalism'?

These are the words of feminist writer Meg Stacey: 'Tidying away some hereditable diseases will not make society tidy, nor will it eliminate suffering. Has the time perhaps come when it is necessary to revise the scientific goal to one which would work with nature rather than attempting to beat it?'[38]

We shall look at Christian responses to the issues raised by fetal screening in chapter 7, but in the next chapter we will examine in more detail some recent advances in biotechnology, and the opportunities and challenges that they bring.

5. BRAVE NEW WORLD: BIOTECHNOLOGY AND STEM CELLS

Developments in biotechnology over the last ten to twenty years have contributed to a remarkable sense of uncertainty amongst policy makers and so-called opinion formers. There is a sense of being cut loose from familiar ethical moorings, a feeling of unease at the abyss of runaway technological development, coupled with ethical relativism which threatens to swallow us all. If it is technically feasible to generate an unlimited supply of human embryos for research, should we prevent it or encourage it? If it is possible to choose the sex and to enhance the genetic potential of our children, should this be opposed or regulated? If it is possible to create human-animal hybrids or cloned embryos to provide vitally needed human tissue or genetically matched organs for transplant, why should we oppose it? When the potential medical and human benefits are so enormous, what possible grounds can be found to resist?

In this chapter we will look at some recent developments in biotechnology and then ask how Christian thinking can be brought to bear in this rapidly changing field. It is not possible to cover all the developments of the last few years in the space available, but more material is available on the website.

Sex selection

One of the many options which has become available for parents is the selection of the sex of their future child. Philosopher John Harris of Manchester

University has argued neatly that, within a liberal secular worldview, parental choice should be paramount. Parents should be able to choose the sex of their child, rather than leave it to chance: 'Either the sex of your child is morally significant in which case it's much too important to be left to chance, or it's morally insignificant, in which case it doesn't matter if we let parents choose.'

The logic is impeccable. Leaving something as important as the sex of your future child to chance makes no sense at all in a secular universe. It only makes sense in a theistic worldview, where a child can be viewed as a mysterious gift, and not as a product of human planning and ingenuity. And yet several surveys within the UK have demonstrated that the majority of the public are strongly opposed to sex selection, except on strictly medical grounds, where it may be used to avoid sex-linked diseases. Although there are pragmatic reasons to oppose sex selection, such as a possible shift in the balance of males and females in society, it seems that the main reason for this opposition is because choosing the sex of one's child still feels wrong, at least to most of us. It goes against a basic intuition of many in our society. Currently the HFEA is opposed to sex selection for social reasons. But for how long?

Sex selection for social reasons using PGD is now widely available in commercial fertility centres in the US and in many countries across the world. One clinic advertising in the UK introduces its service with the words, 'There are many different medical, social, economic or cultural circumstances which put couples under the most intense pressure to produce a child of a specific gender.'[1] In the USA, surveys suggest that there is an approximate overall balance between the numbers of males and females who are selected. However, there is a strong tendency for parents to select a male for their first born.

Of course, sex selection using PGD is a high-tech version of a process which has been going on for thousands of years. There are many people across the world who are under 'the most intense pressure to produce babies of a specific gender'. In 1990, the economist Amartya Sen estimated the number of 'missing women' worldwide, lost to neglect, infanticide, and sex-specific abortions, at one hundred million.[2] In India, pregnant women are often forced by relatives to undergo antenatal tests such as high-resolution ultrasound scanning or even amniocentesis to identify the sex of their fetus. If it is found to be female, an abortion is performed. In Punjab state, selective abortion has led to the lowest sex ratio in India, with 776 girls for every 1,000 boys up to the age of six years. Although sex selection is technically illegal, it appears that tens of thousands of females are covertly aborted every year in a highly profitable commercial operation. A local journalist said, 'Although everyone is aware this is illegal, most people do not think anything about aborting a female child and trying again for a boy ... Female <u>feticide</u> is rampant in all the small towns here. Most nursing homes do such work at night and everybody – the police, the health authorities and the civil administration – knows this is happening.'[3] The main forces behind this practice were said to be 'intensely patriarchal attitudes', combined with the dowry system. Another commentator said, 'Girls are seen as an economic burden by parents because they need a dowry for marriage. They are also seen as a potential embarrassment because they are vulnerable to sexual harassment.'

There are now large numbers of South Asians living in European and North American countries, and sex selection ads in newspapers for Indian groups have specifically targeted them. South Asian feminists in these communities fear that sex selection could take new hold among immigrants who retain a preference for sons. They decry the numerous ways it reinforces and exacerbates misogyny, including violence against women who fail to give birth to boys. If the selection of boys is unacceptable in South Asia (and elsewhere), should it be allowed among Asian communities in the West?

In 1994 a black woman in Italy received an embryo created from white sperm and egg donors because she wanted to have a white child, which she felt would be free from the prejudice a black child would face. Although many opposed this practice, John Harris defended it on the grounds of individual autonomy. 'Previously people have got gametes from their procreational partners and that's been treated as the norm. Technology has given us the power to change that.' For Harris, the key issue is the right to choose. After all, he points out, when people request gametes of the same race they are making a race choice: 'It seems suspect that when people choose the same race gamete they are not choosing the race of their child. Why should it be more problematic to choose a different race gamete?'[4]

Embryo selection of desirable characteristics

At present PGD with embryo selection is mainly restricted to the detection of childhood diseases, such as sickle-cell anaemia or cystic fibrosis, that are regarded as having a severe and immediate impact on life. However, increasingly, PGD is being extended to late-onset disorders, and in the future it may be possible to detect genetic variants that have a less severe impact on a child's life, such as predispositions to obesity, diabetes, heart disease, asthma and various forms of cancer.[5] It seems likely that genetic variations which increase resistance to infective diseases will also be identified. The identification and modification of genes which may predispose to 'socially desirable characteristics' is much more speculative and still belongs to the wilder reaches of science fiction. However, the speed of progress in molecular genetics and reproductive technology is enough to dispel complacency.

A distinction is commonly made between *negative* selection, against embryos which carry genetic variations likely to cause a disease, and *positive* selection, in favour of embryos which are found to carry genetic variations which are socially desirable. In reality, the distinction is less clear than it seems at first. If we choose not to select an embryo with a genotype likely to cause a disease, should we refuse to select an embryo with a genotype who will be an unaffected carrier of the disease, but who may pass it on to any future offspring? Should we select for a genetic variation which is found to be associated with a *reduced* risk of disease compared with the general population. Of all the embryos available, surely it would be rational to select the ones that have the least risk of disease, and the best chance of future well-being.

Some have predicted that embryo selection is here to stay, at least in American society, where the majority 'hold fast to the overriding importance of personal liberty and personal fortune in guiding what individuals are allowed and able to do'. Although embryo selection is currently used by a tiny fraction of prospective parents to screen for a tiny number of disease genotypes,

> with each coming year, the power of the technology will expand, and its application will become more efficient. Slowly but surely, embryo selection will be incorporated into American culture, just as other reproductive technologies have been in the past . . . Environment and genes stand side by side. Both contribute to a child's chances for achievement and success in life, although neither guarantees it. If we allow money to buy an advantage in one, the claim for stopping the other is hard to make, especially in a society that gives women the right to abort for any reason at all.[6]

Cloning and nuclear transfer

On 23 February 1997, the news of the creation of Dolly the sheep transfixed the world media and the scientific community alike. Dolly was created using DNA taken from a cell-line cultured from a mammary gland cell from an adult sheep. The nuclear material was transferred into an unfertilized egg from which the original nucleus had been removed. The newly created embryo was then inserted into the uterus of another sheep where it grew into Dolly – whose genetic structure was identical to the original sheep from whom the mammary gland cell was taken.[7] Although cloning using cells from embryos had been reported previously, the scientific community was surprised and even shocked that it was possible to use nuclear material from an adult cell.

Commentators and ethicists seized on the possibility that the same procedure could be undertaken in humans. It was not a new idea. Aldous Huxley, in his novel *Brave New World*, had introduced the concept to a mass audience: 'Bokanovsky's Process ... one egg, one embryo, one adult – normality. But a bokanovskified egg will bud, will proliferate, will divide. From eight to ninety-six buds, and every bud will grow into a perfectly formed embryo, and every embryo into a full-sized adult. Making ninety-six human beings grow where only one grew before. Progress.'[8] In 1970 Alvin Toffler produced his influential book, *Future Shock*, which predicted, 'One of the more fantastic possibilities is that man will be able to make biological copies of himself ... Cloning would make it possible for people to see themselves anew, to fill the world with twins of themselves.'[9] Woody Allen brilliantly parodied the idea in his movie *Sleeper*, where a surgeon, transported 200 years into the future, is given the task of cloning the recently deceased leader from his nose, which had been kept alive for the purpose. Ira Levin's *The Boys from Brazil* was based on the use of cloning in a conspiracy aimed at duplicating an army of neo-Nazi thugs.

Therapeutic or research cloning

Where the dystopic visions of Huxley and Levin are misleading is that the technology is unlikely to be used in the foreseeable future by totalitarian governments or neo-Nazi dictators. Instead, the demand for human cloning has come from the strictly medical arena. The 2008 HFE Act has upheld the legality of 'therapeutic' or 'research' cloning – the generation of cloned human embryos for research purposes within the UK. The aim is to research the mechanisms of human diseases leading ultimately to the development of new embryonic stem cell therapies. The Act prohibits embryonic development beyond the fourteen-day stage, although the rational justification for this limit is unclear.

Genetically matched stem cells offer the prospect of remarkable new treatments for a range of medical diseases. Blood, skin, muscle, and brain cells could be grown in the laboratory and implanted without the need for anti-rejection treatment. If we are prepared to accept the generation, manipulation and destruction of large numbers of human embryos, we may have access to an unparalleled range of new treatments for inherited, degenerative and cancerous diseases.

Another suggested use of nuclear transfer techniques is to prevent the inheritance of rare disorders (affecting a component of the cell known as the mitochondria) which are passed on in the cytoplasm of the mother's egg. If the nuclear DNA from the mother was inserted into a donor egg from which the nucleus had been removed, followed by IVF, it would be possible for the mother to have a genetically related child without the risk of mitochondrial disease being passed on to the next generation.

Reproductive cloning

Reproductive cloning also carries the possibility of medical benefit. For instance, the success of bone marrow transplantation for leukaemia depends critically on the availability of a genetically matched donor. Sometimes, when bone marrow transplant remains the only hope of treatment, a prolonged search of related and unrelated donors fails to find a suitable match, condemning the leukaemia sufferer to death, without the prospect of a cure. The cloning of a child from genetic material taken from the leukaemia sufferer would provide a genetically matched donor for a bone marrow transplant. Is it wrong for a couple to use reproductive technology to have a second child who will not only be loved for themselves, but will also have the capability of saving their first child's life? Informal surveys conducted by organ transplantation centres suggest that it is not unheard of for couples to have another child by normal means, in order to act as a potential donor for an older sibling, although this is rarely acknowledged in public.[10] The availability of cloning would enable parents to reproduce knowing that an exact genetic match would result.

A third possible scenario is that of the mother who, after giving birth to a baby, receives chemotherapy for cancer which means that she becomes permanently sterile. If her baby were then to die, cloning from cells taken before or even after the baby's death would enable her to have another child who was still genetically her own.

Cloning might even allow lesbian couples to share biological parentage of a child, and avoid introducing alien genes into their relationship. One member of the couple could provide the donor cell, and the other could provide the unfertilized recipient egg. The newly formed embryo could then be introduced into the uterus of the second woman, allowing the child to be biologically related to both women.

Although reproductive cloning is illegal in most countries, there are persistent reports that it is being attempted. The equipment and facilities are standard in laboratories and assisted conception clinics around the world. There are thousands of professionals who possess the necessary skills to undertake the procedures. In April 2009, an American fertility expert, Dr Panayiotis Zavos, claimed that he had undertaken attempts at human cloning in four individuals, using a secret laboratory. 'To date we have had over 100 enquiries and every enquiry is serious ... [they] consider human reproductive cloning as the only option available to them after they have exhausted everything else.' Dr Zavos also claimed that he had produced cloned embryos of three people who had died, including a ten-year-old child.[11] From a utilitarian viewpoint, the only rational argument against reproductive cloning appears to be uncertainty about the safety of the procedure.

Regenerative medicine and embryonic stem cells

Rapid advances in stem cell biology have underpinned the development of regenerative medicine, a new medical speciality. A 2008 review paper in the medical journal, *The Journal of the American Medical Association* (*JAMA*), listed 323 published scientific reports on stem cell therapies between 1997 and 2007.[12] Already, more than seventy different therapeutic approaches using stem cells have been trialled in human patients, and several, such as bone marrow transplantation, are now a matter of routine. All the clinical approaches to date have employed so-called 'adult' stem cells, obtained from a range of sites, including bone marrow, skin fibroblast cells or umbilical cord blood. Recently, cells derived from adult skin have been shown to be capable of providing a wide range of different types of stem cells with remarkable therapeutic potential. In contrast, stem cells derived from human embryos have provided no proven therapies to date, and it seems it may be many years before any viable treatment becomes feasible.

Yet in the UK there has been a sustained scientific and media campaign to remove any restrictions from research on stem cells obtained from human embryos. The argument has been that without embryonic stem cell research, treatments for incurable conditions will never be possible. On the eve of the parliamentary vote about the HFE Bill in May 2008, the Prime Minister Gordon Brown gave an emotional appeal to support the use of embryonic stem cell research, claiming it would ' ... save and transform millions of lives'.[13] Similarly, the UK government has strongly defended and supported the creation of a range of human and animal hybrid embryos, to derive stem cells for potential therapies, despite serious concerns about the practicality, safety and ethics of this approach.

Behind the scenes, a loose coalition of academic scientists, politicians, commercial biotechnology companies and journalists has mounted a highly successful public campaign for the liberalization of UK laws. Their efforts have

led to the UK adopting arguably the most liberal legislative framework on reproductive and embryo technology in the world.

Saviour siblings

A recurring theme in the history of ethics is the sanitization and corruption of
language which frequently precedes and justifies the introduction of morally
questionable acitivities. The newly coined phrase 'saviour sibling' is a striking
example. It seems so noble, so virtuous, so transparently worthwhile. Yet the
reality is more ambiguous. The case of Zain Hashmi (in the Introduction) highlights the desperation which leads parents to attempt to create a sibling who
will act as a tissue donor. But what about the child that is created to be a donor?
We have all agreed that adults should never be coerced to become donors. They
offer their organs and tissue voluntarily as an act of compassion and solidarity.
But the child that is created to be a tissue donor has no choice. If bone marrow
donation is required, he or she may be forced to undergo repeated painful, and
potentially dangerous, procedures. The novel, *My Sister's Keeper*, by Jodi Picoult
gives a fictional and striking account of the family conflict and trauma which
the creation of a 'saviour sibling' might bring.[14] Perhaps 'forced donor creation'
is a more accurate phrase.

The new biotechnology has enormous potential for bringing health benefits
to all human beings. But it always carries within it the ominous potential for the
manipulation and instrumentalization of vulnerable human beings. In the
prescient words of C. S. Lewis written in 1948, 'Man's power over Nature turns
out to be power exerted by some men over other men.'[15]

So is there no ethical alternative to the creation of donor children? Well, yes
there is. It is likely that the Hashmis could not find a matched bone marrow
tissue donor for their son because few donors from their racial group have been
tested and registered. The answer is the development and encouragement of
large international donor registries, using adult volunteers from all ethnic and
racial groups, which will greatly increase the chances that a suitable donor will
be found. (Other issues of biotechnology including gene therapy and human-
animal hybrids are discussed on the website.)

Public acceptability of genetic technology

Many scientists believe, in private, that there will be a gradual acceptance of
human genetic selection and manipulation by the community as a whole. They

point to the initial media furore and ethical disquiet that has greeted many advances in medical technology over the last forty years. In 1966, two American reproductive specialists wrote presciently about fertility treatments: 'Any change in custom or practice in this emotionally charged area has always elicited a response from established custom and law: horrified negation at first; then negation without horror; then slow and gradual curiosity, study, evaluation, and finally a very slow but steady acceptance.'[16] Many scientists believe that the main role of official bodies, such as the Human Fertilisation and Embryology Authority, is to gauge the public mood and ensure that approved activities remain within broad limits of public acceptability. As one IVF clinician put it, 'I think ethics is what the public is comfortable with.'

At the same time, it may be argued that, ultimately, governmental control of reproductive technology is doomed to failure. Small clinics can be set up in any part of the world, including off-shore islands. Many people in our society have an overwhelming desire to raise healthy children, and in a free-market economy, the financial rewards that are available for those who satisfy that desire are enormous. As Silver puts it, 'If there are people who desire reprogenetic services, there will be others willing to provide them ... Whether we like it or not, the global marketplace will reign supreme.'

Promises and dangers of the new biotechnology

Even if we penetrate the hyperbole, there is no doubt that the new biotechnology offers real promises for the future. There is the possibility of new biological insights which will have far-reaching consequences for medicine. By understanding the complex links between genetic variations and the complete range of human diseases, scientists are already discovering new insights which are likely to lead to completely new medical treatments. Gene therapy, despite disappointing results so far, clearly has great potential for the future, and genetic analysis may enable genetically vulnerable individuals to be identified early in life, so that exposure to damaging environmental factors can be avoided. Stem cell therapies using non-embryonic sources are already bringing new hope for sufferers from incurable diseases, and will undoubtedly make an increasing contribution to medicine in the future.

But, at the same time, there is a dark side to this technology. Widespread use of genetic screening is likely to lead to increased stigmatization of genetically abnormal individuals. In the past, medicine has been limited in both diagnostic precision as well as therapeutic possibilities. What new genetic understanding is starting to provide is a very much more precise means of predicting the future, while the possibility of any specific treatment remains many years away. For some individuals, the ability to predict the future may be a curse as much as a blessing. The identification of a genetic mutation may mean that an individual is unable to obtain a job, purchase life or health insurance, obtain a mortgage, or find a marriage partner. Increased antenatal screening may lead to loss of respect and victimization of the disabled and their parents. The use of genetic techniques to select and enhance embryos may encourage parents to regard their children as commodities. Commercial exploitation of genetic information will allow large multinational corporations to exert enormous financial pressures on individuals and on health-care systems, including the National Health Service. Biotechnology may concentrate limited resources on the diseases of wealthy groups, and divert resources away from low-tech solutions to the diseases associated with poverty and deprivation. Finally, unscrupulous politicians and dictators may be tempted to use the technology to increase control over their people, engage in eugenic social engineering, or even use genetic 'bombs' to wipe out unwanted racial groups.

Christian responses

How can we respond to these issues from the perspective of the Christian worldview? I have no neat solutions or obvious panaceas to the challenges and questions raised by advances in biotechnology. We need to struggle together as a Christian community to try to understand more clearly the rapid changes which are occurring in our midst, and to try to discern how to respond from a position of Christian faith.

What are the fundamental principles which should inform our thinking and our practice? As we try to think Christianly about developments in genetics, we must steer between two fallacies. On the one hand there is the fallacy of *genetic determinism*. This is the popular fallacy of the simplistic biological reductionist. According to this view, genetics explains everything. I am programmed by my genes as a computer is programmed by its software. Everything I am, everything I do, is determined, a product of an immutable genetic code which was randomly generated at my conception. This attitude is encouraged by much of the sensationalism generated by the media, and by some of the genetics industry itself. The implication is that detailed genetic analysis and the introduction of gene therapy will usher in a new age of health, wisdom and benevolence. Similarly, much of the shock-horror publicity about advances in genetics encourages a popular belief in genetic determinism. It implies that, once scientists have unravelled the entire human genome, they will have insight into all the mysteries of the human condition, and will be able to control and manipulate human beings at will. The furore generated about the possibility of human cloning is another example. At the time that Dolly's birth was announced, a number of journalists and commentators speculated that, if a genetically identical individual was created in this way, it might not be a real human being and would have no 'soul'. Again this is nonsense. Identical twins conceived naturally are 'clones', and yet no-one would suggest that they are any less than human because of the existence of their identical twin.

The truth is that genetic determinism is both scientific rubbish and spiritual idolatry. Human beings are far greater than the product of their genes. At a physical and psychological level, we are formed continuously by the interaction between our physical and genetic structure, and the constantly changing environment to which we are exposed. At a spiritual level, we have a unique relationship with God who calls us into existence and into relationship with him.

The opposite fallacy is that of *philosophical dualism* which says that my physical body and structure is of no importance compared to the real me, the immaterial thinking mind and spirit. My genetic structure is irrelevant to my identity. I am free to manipulate the physical structure of my body and its genetic code at will because my identity is defined by my mind, or by my relationship with God. Dualism has obvious attraction for biological scientists and doctors. It allows us to participate in biological research, or in reproductive and other forms of biotechnology, without having to be too concerned about the spiritual consequences. After all, biological science and medicine only deal with the physical stuff of humanity, whereas the true identity and value of human beings is in their relationship with God.

But dualism, like determinism, is based on a fallacy, on a false view of reality. Orthodox Christian thought has always affirmed that in the complex and mysterious unity which constitutes the human person, *both* the physical structure of my body *and* the immaterial spiritual aspects of my being are important and inextricably intertwined. The givenness of my genetic inheritance, expressing in a physical form the web of relationships into which I have been born, is as much a part of my identity as my mind and my personality. Yes, the body does matter and, yes, my genetic heritage is important in determining my identity, but no, I am not merely programmed. The human self, known and loved by others and by God himself, is greater than my genes.

So, if my genetic inheritance is important, how should we think about medical treatments which manipulate the genetic code? Within the perspective of medicine as art restoration, is gene therapy an appropriate form of technology for 'flawed masterpieces'? In my view, genetic manipulation which is intended to be *restorative*, recreating a damaged length of DNA, or replacing an abnormal gene variant with a normal counterpart, seems consistent with normal medical practice. The aim is to preserve and restore the original artist's design. There seems to be no fundamental difference between providing artificial thyroid hormone for a patient with congenital hypothyroidism and replacing a segment of DNA with a new portion, so that the patient is able to synthesize their own thyroid hormone. Both actions are aimed at preserving the original design. However, therapy which is intended to be *enhancing*, aimed at providing children who have stronger limbs, better growth, happier personalities and quicker brains, seems to me to step over the limits of human responsibility. Enhancing gene therapy is the attempt to improve on the original design. But Christians must take creation order seriously. Within ethical art restoration, the intention of the original artist must be normative.

Of course, the distinction between restorative and enhancing therapy is not always clear-cut. What about gene therapy which is intended to lead to an improved resistance to infectious diseases, such as HIV infection? What about enhancement of cellular repair mechanisms which will prolong human lifespan maybe to 120 years and beyond? What about psychoactive medication which improves concentration, vigilance or memory well above normal level? Should these be regarded as therapies that are restoring the original design, or do they represent a fundamental change? Because of the impact of new biotechnology, we need to reflect more deeply on the natural order given at creation. What does it mean to be human? What are the limits which are laid down by the givenness of our creation?

Similarly, the selection of embryos, to choose the sex or the genetic makeup of a child, seems fraught with problems. In the original creation order, a child can be seen as a gift, a mysterious other who is equal to us in status and significance. But with embryo testing and selection, our child becomes a commodity, the one we have chosen, the one which reflects our wishes and desires. To me this seems to change the nature of parenthood. It is to surrender to the controlling spirit of the age. William May has drawn a helpful distinction between two aspects of parental love – accepting love and transforming love.[17] Parents are called both to accept the child they have been given, while at the same time encouraging and supporting them to develop and transform into something greater. There is always a creative tension between accepting and transforming love. (For Christians there is a fascinating parallel here with the fatherly actions of God in our own lives.) But modern parents are in danger of being control freaks. Transforming love has overwhelmed acceptance. We want to control and design our children to fulfil our deepest desires. Maybe we want to live out unfulfilled expectations in them. But a biblical perception of parenthood teaches us that we must let go. Although we have a responsibility to protect, nurture and educate, we must *respect* our children as mysterious others, those who are equal to ourselves at a fundamental level. In the words of Gilbert Meilaender, 'We are very reluctant to let the mystery of personhood – equal in dignity to our own – unfold in the lives of our children.' Instead, 'We need the virtue of humility before the mystery of human personhood and the succession of generations. We need the realisation that the children who come after us are not simply a product for us to mould.'[18]

As Christians we are called to empathize with the human suffering caused by devastating genetic diseases and chronic degenerative conditions. It is the reality of this pain and the quest for technological solutions which drives much of the research and development in the new biotechnology. So often, it is the failure of practical caring in our society which seems to drive a desperate quest for technological fixes to the painful realities of the human condition.

At the same time, as a Christian community, we must challenge the reductionist mentality which is starting to pervade modern society and the health-care systems within it. We need to oppose and inform the naive and dangerous concepts of biological and genetic determinism which are sometimes perpetrated by popular science and by the media. At a social level, we need to challenge the economic and political power base which the new biotechnology is creating, and demand democratic accountability, transparency, and justice in the actions of those who control the technology. There are hidden vested interests and power plays which rarely come under public scrutiny. Some of the scientists and technologists who have vociferously promoted the use of stem cell therapies as a life-saving solution have extensive investments and personal financial interests in the exploitation of the technology, but these obvious conflicts of interest have not been exposed or scrutinized.

Finally, and perhaps most importantly, I passionately believe that, as a Christian community, we need to demonstrate the reality of our belief in the value and dignity of every human life, by practising and encouraging the highest possible standards of practical, respectful caring for those whose lives are blighted by incurable diseases. There is a recurring theme here. It is often because of the failure of practical caring that desperate people feel driven to consider unethical solutions. It is because of our failure to provide adequate care for disabled people that pregnant mothers feel such pressure to abort their unborn baby who has a disabling condition, or to undergo PGD. It is because of our failure to care for dying people adequately that people feel driven to ask for euthanasia.

We will return to these themes in later chapters, but first, we turn from the ethical dilemmas raised by recent biotechnology advances to the painful issue of the unwanted pregnancy and the ancient ethical debate about abortion and infanticide.

6. ABORTION AND INFANTICIDE: A HISTORICAL PERSPECTIVE

At first glance, abortion (the intentional termination of pregnancy with the destruction of a fetus) and infanticide (the intentional killing of a newborn baby) seem starkly different. Yet, as we shall see, on both historical and ethical grounds, they belong together. Our aim in this chapter is to look first at the ancient history of abortion and infanticide, and secondly to review the contemporary scene.[1]

Abortion and infanticide in the ancient world

'If you don't know where you are going,' Archbishop William Temple once said, 'it is sometimes helpful to know where you have been.'[2] As moderns, we tend to imagine that our problems are unique to our generation. Yet the debate about abortion and infanticide is an ancient one in the history of Western civilization, and in the history of the Christian church. By delving into some musty history, we may gain a fresh perspective on the debate which is still raging.

Both abortion and infanticide have been common practices since the earliest records of human history. Far from being confined to primitive, unsophisticated communities, both were well known in the cosmopolitan and advanced civilizations of Ancient Greece and Rome.[3] In the city states of Greece and throughout the Roman Republic, abortion was widely available. It was a service provided by both professional and amateur abortionists, and by some physicians. The methods included manipulation of the abdomen and uterus, herbal medications given by vaginal pessaries or by mouth, and a range of surgical techniques using tools specially designed for the purpose.

In most regions, abortions were readily available, although at a price. They were thus more common amongst wealthy women than among the poor. Probably the commonest reason for obtaining an abortion was so that a woman might conceal illicit sexual activity, but it is well attested that wealthy women would obtain abortions, merely to preserve their figures and their sexual attractiveness.[4]

The practice of abortion was endorsed by many prominent philosophers and writers. In discussing the role of women in his ideal *Republic*, Plato stated forcefully that women should have an abortion above the age of forty years, presumably because of an increased risk of maternal death and fetal abnormality. Aristotle, in his work *Politics*, recommended both infanticide and abortion if there was a risk of a 'deformed child', or an excess number of existing children in a family. He recognized, however, that infanticide by exposure of normal children might not be acceptable in certain regions, and therefore recommended an abortion in these cases:

> On the ground of number of children, if the regular customs hinder any of those born being exposed, there must be a limit fixed to the procreation of offspring, and if any people have a child as a result of intercourse in contravention of these regulations, abortion must be practised on it before it has developed sensation and life: for the line between lawful and unlawful abortion will be marked by the fact of having sensation and being alive.[5]

A major concern of the leaders of Greek city states was overpopulation leading to famine and social breakdown. Both abortion and infanticide were seen as entirely rational and reasonable approaches to this danger. The attitudes to babies and children within the classical Graeco-Roman world were startlingly different from our own.[6] Contemporary Graeco-Roman society was fundamentally hierarchical. At the top of the pile were the elite: politicians, philosophers, athletes. Next down were ordinary decent working people: farmers, soldiers, tradespeople. Further down were women. And then there was the riff-raff: children, slaves, the disabled, the leper, and other undesirables. It was a society that prized athleticism, strength, and what were called 'the masculine virtues', so it was natural for children to be despised because of their weakness, dependence and immaturity. The significance and worth that society tended to place on an individual child was in proportion to his or her future contribution to the state as an adult.

Like abortion, the intentional killing of malformed or unwanted newborn babies, by exposure, strangling or drowning, was a widespread practice. In fact, the practice was so common that one contemporary historian, Polybius, writing in the second century BC, concluded that it had contributed to the serious depopulation that had occurred in Greece at the time. There were no laws prohibiting the killing of malformed or sick infants, and even healthy newborn babies were frequently unprotected by legal statute or social custom. Infanticide was such a natural and common event that it is mentioned frequently in comedies and plays of the period.[7]

It seems that the majority of philosophers and writers of the period supported both abortion and infanticide. In Plato's *Republic* infanticide is regarded as essential to maintain the quality of the citizens: 'The offspring of the inferior and any of those of the other sort who are born defective, they will properly dispose of in secret, so that no one will know what has become of them.' For Plato, children were valued according to their approximation to the ideal adult. They must be 'malleable, disposed to virtue and physically fit'.

Aristotle supported a law to ensure the compulsory exposure of all malformed babies: 'As to exposing or rearing the children born let there be a law that no deformed child shall be reared.' Seneca, in his treatise *On Anger*, wrote, 'Mad dogs we knock on the head; the fierce and savage ox we slay; unnatural progeny we destroy; we drown even children who at birth are weakly and abnormal. Yet it is not anger, but reason that separates the harmful from the sound.'

In the Roman republic, power was enshrined in the head of the family, the *paterfamilias*. He had, quite literally, the power of life and death over all his lawful possessions, in other words his slaves, children and wife. The earliest Roman law code permitted a father to expose any female infant he wished, and a deformed baby of either sex. Interestingly, abortion came under greater official disapproval than infanticide. This was probably partly because it involved a risk to the mother's life and health, but also because it allowed married women to commit adultery without being discovered by their husbands, and perhaps because it was common practice of professional prostitutes. The secret performance of an abortion on a woman without the knowledge of her husband was viewed as a major offence against the 'property' of the husband. Nevertheless, abortion was extremely common in Rome and its dependent states from the first century BC onwards. Handbooks on techniques for abortion circulated quite freely.

Within the orthodox medical world, gynaecology developed as a separate discipline and a number of female physicians specialized in this art. Soranus, a Roman physician in the first and second centuries AD, wrote the earliest known treatise on gynaecology, which has been recently reprinted.[8] He maintained that abortion was improper to conceal adultery or to maintain feminine beauty, but that it was permissible to save the woman's life. He also included a chapter entitled 'How to Recognise the Newborn That is Worth Rearing'. In it Soranus gives practical advice for midwives on the assessment of newborn babies immediately following delivery. First, the mother's health during pregnancy should be assessed, together with the gestational age of the infant. Subsequently, the newborn baby is examined to see if 'when put on the earth it immediately cries with proper vigour', and also to ensure that 'it is perfect in all its parts, members and senses; that its ducts, namely of the ears, nose, pharynx, urethra, anus are free from obstruction; that the natural functions of every member are neither sluggish nor weak; that the joints bend and stretch; that it has due size and shape and is properly sensitive in every respect . . . And by conditions contrary to those mentioned, the infant not worth rearing is recognised.'[9]

Not all the classical philosophers and writers approved. In particular, the Hippocratic oath prohibited the use of a pessary to procure an abortion, and we shall return to this notable exception in chapter 11. But it is clear that both abortion and infanticide were widely accepted.

It is possible to identify three underlying assumptions in the culture of the time. First was the belief that the value of an individual human life was not inherent, but was acquired some time after birth. No fetus or newborn child had an intrinsic right to life after birth. Second, it was assumed that the value of a life lay primarily in its usefulness, partly to the parents, but especially to the state as a future citizen. The healthy fetus or newborn baby was a future farmer, soldier or mother. Thus the value of the fetus or the newborn resided entirely in their *potential* to make a future contribution to society. If you could make no contribution then you were worthless. Finally, there was the generally accepted belief that health and physical wholeness were essential, not only to survival, but also to human dignity. In a culture that gloried in the 'masculine virtues', the weak, the disabled and the malformed were always likely to be seen as less than fully human.

If abortion was regarded as wrong, it was generally because of the risk to the mother's life, or because of the infringement of the father's property rights, or the rights of some other interested party. If infanticide was wrong, it was because of the risk of depopulation. No author seems to have raised the possibility that there was an *intrinsic* value to the life of a fetus or even of a newborn baby. It is clear that the apparent value to society of an unwanted fetus or a malformed or diseased newborn was minimal. It is interesting that, whereas abortion was criticized from time to time, the morality of killing sickly or deformed newborns was hardly questioned. It is perhaps understandable that the medical treatment and care of sick or defective babies appears to have been of no concern to the medical profession, and that the physicians of the period concentrated their efforts on the adults whose lives were of obvious value and significance.

The Judeo-Christian world

The Old Testament period

The Jewish world of the same period displayed a radically different attitude to the fetus and newborn infant. There is no doubt that this stemmed from the teaching of the Old Testament law, the Torah. In the next chapter we shall return to the biblical teaching in more detail, but here we shall sketch over the outlines. At the heart of the Jewish law was the doctrine of the image of God. Every human being, newborn or adult, deformed or healthy, slave or free, had an *intrinsic* value as a unique expression of God's image. As we have seen, the Torah taught that the deliberate destruction of any human life was an affront to the dignity of God (Genesis 9:6). The Mishnah, which enshrined traditional rabbinic teaching, declared that God created but a single man in order to teach mankind that 'whoever destroys a single individual God imputes it on him as if he had destroyed the entire world, and whoever saves the life of a single individual God imputes it on him as if he had saved the entire world'.[10]

In ancient Jewish thought, the high value attached to human life extended to the fetus, which was the unique creation of Yahweh, formed for his own purpose. Nevertheless, the protection afforded to the fetus was not absolute. The rabbis taught that the fetus could be destroyed before birth if it was necessary to save the life of the mother. But from the moment of birth, once the head had emerged from the body of the mother, the baby was regarded as a full member of society with the same rights and protection as any fully grown person.

The second element in the condemnation of abortion and infanticide was the requirement given by God for the strong to protect the defenceless. Although the Torah does not contain many specific references to fetuses or babies, there is no doubt that they were seen as especially vulnerable, and therefore they were those whom God was concerned to protect from abuse. The pagan ritual of sacrificing children was explicitly condemned in the Old Testament law (Deuteronomy 18:10), and the practice of infant exposure was, not surprisingly, viewed with abhorrence within Israel. Yet it was a sufficiently common practice in the surrounding nations to be referred to by the Old Testament prophets. In the book of Ezekiel, the infant nation of Israel, rejected by the surrounding nations, is graphically compared to a newborn baby 'thrown out into the open field, for on the day you were born you were despised', and as lying on the ground 'kicking about in your blood' (Ezekiel 16:4–6).

Philo, a well-known Jewish apologist, writing at the time of Christ, confirmed the orthodox Jewish view of child exposure when he stated that 'infanticide undoubtedly is murder, since the displeasure of the law is not concerned with ages but with a breach to the human race'. The Roman historian Tacitus, who frequently commented on the strange and exotic practices of foreigners, felt that the unusual attitude of the Jews to newborn infants was worthy of comment. He wrote, with an unmistakable air of astonishment, that infant exposure was unknown among Jews; in fact 'they regard it as a crime to kill any recently-born child'.[11]

Jesus and the Early Church

Jesus affirmed the Old Testament view of the significance of babies and young children, and in some senses he took a more radical position. Living in our modern child-orientated society, we find it hard to appreciate just how revolutionary was Jesus' teaching that unless you become like a little child you cannot enter the kingdom of God (Matthew 18:1–4). Jesus taught that the 'welcoming' of a little child in Jesus' name was equivalent to welcoming Christ himself and the Father who sent him (Matthew 18:5, Mark 9:36, 37). Conversely, those who caused a little child to 'stumble' would be punished with great severity (Matthew 18:6). Jesus rebuked his disciples for preventing children from coming to be blessed by him and went out of his way to make time for them (Matthew 19:13–15, Mark 10:13–16).

Although there is no explicit reference to abortion or infanticide in the New Testament, the technical term *pharmakeia*, is found in lists of evil practices which are incompatible with Christian truth (e.g. Galatians 5:19–21, Revelation 21:8). The word is normally translated as 'sorcerers' or 'those who practiise magic arts' in translations of the New Testament. But *pharmakeia* was, in fact, a technical term referring to the use of drugs, and it may well refer to those who employed herbal potions to poison or to obtain an abortion.[12]

The *Didache* and the *Epistle of Barnabas* are early treatises on practical Christian living which date from the first two centuries AD. They contrasted two ways to live: the way of light and the way of darkness. The way of light was the way of neighbour-love and care for human life in all its forms. The way of darkness included murder, adultery, sodomy, fornication, the use of magic, and child destruction by abortion or infanticide. Abortion and infanticide are seen as clear examples of offences against the two great commandments referred to by Jesus: love of God and love of the neighbour.[13]

The Early Church Fathers uncompromisingly attacked the contemporary Graeco-Roman morality, with its acceptance of the elimination of unwanted human life and its cruelty to the weak and despised. Whereas the Romans drew a distinction between abortion and infanticide, early Christians tended to speak of them both as 'parricide'. In the Roman world, 'parricide' was the name given to the killing of a parent or close relative, and it was regarded as the most shocking of crimes, because it was the most unnatural.[14] It is very significant that Christians applied this scandalous term both to abortion and infanticide, equating the destruction of an unwanted child to the murder of a close relative.

The Early Church responses to abortion and infanticide

The consistent Christian teaching of the first three centuries, then, was total opposition to the pagan practices of abortion and infanticide. But the early Christians did not only oppose these practices, they saw the need to create practical alternatives. The rescue of orphans and foundlings was regarded by early Christians as a particular Christian duty, since it involved in many cases saving those babies who had been exposed by their parents. As the local population got to know about those Christians with their 'crazy' ideas, it was apparently quite common for mothers to leave their unwanted babies at the doors of churches, in the hope that they would be cared for. Christians frequently adopted foundlings into their families, as shown by inscriptions on tombs, but as the numbers grew, Christian orphanages were set up in the third and fourth centuries.[15]

It is fascinating to see how the laws of the Roman Empire gradually changed in the third and fourth centuries, at least partly in response to the growing Christian witness in their society. In AD 374 infanticide and infant exposure were made punishable by law, and every parent was required to care for their own offspring. Christian hospitals began to be established towards the end of the fourth century AD and many of the hospitals had a section (called the *Brephotropheion*) specifically set apart for foundlings.[16]

In summary, the consistent teaching of the Old and New Testament, and of the Early Church Fathers, is first that the value of the lives of all human beings, including fetuses and newborn babies, is *intrinsic* to their creation by God, and secondly that there is an overwhelming duty on the followers of Christ to act with neighbour love towards the weak and vulnerable in society.

Abortion in the modern world

As we turn to the battleground which abortion has become in our society, our Christian task is first to listen and to understand, to empathize. Only in this way are we going to be able to speak with integrity, with authenticity and with compassion.

In Britain, as in most countries, intentional abortion was illegal from the medieval period. The Offences against the Person Act 1861 made abortion a felony, with a maximum sentence of penal servitude for life. The Infant Life (Preservation) Act of 1929 made it an offence to 'destroy the life of a child capable of being born alive'. The Act made a gestational age of twenty-eight weeks the point at which there was prima facie proof that this stage had been reached. The only exception allowed under the 1929 Act was an abortion carried out in good faith to preserve the life of the mother.

Up until the 1960s medical abortion was being practised on a small scale by gynaecologists, but it was not widely available, except for the wealthy. On the other hand, everybody knew that there were a large number of criminal abortions being performed by 'back-street' abortionists who could be found in every part of society. Many women suffered from the consequences of criminal abortion, with the risk of serious infections and infertility, and a few died. In the nature of things, the exact number of criminal abortions was not known, and estimates have varied wildly. Probably the most authoritative estimate is that from a 1966 report from the Royal College of Obstetricians and Gynaecologists which concluded that the annual number of abortions at that time was about 14,600, although other estimates were much higher. In 1967, the number of maternal deaths which were known to be due to criminal abortion was thirty–two.[17]

The 1967 Abortion Act

David (now Lord) Steel introduced his Private Member's Bill to reform the abortion law in 1966 and it was passed in 1967. It is clear that the motivation of David Steel and many of the original framers of the Bill was genuinely humanitarian. The great concern that was expressed at the time was the need to prevent the litany of death and misery from criminal abortions and illegal abortionists, and to provide a legal remedy for the victims of rape and those found to be carrying seriously malformed infants. The abortion debate was also coloured by the thalidomide tragedy, in which hundreds of fetuses were severely damaged by a sedative taken by their mothers. Medical abortion was seen as a way of reducing the number of severely handicapped children being born every year. Another quoted reason was to reduce the terrible evil of child abuse (which was being increasingly recognized by paediatricians), by reducing the number of unwanted children.

Some of the 1967 Bill's supporters claimed that it would not make abortion easily available, but rather that it would reform and clarify the law, enabling doctors to carry out abortions in 'hard cases' without fear of prosecution. Interestingly, the radical liberal argument that women had the right of abortion on demand, out of respect for their moral autonomy, was not a feature of the parliamentary debate. David Steel stated explicitly: 'It is not the intention of the promoters of the Bill to leave a wide open door for abortion on request.'

Forty years later, in 2008 David Steel wrote, 'We did not create abortion on request, we created a state of law where there is a balance between the right of the fetus to develop to full life and the right of the women to have what I would call in the biblical phrase "abundant life". And that is a balance which only the medical profession can make.'[18]

Although the 1967 Act was amended by Parliament in 1990, the core of the legislation remains unchanged. It states that an abortion is legal if two doctors agree in good faith on one of the following grounds:

a) the continuance of the pregnancy would involve risk to the life of the pregnant woman greater than if the pregnancy were terminated;
b) the termination is necessary to prevent grave permanent injury to the physical or mental health of the pregnant woman;
c) the continuance of the pregnancy would involve risk of injury to the physical or mental health of the pregnant woman, greater than if the pregnancy were terminated;
d) the continuance of the pregnancy would involve risk of injury to the physical or mental health of any existing child(ren) of the family of the pregnant woman, greater than if the pregnancy were terminated;
e) there is a substantial risk that if the child were born it would suffer from such physical or mental abnormalities as to be seriously handicapped.

or in the rare conditions of a genuine medical emergency:

f) to save the life of the pregnant woman;
g) to prevent grave permanent injury to the physical or mental health of the woman.

Abortion statistics

The Abortion Act came into force in 1968, and the numbers of legal abortions in England and Wales rose steadily from 54,000 in the first complete year to over 169,000 by 1974. Since then the total number of abortions has continued to rise inexorably, and in 2007 the number was approximately 205,500. For comparison, the number of live births in 2007 was 690,000, indicating that about one in five established pregnancies end in an induced abortion. (It's estimated that 10–20% of pregnancies end in a spontaneous miscarriage but the precise numbers are uncertain.) To the despair of sexual health professionals, despite the almost universal availability of contraceptives and compulsory sex education in schools, the rate of abortions per 1,000 of population continues to rise inexorably year on year.

Although the intention of the original supporters of the Bill may not have been to allow abortion on request, the wording of the Bill was capable of remarkably elastic interpretation. In particular, because the risk to the mother of a completely normal delivery at term is greater than the risk of an early abortion, ground 'c' can be interpreted to allow abortion in any pregnancy. In fact, it is very difficult to conceive of a situation in which an abortion would not be 'legal' under the current wording of the Act.

In 2007, abortion in England and Wales was commonest in the 20–24 age group, whilst 10% were in women under 18 years. Single women represented 81% of the total, and 32% had had one or more previous abortions. Seventy per cent of abortions were performed at less than ten weeks' gestation and only about 1.5% at twenty weeks or more. About 1% of abortions were performed because of clause 'e', a 'substantial risk' of a child who is 'seriously handicapped'. Less than one in 1,000 of all abortions were performed because of a risk to the life of the mother.[19] Nearly 80% of all abortions in England and Wales were funded by the NHS although the majority were carried out in private clinics.

The reality of the current situation in the UK is that abortion is available for most women on request. In other words, the stated intention of the 1967 Act is being widely flouted, even if doctors can claim to remain technically within its wording. It is estimated that, on average, three to four out of every ten women in the UK will have an abortion in their lifetime. What this means is that abortion touches virtually all of us in UK society, not just women, but their partners, husbands, friends. And yet it is rarely, if ever, talked about. We can talk about our sexual experiences, about cancer, about Alzheimer's disease, even our experiences of child abuse. But we can't talk about our personal experience of abortion. It's like an unseen, unhealed wound penetrating our society.

The experience of abortion

It's vitally important to listen to the first-hand accounts both of women who have had abortions and of their partners. Otherwise it's easy for our opinions to be formed by popular stereotypes and prejudices. The Care Confidential website (http://www.careconfidential.com) provides a forum for people to describe their experiences of abortion, and the accounts are unedited, honest, moving and sometimes searingly painful. I can only give brief extracts from a few of the accounts here and strongly recommend that the originals are accessed online:[20]

> After the abortion I felt relief. I was just pleased to have made a decision. However, as time goes by, I realise what I have lost. I miss my child. I feel empty and guilty. It was a horrific experience which will stay with me for a long time. I don't blame myself because I know I was upset and confused . . .
>
> On the day of the procedure I was petrified, and I cried for hours. I felt like the worst person in the world. I couldn't understand how I was about to murder my own child? I loved children dearly and had previously worked as a nanny. I just didn't know where all my emotions were coming from . . . After the procedure for the next three days, I felt a great sense of relief, like the burden had been lifted and I had a chance to start living my life again. Sadly this lasted no longer than about a week . . . Now I think about it every day. I think about how selfish I am. I have nightmares of giving birth, of looking for my lost child. I fear that this has been made worse by the lie to my partner, and the guilt I feel as he too is struggling with the situation.
>
> The day I 'terminated' my baby is the day my life changed forever. I have three beautiful children and whenever I say that to people, I always feel a lump in my throat as I so want to say 'four'. When I look back (four years ago now), I see so clearly the huge mistake my husband and I made, but it is so weird that at the time you just don't see it. Maybe your mind is fogged with sickness, financial worries, or lots of other 'reasons' that seem so acceptable at the time. As soon as I woke from the anaesthetic I cried and cried, not from relief but from regret . . . I carried on, though, to the outside as if nothing had happened, but it really doesn't take all that long for the effects to surface one way or another. My husband tried to understand but kept saying I needed to move on, 'we have three beautiful children', and I would say 'yes, but we should have four.'
>
> I spent the next ten years crying and hating myself, drinking and getting drunk to temporarily blot out the feelings of hate and loathing I had developed about myself. Fourteen years on, I went on to have a beautiful baby boy and have been in a lovely supportive relationship for the past seven years, and we are trying for another baby.

A male account:

> All I could think was, what have I done? What have I done to the girl I love, and the baby I could've had? The reason I wrote so much about what happened at the

clinic is because, that's the reality. If anyone reading this is considering abortion, go to a clinic and just sit, and watch the people waiting for a loved one. No one says a word, the silence is scary. I will always regret this one thing.

When I read these accounts, I feel a deep sadness at the sense of silent despair and grief carried by so many in our society. The statistics demonstrate just how many people in our community are touched by abortion, although for most the pain is never revealed, not even to their closest friends and confidants. This is why the violent rhetoric of the public abortion debate is so unhelpful, if not positively damaging. Whenever the evils of abortion are declared in a harsh and condemnatory fashion, it is as though a knife was being silently twisted in the hearts of so many who listen.

I also feel deeply ashamed for my gender: ashamed at the cynical psychological abuse perpetrated by men on women who find themselves in the exquisitely vulnerable position of an unwanted pregnancy. The tragic irony is that abortion on request, effectively legalized by the 1967 Abortion Act, was hailed by feminists as empowering woman, and liberating them from patriarchal oppression. Yet the paradoxical effect of the emphasis on the woman's autonomy is the disempowerment and disengagement of men from the entire issue of abortion. When a women tells her boyfriend that she is unexpectedly pregnant, the boyfriend, well-educated in the liberal attitudes of the age, will usually respond, 'Well it's your choice, it's your body. Whatever you decide I will back you up.' But, in reality, what she hears is, 'You're on your own, darling. Don't expect me to take responsibility.' So at the moment of a crisis pregnancy, when many women feel acutely vulnerable, they are met with male disengagement, even abandonment.

When a women chooses to have an abortion because her partner has said, 'I'll leave unless you get rid of the baby', when the firm says 'Promotion is only available to those who work full time', when social services says, 'Sorry, we can't support single mothers', when society has discriminatory and prejudiced attitudes to disabled people, is it really a triumph of reproductive autonomy? The focus on personal autonomy masks the powerful distorting societal forces under whose influence women make choices about pregnancy and childbirth. The context of the decision about abortion is not neutral – it is predetermined by society, and in particular by the dominant male interests and power relations within that society. Women end up making apparently autonomous choices which frequently serve other people's interests.

The truth is that abortion on request has become a means for others, principally men, cynically to exploit and manipulate pregnant women. Most women, confronted with an unplanned pregnancy are not able to exercise free choice, unconstrained autonomy as expounded by the philosophers. Once abortion is freely available, women must provide their partners with a reason, not for having an abortion, but for the reverse, an adequate reason for *continuing* with their pregnancy. The prominent feminist lawyer Professor Catharine MacKinnon agrees that liberal abortion rules allow men to use women sexually with no fear of any consequences of paternity. Against the reasoning that abortion should be regarded as a private matter for women to decide, she argues that this supposes that women really are free to make decisions for themselves within the private space they occupy. In fact, she insists, women are often very unfree in the so-called private realm. Men often force sexual compliance upon them in private.[21] In the brutal language of another feminist, a liberal abortion policy allows men 'to fill women up, vacuum them out, and fill them up again'.[22]

The emotional consequences of abortion

According to gynaecologists and abortion providers, psychological problems following abortion are generally uncommon and minor. But this contrasts markedly with the experiences of many who offer counselling and support for those who seek help following an abortion.[23] For understandable reasons, many women are reluctant to return to the clinic where an abortion was performed, or to the doctor who authorized the procedure, and hence medical staff and abortion clinics are frequently unaware if long-term distress occurs.

The desire to minimize the psychological trauma of abortion has led to divergent views on how to improve practical abortion arrangements. Those in favour of a liberal abortion policy have argued that abortion should be made as straightforward and uncomplicated as possible. Some clinics offer a one-stop walk-in walk-out abortion service where women are able to leave the clinic after sixty minutes.

Here is another example of medical science being employed as a quick technological fix to meet complex human and social issues. The adverse implications of an unwanted pregnancy in our modern society are due to a complex mix of psychological, relational, spiritual, social, financial, employment, and gender issues. Abortion seems to offer a neat, apparently uncomplicated technological solution to a complex problem. But, as so often, the solutions offered by technology come with a high price tag.

The well-known American feminist Naomi Wolf published an uncompromisingly honest account of growing up as a young woman in the sexually liberated atmosphere of Los Angeles in the 1960s, entitled *Promiscuities*.[24] She interviewed many of her friends and contemporaries about their experiences: 'Among the events described by the women I interviewed, it was only the accounts of their teenage abortions that they insisted on confiding anonymously, compartmentalised from the rest of their stories. Out of all the difficult sexual events the women experienced, it was the abortions alone that seemed, even twenty years later, just too painful to integrate.'

One of the women recounted the story of her abortion at seventeen: 'We were so young . . . Logically I thought, OK, this is what you do in this situation. I had no idea what the emotional ramifications would be. It was the strong, smart, emancipated thing to do. We had no idea of the enormity of it. We were just kids.'[25]

Adoption figures

Adoption has always been an alternative to abortion when a mother feels unable, for whatever reason, to raise and care for her baby. The number of legal adoptions in England and Wales was rising in the 1950s and 1960s and reached a peak of 24,800 per year in 1968, the year that the Abortion Act became law. Since then, the number of adoptions has been falling steadily year on year, and in 2006, 5,294 adoptions were legalized. Of these only 190 babies were adopted under the age of one year. At the same time 60,000 children were in the care of the local social services.

Perhaps it is inevitable that, as abortion has become more common and socially accepted, the number of babies being offered for adoption has fallen. Yet this trend has meant that it has become progressively more difficult for childless couples to adopt a child. Of course adoption is not without problems, and adopted children may suffer complex emotional difficulties in later life. But the lack of babies for adoption has undoubtedly contributed to the pressure on health professionals and medical services to develop and provide new techniques and treatments to help infertile couples. To health professionals, it sometimes seems as though half the world is desperately trying to have a baby, while the other half is equally desperately trying to get rid of one. This is the practical reality of what philosophers have called the right to 'procreative autonomy'.

Late abortion or 'feticide'

 In 1990, the UK Parliament amended the 1967 Abortion Act. The gestational age at which abortion could be carried out under the 'social' clauses (grounds 'c' and 'd') was reduced to twenty-four weeks. However abortion for strictly 'medical' reasons (grounds 'a', 'b', 'e', 'f' and 'g' could now be carried out at any gestational age, up to and including term.

Thus, abortion can be performed at any stage of pregnancy if 'there is a substantial risk [undefined] that if the child was born it would suffer from such physical or mental abnormalities as to be seriously handicapped [undefined]'. The wording of the Act seems deliberately vague, allowing considerable latitude for interpretation by doctors and lawyers. What exactly is a 'substantial risk'? In private conversation, an experienced lawyer told me that a court would probably conclude that a risk of 10% was within the definition of 'substantial'. Similarly the definition of 'serious handicap' is open to considerable variation in interpretation, and might include abnormalities such as achondroplasia.

The case highlighted by Joanna Jepson was of a late feticide carried out at twenty-eight weeks in a fetus with bilateral cleft lip and palate. She asked the High Court to declare that cleft lip and palate did not constitute a 'serious handicap' in the context of the Abortion Act, but the Crown Prosecution Service declined to continue the case. In practice, the decisions of doctors on the interpretation of this aspect of the Act have never been put to legal test. In 2007, 135 abortions were performed beyond a gestational age of twenty-four weeks, of which 58 were performed beyond twenty-eight weeks.[26] The commonest abnormalities were of the central nervous system followed by chromosomal abnormalities. Although late feticides are uncommon compared to the large numbers of 'social' abortions performed each year in the UK, nonetheless they cause great unease and emotional distress to obstetricians, paediatricians, and to the staff of neonatal intensive care units.[27] The paradox is that late feticides may only be performed in major NHS hospitals, and it is those very same hospitals which have seen dramatic improvements in my own specialist area of intensive care for premature babies.

The practice of late feticide has led to a somewhat surreal situation. Imagine the scene in two adjacent operating theatres in one of our major National Health Service hospitals. In one operating theatre a group of highly trained professionals are engaged in a sophisticated medical procedure, the sole aim of which is to salvage an unborn baby whose life is seen as precious and uniquely valuable. Paediatricians and neonatal nurses are present to resuscitate the infant immediately after birth and commence sophisticated intensive care. Yet, in the adjacent operating theatre a group of highly trained professionals are engaged in a sophisticated medical procedure with the sole aim of destroying an identical unborn baby who is seen as disposable, and whose life has effectively been rejected by both parents and society.

The contradictory activities in the two operating theatres may collide in an even more startling way. Suppose the fetus in the second operating theatre, instead of being killed within the womb, should accidentally be delivered alive. There is now a living but critically unwell baby whose life is technically protected both by law and by traditional medical ethics. Do the doctors have a duty to preserve his or her life now that the baby is delivered? Should the paediatricians from the first operating theatre be called to initiate intensive care of this baby, who just moments previously was under sentence of death? How is it possible for one medical system, one body of law and one society to encompass and approve of such mutually contradictory procedures?

It seems to me that one way of understanding this paradox is to recognize that it is as if the two operating theatres are functioning under two mutually contradictory ethical traditions. In the first operating theatre, the view of the newborn is derived ultimately from the Judeo-Christian tradition, whereas in the adjacent theatre the ethical viewpoint is much closer to the ancient Graeco-Roman perspective.

And what is the ultimate reason for the different activity in the two theatres? Answer: the wishes of the parents. In fact, it is ultimately the wish of the mother alone, as, in this particular area fathers have few legal rights. It is the philosophical principle of autonomy, the right to choose within a liberal society, being worked out in practice. It is a view which regards the value of unborn life as a social construct. The value of your life is the value I give to it.

In response to public and professional unease, and occasional tragic cases in which botched abortions have led to the birth of live babies, the UK Royal College of Obstetricians and Gynaecologists published guidelines entitled *Termination of Pregnancy for Fetal Abnormality* in January 1996. The document makes rather grisly reading:

> Abortion . . . is the deliberate termination of a pregnancy for the benefit of the woman. The intention of an abortion is that the fetus should not survive – that the process of abortion should result in its death. A fetus that is born alive becomes a 'child' even if the reason for the birth was a legal abortion procedure. A deliberate act that causes the death of a child is murder . . . Consequently a doctor could be accused of murder when the deliberate act in question was the performance of a lawful abortion by a method that was followed by a live birth and the subsequent death of the child, perhaps because of immaturity. Consequently, a legal abortion must not be allowed to result in a live birth. Within defined limits the law allows the destruction of a fetus but not of a child.
>
> The fetus is entitled to respect throughout the pregnancy. Up to 26 weeks gestation the method of abortion should be selected to minimise the physical and emotional trauma to the woman. After 26 weeks it is not possible to know the extent to which the fetus is aware. So, in the later weeks of pregnancy, methods used during abortion to stop the fetal heart should be swift and should involve a minimum of injury to fetal tissue.[28]

As these quotations reveal, the procedure of medical feticide in a mature fetus is disturbingly close to an execution. I have witnessed at first hand the psychological unease and distress which may be caused, not only to parents, but also to health staff who are involved, sometimes rather unwillingly, in these distressing procedures.

A 1995 survey of obstetricians in the UK found that over 95% would perform an abortion at beyond twenty weeks of gestation for Down's syndrome or spina bifida, and the percentage who would perform an abortion beyond twenty-four weeks was 13% for Down syndrome, 21% for spina bifida and 64% for anencephaly.[29] Thirteen per cent also agreed with the statement that 'the state should not be expected to pay for the specialised care of a child with a severe handicap in cases where the parents had declined the offer of prenatal diagnosis.' The opposite view, that late abortion is only justified for conditions which are inevitably fatal, has also been forcibly stated by several obstetricians.[30] It is clear that many obstetricians feel uneasy about agreeing to a request to perform a late abortion under these circumstances, and some anonymous comments have been published.[31] However, the widespread availability of abortion of perfectly normal fetuses for social reasons may mean that some obstetricians find it hard to refuse to perform an abortion at the request of parents when the fetus is abnormal.

Philosophical reflection on abortion and infanticide

Ronald Dworkin

In chapter 1 we looked at Professor Ronald Dworkin's book, *Life's Dominion – an argument about euthanasia and abortion*, a highly influential and beautifully written exposition of a modern liberal position. It is important to understand that Dworkin is writing out of the American experience of violence and social unrest over abortion. He is concerned that these deep-rooted divisions in society will continue to fester, leading ultimately to civil breakdown and widespread violence. How can we live together as a society when we differ about such a fundamental issue as to whether the life of a fetus is sacrosanct? According to Dworkin, there is only one answer: we must agree to disagree. He argues that although abortion is an extremely divisive issue in Western societies, in fact nearly all members of those societies hold fundamental convictions about the sacred and 'inviolable' nature of human life. It is just that we have very different ideas of in what that 'sacredness' consists.[32]

The 'conservative' position sees the sacredness of human life in its natural creation, in its biological origin and make-up. On the other hand the 'liberal' position perceives the sacredness of any individual human life in terms of the human investment and contribution which that particular life represents. Dworkin writes strikingly of the process of self-creation which a human life entails. As soon as a pregnancy is planned, creative decisions are being made,

'... because a deliberate decision of parents to have and bear a child is, of course, a creative one. Any surviving child is shaped in character and capacity by the decisions of parents and by the cultural background of community. As that child matures, in all but pathological cases, his own creative choices progressively determine his thoughts, personality, ambitions, emotions, connection and achievements. He creates his life just as much as an artist creates a painting or a poem ... We can – and do – treat leading a life as itself a kind of creative activity, which we have at least as much reason to honour as artistic creation. The life of a single human organism commands respect and protection, then, no matter in what form or shape, because of the complex creative investment it represents, and because of our wonder at the divine or evolutionary processes that produce new lives from old ones, at the processes of nation and community and language through which a human being will come to absorb and continue hundreds of generations of cultures and forms of life and value, and, finally, when mental life has begun and flourishes, at the process of internal personal creation and judgment by which a person will make and remake himself, a mysterious, inescapable process in which we each participate and which is therefore the most powerful and inevitable source of empathy and communion we have with every other creature who faces the same frightening challenge.'[33]

In Dworkin's view, 'conservatives' view the destruction of human life as wrong because of the intrinsic or innate value of life. 'Liberals' view the destruction of human life as wrong because of the frustration of all the human contribution to that life. There is a spectrum of belief between those who put all the emphasis on the intrinsic element of the sanctity of life and those who put all the emphasis on the human contribution to the sanctity of life.

He illustrates this by giving the example of a young single woman who has an unwanted pregnancy, and who has to face either an abortion or abandoning her education to care for the child. The 'conservative' person views the abortion as wrong because it frustrates the intrinsic natural value of the human life of the fetus. The 'liberal' regards continuing the pregnancy as wrong because the life of the fetus has had very little human contribution, and therefore its destruction causes little frustration of human life. Moreover, the forced abandonment of the mother's education frustrates her life, and is therefore an offence against the 'sacredness' or inviolability of the mother's life. So an abortion should be performed to respect the sanctity of the mother's life! 'It may be more frustrating of life's miracle when an adult's ambitions, talents, training, and expectations are wasted because of an unforeseen and unwanted pregnancy, than when a fetus dies before any significant investment of that kind has been made.'[34]

It is the difference in conservative and liberal conceptions of the sacredness of human life that leads to very different views about the morality of abortion.

Dworkin then goes on to argue that, at root, the difference between the 'conservative' and the 'liberal' position is a religious or spiritual difference. As we saw in chapter 1, Dworkin argues that the atheistic, secular liberal's system of beliefs has 'a place in the life of its possessor parallel to that of the religious person's belief in God'. The liberal's beliefs affirm an essentially religious idea, that the importance of human life transcends subjective experience. Both the secular liberal and the Christian believer hold religious or spiritual beliefs about human life. It is just that they differ in those beliefs. Dworkin hopes that this insight will mean that real community is possible across deep religious divisions. 'We might hope for even more – not just for greater tolerance but for a more positive and healing realization: that what we share – our common commitment to the sanctity of life – is itself precious, a unifying ideal we can rescue from the decades of hate.'[35]

If beliefs about abortion are essentially religious beliefs, then the modern state should not *coerce* its citizens to adopt one particular set of beliefs. Arguing from major constitutional debates taking place particularly in the USA, Dworkin concludes that the right of privacy of individuals gives them the right of *procreative autonomy*.[36] Because beliefs about abortion are fundamentally religious issues, the state must allow citizens to exercise freedom of religion. 'If we have a genuine concern for the lives others lead, we will also accept that no life is a good one if lived against the grain of conviction, that it does not help someone else's life to force values upon him he cannot accept.'

Dworkin puts forward a hypothetical example. Suppose that in some country or state a majority of voters decide that it shows *disrespect* for the sanctity of life to *continue* the pregnancy if there is severe fetal malformation. 'If a majority has the power to impose its own views about the sanctity of life on everyone, then the state could *require* someone to abort, even if that were against her own religious or ethical convictions.'[37] We would rightly think that was intolerable. But Dworkin states that the argument applies with equal force in the opposite direction. A government just as seriously insults the dignity of a pregnant woman when it forces her to continue a pregnancy against her deeply held convictions. The democratic majority should not be able to *coerce* people to act against their 'religious' beliefs.

This brings Dworkin to his conclusion. Modern liberal societies have shown how different religious groups can live together, by differentiating between 'public' and 'private' matters. The laws of the state are able to direct and coerce citizens on public issues, but freedom of conscience must be allowed on private matters. Private matters are those which are a matter of individual preference and belief. By removing religion from the public sphere, and putting it in the private sphere we are able to live together in harmony despite our religious differences. We can respect one another's differences without threatening social harmony. Since beliefs about abortion (and for that matter, euthanasia) are essentially religious beliefs, they should be removed from the public sphere and placed in the private sphere. We can respect one another's ethical views as essentially religious differences. If a liberal society is going to survive, the law must allow abortion whenever a mother's individual autonomy demands it.[38]

The hypothetical example of the two operating theatres side by side, mentioned above, is a startling illustration of procreative autonomy being worked out in practice. Dworkin would argue that the existence of the two mutually contradictory operating theatres is a triumph for the democratic principle of individual autonomy. The procedure in one operating theatre is likely to be based on the 'conservative' philosophical view that the value of a fetal life is intrinsic. The adjacent operating theatre is working on the alternative 'liberal' philosophical position. In any genuinely democratic society, both operating theatres should be made available. Any individual woman is free to decide which operating theatre she opts for, and thus whether she wishes her fetus to be saved or destroyed. You pay your money and you take your choice.

There is clearly some force to Dworkin's arguments. We do have to live together as a pluralistic society, a society in which there are deep divisions in religious and philosophical beliefs. But deep down, many of my professional colleagues and many other lay-people in our society feel uneasy about the situation in the two operating theatres. Can a society survive in which such totally contradictory activities are being officially approved and carried out with state help? Can a society survive in which some state employees are saving lives, and other state employees are destroying identical lives? What kind of vision of society is this?

Does it make no difference to me what practical decisions you make about the ultimate value of life and vice versa? Is society just a collection of private individuals all doing their own thing? The very fact that disabled people like Marsha Saxton and Christy Nolan want to protest against the abortion of affected fetuses is evidence that this is an inadequate view of society and of the value of human life. It seems to me that the liberal individualistic concept of society as a series of autonomous individuals is a modern mythical construction. It does not fit with reality, and it does not fit with our deepest human intuitions.

As we have seen in chapter 2, the Christian perspective on society is very different. Christian thinking views us as locked together in mutual dependence with bonds of loyalty and responsibility to each other. Of course we may differ fundamentally in our beliefs, we may have unique attributes and personalities, but even so we are not just a collection of autonomous individuals. What I do affects you, and what you do affects me. If we treat the abnormal fetus with contempt, it does have an undeniable effect on disabled people in our midst. In Christian thought, human beings are one family and the rules that should govern our relationships are family rules, rules of duty, loyalty, responsibility and care for all of God's creation.

Peter Singer

As we saw in chapter 1, to Peter Singer it seems self-evident that the life of a fetus is worth less than the life of a healthy adult, and the life of a handicapped child is not as valuable as that of a healthy child. Neither the fetus nor the newborn baby can be regarded as a 'person', an autonomous, choosing individual. Singer concedes that there are some differences between the fetus and the newborn baby, in that the baby is no longer dependent on the mother's body and that, if the baby is unwanted by the mother, it can be cared for by someone else who does want it.[39] However, ultimately both abortion and infanticide are acceptable options. The parent's choice, their free autonomous decision is central. If they want the baby to live, that's fine, but if they don't wish their baby to survive, it is morally acceptable to get rid of it, either before or after birth, provided we do it cleanly and painlessly. Singer quotes with approval the celebrated case of a baby called John Pearson who was born with Down's syndrome in Derby General Hospital in June 1980.[40] When Molly Pearson, John's mother was given the news, she wept and said to her husband: 'I don't want it, duck.' The baby was under the care of the respected paediatrician Dr Leonard Arthur, who prescribed 'nursing care only', together with regular doses of a potent analgesic. The death of John on the fourth day of life led to a celebrated murder trial. The charge was subsequently changed to attempted murder and, after complex legal argument, Dr Arthur was acquitted.

To Singer it is inexplicable and irrational that we are prepared to abort a fetus with Down's syndrome, but are not prepared to kill a newborn baby with the same condition. He argues that this is merely a curious quirk of a society influenced by Judeo-Christian religious ideas. 'Killing unwanted infants or allowing them to die has been a normal practice in most societies throughout human history and prehistory.' It was not only ancient Greek and Roman societies who practised infanticide. Anthropologists confirm that most forms of human societies have approved of the killing of unwanted babies. 'We find it in nomadic tribes like the Kung of the Kalahari desert, whose women will kill a baby born while an older child is still too young to walk . . . Japanese midwives who attended births did not assume that the baby was to live; instead they always asked if the baby was "to be left" or "to be returned" to wherever it was thought to have come from. Needless to say, in Japan as in all these cultures, a baby born with an obvious disability would almost always be "returned".'[41] 'Even in nineteenth-century Europe, unwanted infants were given to foundling homes, run by women known as "angel makers" because of the very high death rates that occurred ... It is worth knowing that from a cross-cultural perspective, it is *our* tradition (original emphasis), not that of the Kung or the Japanese, that is unusual in its official morality about infanticide.' Yet Singer sees an increasing public acceptance of some forms of selective medical infanticide in Western societies. 'Thousands of years of lip-service to the Christian ethic have not succeeded in suppressing entirely the earlier ethical attitude that newborn infants, especially if unwanted, are not yet full members of the moral community.'[42]

As Singer recognizes, our own society has been heavily influenced by Judeo-Christian concepts of the value of fetal and newborn life. In our next chapter we will examine the biblical basis of this perspective and ask how it can be applied practically to the painful issues of antenatal screening and abortion.

7. WHEN IS A PERSON? CHRISTIAN PERSPECTIVES ON THE BEGINNING OF LIFE

When we turn from the complex and painful dilemmas raised by abortion, infertility treatments and antenatal screening to the world of the Bible, we are again struck by the gulf between the biblical world and our own. We cannot look for proof-texts which will provide neat answers to these complex problems. Sometimes Christian writers and teachers have attempted to construct a complete edifice of teaching about abortion on a single text, such as the verses in Exodus 21:22–24, which deal with accidental injury to a pregnant woman. We will look at this passage later, but it is not the place where we should start. Instead, we must attempt to immerse ourselves in the biblical worldview, seeing the world as the biblical writers saw it.

We start with creation design: the way we are made. As we saw in chapter 2, in orthodox Christian thought we are all unique and we are all special in God's eyes because we are made in God's image. Each human being is a unique masterpiece of God's creation: flawed, imperfect, damaged but a masterpiece nevertheless. Philosophers such as Singer and Harris argue that the right to be treated with dignity, the right to be protected, the right to be regarded as a 'person', is a right which has to be earned. It is as though every human has to pass a test before he or she is regarded as 'one of us', a member of the moral community. Are they aware of their own existence as 'continuing selves'? Are they able to choose, to exercise autonomy? Do they display 'morally relevant characteristics'?

But in the biblical Christian worldview, no human being needs to earn the right to be treated with respect or dignity. Our dignity is *intrinsic*: it lies in the way we have been made, in how God creates us, remembers us and calls us to himself.

God's creative involvement with human beings extends to fetal life

The biblical narrative is insistent that God's creative activity does not just start at the moment of birth. Instead, God is intimately involved in the hidden and mysterious process of fetal development within the womb. This is seen most clearly in Psalm 139, which is a wonderful and moving meditation on the awesome intimacy between God and a human individual. The psalmist starts with a profound awareness of God's presence, an unsettling sense that God has invaded every aspect of his life:

> O LORD you have searched me
>   and you know me.
> You know when I sit and when I rise;
>   you perceive my thoughts from afar.
> You discern my going out and my lying down;
>   you are familiar with all my ways.
> Before a word is on my tongue
>   you know it completely, O LORD.
> You hem me in – behind and before;
>   you have laid your hand upon me.
> (Psalm 139:1– 5)

The extent of the divine knowledge is wonderful, bringing a sense of security in God's all-encompassing presence. But this presence is not entirely welcome. There seems to be an element of ambiguity in the psalmist's response, a very human sense of emotional claustrophobia. It is as though he is saying, 'This is all very well, but could you please get off my back, God? I need a little space.' So the psalmist embarks on a thought experiment. Is there any place in the cosmos where I could escape from God's all-invading presence? No. The search for emotional space is doomed to failure.

> Where can I go from your Spirit?
>   Where can I flee from your presence?

If I go up to the heavens you are there;
    if I make my bed in the depths, you are there.
If I rise on the wings of the dawn,
    if I settle on the far side of the sea,
even there your hand will guide me,
    your right hand will hold me fast.
(verses 7–10)

If there is no place in the cosmos where the psalmist can evade God's presence, perhaps there is a place in his personal history. Perhaps if he goes back far enough into his personal origins, he can find a space, a time when, for once, he was free from the claustrophobic presence of God. But no, even if he traces his life story back to his own mysterious origins in the womb, he discovers God's presence:

For you created my inmost being;
    you knit me together in my mother's womb.
I praise you because I am fearfully and wonderfully made;
    your works are wonderful,
    I know that full well.
My frame was not hidden from you
    when I was made in the secret place.
When I was woven together in the depths of the earth,
    your eyes saw my unformed body.
All the days ordained for me
    were written in your book
    before one of them came to be.
(verses 13–16)

Wonderfully and terrifyingly, the search for a space from God is doomed to failure. The narrative of a human life is invaded by God from its intrauterine origins. Of course, this is poetry and not a textbook of embryology. The fetus is woven together as on a divine loom, hidden in the depths of the earth. The psalmist was not a fool. He knew that babies were not dug up like potatoes from the soil. But in the Old Testament world, virtually nothing was known about the biological processes which occurred in the womb. In a world where abdominal surgery was unheard of, and post-mortems were taboo, what was actually happening within the pregnant abdomen was a complete mystery. Of course, people knew that a man and a woman had intercourse, and nine months later there was a baby, but what happened in between was an enigma, one of the greatest riddles of human existence. In the words of the Preacher: 'As you do not know the path of the wind, or how the body is formed in a mother's womb, so you cannot understand the work of God, the Maker of all things' (Ecclesiastes 11:5).

By contrast, we moderns know a great deal about the biological process of fetal development. Antenatal ultrasound in particular allows us the privilege of seeing what the psalmist could only dream of. Many parents, myself included, have experienced a mysterious thrill at the first glimpse of their unborn child. It is a glimpse into the hidden creation chamber where God is bringing another wonderful but flawed masterpiece into existence.

What then can we learn from Psalm 139 about God's involvement with the unborn child? How can we relate this ancient poetry to the world of the ultrasound scan and the assisted conception unit? John Stott, in his book *Issues Facing Christians Today*,[1] helpfully draws out three headings.

The first is *creation*. The clear emphasis of the passage is on God's individual and minutely detailed creative activity within the womb. Human development is not just an anonymous, deterministic, biological mechanism, a routine proliferation of cells. Of course, molecular biology is uncovering many of the cellular mechanisms which control the formation of the human organism, but we must avoid a crude biological or genetic determinism. The language of developmental biology implies that fetal development is impersonal, mechanistic and ultimately random. But in contrast, the language of the psalm emphasizes that what is occurring in the womb is *personal* and *intentional*. At the same time that the biological mechanisms are ticking away, the divine artist is creating a unique masterpiece.

It seems to me that the psalmist is consciously echoing the creation narratives of the first chapter of Genesis. The womb is dark, mysterious, the secret place; the action takes place in the depths of the earth; the body is unformed. This is the secret creation chamber of the infinite God. Inside this womb is a microcosm of the miracle of the creation of the universe. God's guiding hand is creating; God's voice is calling a unique being into existence and into relationship with him. God is the potter who is working the unformed clay; God is the artist weaving his unique tapestry on the divine loom. That is why we must treat even the unborn baby with wonder. One possible reading of the Hebrew of verse 14 says, 'I praise you because, being made, I am wonderful.'

The second is the theme of *covenant*. Throughout the psalm the writer is self-consciously using the language of covenant, unconditional commitment. God the Creator is in covenant relationship with the psalmist. 'You *know* me God.' This is not just an intellectual awareness, because of course God knows everything. This kind of knowledge implies a committed intimate involvement, as when Adam *knew* Eve in the act of sexual intercourse (Genesis 4:1 literally). 'Your eyes saw my unformed body.' 'You *knew* me; you were involved with me.' The emphasis is not on fetal awareness of God, as if the psalmist was saying when I was in the womb, I knew you were there God. No, what matters is that God knew the fetus. God was involved. God was calling me into existence and into a relationship with him. Here is an example of a unilateral covenant based on God's grace, a covenant of creation which God initiates and upholds to all eternity.

The third is the theme of *continuity*. The psalmist meditates on his own personal history, the narrative of his unique, individual life. There is the past ('you searched me'), the present, ('you know when I sit and when I rise'), the future ('your hand will guide me, your right hand will hold me fast'), and the antenatal history, ('when I was woven together in the depths of the earth'). The psalmist looks back to his mother's womb and says, not that there was a mysterious being in there which later became 'me', a person. 'No,' he says, 'that was me in there.' I, the adult human, am in direct continuity with the fetus. This is all *my* story, the narrative structure of a human life.

These same themes can be traced in many parts of the Bible. In the book of Job, the common creation of all human beings in the womb is used as a symbol of the need for equality and justice in human relationships. 'Did not he who made me in the womb make them? Did not the same one form us both within our mothers?' (Job 31:15). The suffering servant of Isaiah also refers to God's intrauterine call: 'And now the LORD says – he who formed me in the womb to be his servant . . . ' (Isaiah 49:5). Here are the same themes of creation, covenant and continuity.

The fetus is an actor within the human drama

Luke, the physician, records in his Gospel a domestic incident: the excited meeting of two pregnant women, to share their experiences (Luke 1:39). Mary, having just received the visitation from the angel and being in the earliest stages of pregnancy, hurries excitedly to visit her relative Elizabeth, also pregnant, but close to term. 'When Elizabeth heard Mary's greeting, the baby leaped in her womb and Elizabeth was filled with the Holy Spirit. In a loud voice she exclaimed: "Blessed are you among women and blessed is the child you will bear! But why am I so favoured, that the mother of my Lord should come to me? As soon as the sound of your greeting reached my ears, the baby in my womb leaped for joy."' (Luke 1:41–44)

I have sometimes wondered why, out of all the eyewitness accounts of Jesus' life that Luke must have accumulated before he wrote his Gospel, did he choose to record such a commonplace domestic incident. Was it because Luke wanted to emphasize that Jesus' earthly ministry commenced even before birth? At first glance there are only two people in that room in Zechariah's home. But Luke implies that in fact there are four. Elizabeth and the unborn John, Mary and the unborn Jesus. And perhaps what captivated Luke was the recognition that John leapt for joy at Jesus' presence, only a few weeks after his conception, in the same way that lepers and paralysed men and blind beggars will leap for joy as Jesus passes by in future.

Jesus shares the narrative of a human life, including all the stages of fetal life. He has become like us, as the letter to the Hebrews says, 'in every way' (Hebrews 2:17). In fact, to use a phrase of Paul Ramsey, Jesus was a fellow-fetus – or, in words we have looked at already, 'Jesus has been with us in the darkness of the womb as he will be with us in the darkness of the tomb.'[2]

Luke uses the same Greek word, *brephos*, for the unborn John, as he does for the newborn baby Jesus (Luke 2:12), and for the little children who were brought to Jesus for his blessing (Luke 18:15). The consistent witness of the biblical writers is that the fetus is part of the human drama, a hidden actor on the human stage; one whom God is creating in secret, calling into existence and into relationship with himself. The same concept of continuity throughout all the stages of the human narrative is evident in the Apostles' Creed which states that Jesus was 'conceived by the Holy Spirit, born of the Virgin Mary, suffered under Pontius Pilate, was crucified, dead and buried . . . [and] rose again'.

Is there a biblical distinction between the early stages of conception and the later fetus?

Some, such as Professor R. J. Berry, have argued that the biblical material such as Psalm 139 can be used only to argue in retrospect: If I know that I exist, then I know that God must have been involved with me when I was a fetus: 'Once a person exists, one must reckon with his or her whole life history as a linked sequence of divinely guided and appointed processes and events. But Psalm 139 says nothing whatsoever about those who are not "persons".'[3] In other words, we cannot use this psalm or other similar passages to argue that God is involved with *every* fetus or embryo, including the numerous embryos and fetuses which have been spontaneously lost during the early stages of prenatal development.

As Professor Berry and other distinguished commentators, such as Professor Gordon Dunstan[4] have pointed out, there is a long-standing Christian tradition which made a distinction between the 'formed' and 'unformed' fetus. The story is rather tortuous but it remains an important feature of contemporary Christian debate. The historical evidence suggests that ancient Judaism was strongly opposed to deliberate abortion, except in rare cases which were performed in obstructed labour, in order to save the mother's life.[5] The Exodus law, however, did contain a statute dealing with accidental injury to a pregnant woman (Exodus 21:22–24). A literal translation of the Hebrew is as follows: 'If men strive together, and hurt a woman with child, so that her fruit depart, and yet no injury follow: he shall surely be fined, according as the woman's husband shall lay upon him; and he shall pay as the judges determine. But if any injury follow, then thou shalt give life for life . . . '

The problem is that the meaning of the text seems fundamentally ambiguous. The phrase 'her fruit depart' could refer to miscarriage leading to fetal death, but it could also refer to premature birth with survival of the baby (as in the New International Version translation). Similarly the 'injury' could refer to injury to the mother or injury to the baby.

When the Hebrew text was translated into the Greek Septuagint version, in the third century BC, the Greek words for 'unformed' and 'formed' were substituted for the phrases referring to injury. Thus the statute prescribed a fine for the loss of an 'unformed' fetus, but the death penalty if there was loss of a 'formed' fetus. This fitted with the Greek philosophy of Aristotle who drew a distinction between (first) the early embryo which had a vegetative, followed by an animal nature, and (second) the fully formed fetus which was recognizably a human being, and which therefore had a 'rational' or 'intellectual' soul.[6]

The Early Church Fathers seem to have been divided on whether to accept a difference in the significance of the destruction of an unformed or a formed fetus. Basil wrote that 'a woman who deliberately destroys a fetus is answerable for murder. Any fine distinction as to its being completely formed or unformed is not admissible among us.'[7]

On the other hand, Augustine accepted the distinction; 'If what is brought forth is unformed but at this stage some sort of living, shapeless thing, then the law of homicide would not apply, for it could not be said that there was living soul in that body, for it lacks all sense, if it be such as is not yet formed and therefore not yet endowed with its senses.'[8] The same tradition was accepted by Aquinas and other medieval theologians. However, it is clear that both Augustine and Aquinas regarded the deliberate destruction of the early embryo as a grave sin and did not in any sense treat the embryo as disposable.[9]

The subject remains a matter of painful controversy and debate between Christians. A number of modern theologians and Christian doctors have argued that this ancient moral tradition should be preserved. In their view, the early embryo and fetus cannot be regarded as a human individual who is worthy of respect and protection until later in pregnancy. They point to other evidence from modern embryology and genetics to support this view. It is now thought that more than 50% of all embryos created naturally following sexual intercourse fail to implant (many have gross genetic abnormalities which are incompatible with life) and are lost during menstruation. Often the mother will not even be aware that she was pregnant. Some early embryos split spontaneously, leading to the formation of identical twins. Very rarely, two separate non-identical embryos which have formed at the same time may fuse to form a single embryo. Most of the tissue that makes up the early embryo does not even go to form the future fetus, but instead becomes the placenta and other supportive structures which are subsequently lost. Even the crucial step of fertilization, when new genetic identity is formed, does not happen instantaneously, but takes place over a matter of hours as the nuclear material from the sperm and the egg remain separate within the one-cell embryo, and only fuse totally following division and formation of a two-cell structure.

In view of this evidence, how can the human embryo and early fetus be regarded as a unique human individual worthy of respect and protection? Professor Donald Mackay argued that in the development of the fetus a critical level of complexity was required before the fetus could be considered a 'conscious personal agency'. In particular, a degree of brain development allowing self-regulation and information processing was necessary.[10]

The implication of this argument is that early abortion, although always painful and less than ideal, may be a Christian action, the lesser of two evils, an act of compassion, and even, at times, a Christian duty.[11] Similarly the creation and destruction of human embryos in research, to help more mature human beings can be seen as worthwhile, provided that significant benefits are likely to accrue in medical advances for the benefit of humanity (see further discussion below).[12]

From a personal point of view, as a medical student and junior doctor in the 1970s, I became convinced by this argument. I felt that abortion could be seen as an act of compassion, the lesser of two evils. But, over the years, as my clinical experience and theological understanding grew, I became increasingly uneasy. Could the intentional destruction of even the early fetus really be consistent with a Christian worldview? What were the arguments that led to my change of heart?

Arguments in favour of protecting the early fetus and embryo

First, I have become convinced that the traditional distinction between the formed, human fetus and the unformed sub-human fetus is not a biblical concept, nor is it consistent with modern biological understanding. It derives ultimately from a dualistic Greek philosophy which regarded the essence of humanity as consisting in a rational, thinking, feeling soul. The soul is seen as a distinct immaterial entity which is implanted in a physical body at a certain stage of fetal development. This does not fit with the thought forms of the biblical worldview. The interpretation of the statute in Exodus 21 remains unclear, but in my view it cannot be used with integrity to support this distinction. Further the statute clearly deals with compensation following *accidental* injury, and cannot be applied to the morality of intentional abortion. It seems that Christian thinkers such as Augustine and Aquinas were using Aristotelian ideas of animation at a later stage of pregnancy, because that was the best empirical information that was available.[13] Now vast improvements in scientific information have made the distinction obsolete. There is no stage in fetal development which represents a biological discontinuity, and which might be interpreted as the transition from an animal to a human form. If there is any discontinuity in the formation of the human individual, it seems to be around the time of fertilization, when a unique human genetic code is created, or implantation in the wall of the womb, when the embryo starts to develop the essential support structures to survive and develop into a mature fetus.

Secondly, it is pointless to expect biology to reveal conclusively the point at which God's covenant involvement with a human individual commences. Biology and genetics can only suggest certain points at which personal identity may commence. Oliver O'Donovan argues that we cannot demonstrate that a person exists by scientific testing for various attributes or capacities, such as rationality or responsivity. Instead 'we discern persons only by love, by discovering through interaction and commitment that this human being is irreplaceable.'[14] In order to know one another as persons we must adopt a mode of knowledge which is based, not on objective scientific analysis, but on brotherly love. 'This implies a commitment in advance to treat all human beings as persons, even when their personal qualities have not yet become manifest to us.'[15] We do not know whether any one particular embryo or fetus will survive the hazards of embryonic development and intrauterine life to emerge as a responsive individual whose personal qualities we can identify, but this does not absolve us from the responsibility to demonstrate a moral commitment in advance to treat each embryo or fetus as though it was destined to manifest its personality in future. We must 'approach new human beings, including those whose humanity is ambiguous and uncertain to us, with the expectancy and hope that we shall discern how God has called them out of nothing into personal being'.[16]

O'Donovan has used a helpful analogy in this regard, taken from an old art film. On a lonely beach, the back of a seated figure is seen, silhouetted against the ocean. The central character of the film walks towards the figure and places a friendly hand on his shoulder. The figure topples forward and crashes face first to the ground. The camera spins round to reveal it is not a living person but a rotting corpse . . . Only by reaching out to the figure in friendship was its true character revealed. In the same way, it is only by reaching out with a prior moral commitment of love and protection to the embryo and fetus that we will discover whether or not a person is there. 'We discern persons only by love . . . '

Thirdly, the thrust of historic biblical theology places the emphasis on what human beings *are* by creation, in the stuff of their being, and not on what they can *do*, on their attributes or functional abilities. It is not necessary to assess what the fetus can do, to look for central nervous system functionality or responsivity, in order to discern the evidence of God's involvement or covenant commitment. God's grace revealed in the Christian gospel is precisely love towards the unresponsive. The covenant relationship of loving commitment does not depend on reciprocity. As parents, we commit ourselves in love to our children long before they are able to respond with self-awareness to that love. As we saw in our brief exploration of Psalm 139, the critical issue is not whether the fetus is aware of God, but whether God is aware of, and committed by grace to, the fetus.

Fourthly, the Bible views all human beings as called by God to share in his life. When God calls us, he calls us *as a person*, he calls us by name. We cannot think of God calling us in any way other than in a personal way. Similarly we cannot think that there was a time in our personal history when we were outside the call of God. In other words, within the confines of our human existence, there was never a time when God was not calling us. As Brendan McCarthy puts it, 'If God calls us, as the Christian faith asserts, then he must have called us, as well as the Old Testament prophets, while we were still in our mother's wombs.'[17] (In fact, since God is outside of time, he knows and calls us even before our conception, as in Jeremiah 1:5.) So our unique human personality derives from God who calls us by name, and God's call is present from the beginning of our human existence, a call to enter into fellowship or communion with him. It is a strange thought that even the embryo has a name, a unique identity, in the sense that no animal or inanimate object has a name, but it is consonant with the biblical worldview.

Fifthly, Christian thinking emphasizes our responsibility to be neighbourly, to a duty of care and protection for vulnerable, weak and defenceless human beings. In the Christian understanding of community, we are locked into bonds of loyalty and responsibility, even to those who appear alien to, and different from, us. The early embryo and early fetus seem to represent par excellence those vulnerable human strangers to whom we owe a special duty of care and protection.

Sixthly, from the point of fertilization, the human embryo has a mother and father. Even if she is unaware of the fact, the person from whom the egg derived has become a mother, the man from whom the sperm came has become a father. In some mysterious way, their identity is changed by the existence of this new being. Within the mystery of the Trinity, the persons of the godhead are constituted by their relations with each other. The Father cannot be who he is without the existence of the Son, and vice versa. Perhaps the person-hood of the embryo, too, can be seen as constituted by its relations with its parents.

Finally, if we recognize a deep uncertainty and ambiguity about the moral significance of the embryo or early fetus, we have to ask the question, 'What is an authentically Christian response to this deep ontological uncertainty?' Surely an appropriate response is to vote in favour of protection and against intentional destruction. It is a standard principle of medical ethics that, if there is any significant degree of uncertainty about life and death issues, for instance in deciding whether to withdraw life-sustaining treatment where the prognosis is hopeless, then we should 'play safe'. We vote in favour of life, and against death. It is only if we are certain *beyond any reasonable doubt* that there is no hope of survival, that the outlook is hopeless and there is no reasonable prospect that our therapy can be helpful, that we can consider the removal of supportive treatment. In the same way, it seems to me that if there is reasonable doubt about the moral status of the embryo or early fetus, then we should vote in favour of protection. Perhaps we can never know with any certainty how God regards any individual embryo or fetus. That profound uncertainty does not give us licence to treat the embryo as a being who is at our disposal. We need an authentic Christian response to uncertainty.

Theological themes and the human embryo

The human embryo is a unique type of being. It is *sui generis*. We cannot think of it simply as a baby who happens not to have been born yet. Nor can we think of it merely as a biological mechanism, a collection of genetic material and intracellular apparatus, a blob of jelly, which happens to have the potential to become a baby. We have to create a new category of thought for this being.

It is neither an unborn baby nor a blob of jelly. It is a human embryo – unique, different in kind from anything else in our experience.

And, in thinking biblically about this strange entity, we must hold onto two familiar tensions which crop up repeatedly in Christian theology. First we must retain the *tension between the physical and the immaterial*. Every human being has a physical aspect, (they are constructed out of the physical stuff of genetic codes, biochemical engineering, intricate plumbing and miles of electrical wiring), and an immaterial aspect, (a person who mysteriously reflects God's character; a strange God-like being who loves and is loved; a unique individual with a unique life history, known by God and destined for eternity). These two aspects of our being are locked together in our humanity. We are, *at one and the same time*, fully physical and fully immaterial. The existence of a physical human body, all that plumbing and biochemical engineering, is a physical sign that an immaterial person is present. That's the way God made us – as 'disgusting hybrids' with the different and apparently contradictory aspects of our being locked together. The reductionist says that human beings are *really* sophisticated self-replicating survival machines who happen to have achieved self-consciousness. On the other hand, the philosophical dualist says that human beings are *really* spiritual beings who happen to be attached to a body for a period of their existence. Biblical anthropology denies both of these alternatives. Human beings are, at one and the same time, fully physical and fully spiritual beings. We hold the two realities in tension.

It is a tension which is familiar to biblical theology. We see it in the doctrine of the Incarnation: Jesus was at one and the same time completely human and completely divine. We see it in the doctrine of inspiration: the words of the Bible are at one and the same time the words of human writers and the words of God. We see it in the doctrine of the sacraments: the bread and wine, and the baptismal water are both physical elements and at the same time a pointer to a hidden, spiritual reality. We see it in the doctrine of divine providence: wicked men chose to crucify God's Son, and yet it was all part of God's plan.

When we think of the embryo within a biblical worldview, then, we have to view this strange being as having both a physical and an immaterial reality. Indeed, I wonder if we cannot think of the embryo within a version of sacra-mentalist theology. At one level, the embryo is just biology. It is a collection of genetic material and cellular machinery. But at the same time, it is a physical sign of an immaterial or spiritual reality, a sacrament of a hidden covenant of creation – a sign that God is bringing forth a new, Godlike being, a unique reflection of his character, a being to whom he is locked in covenant commitment. At the same time that the biological mechanisms are ticking away, the divine artist is creating a unique masterpiece. God is bringing into existence another person and calling him or her into relationship with himself. So we cannot treat the human embryo with contempt because it is 'just' a minute blob of jelly, any more than we can treat the written words of the Bible with contempt because they are 'just' human words. These particular physical words are special: they have a unique spiritual significance. This particular physical blob is special: it is a sign of God's creative covenant.

This way of thinking has implications for the way we think biblically about the human genetic code, and the molecules of DNA from which it is constructed. The biblical revelation views human beings as sons and daughters of Adam and Eve. As we saw in chapter 2, modern genetic analysis suggests that we must treat the biblical narrative with due seriousness. Human beings are both theologically and, it seems, in genetic reality, a single extended family. Not only do we carry the mysterious image of God, we also carry the image of our distant grandparents, Adam and Eve. We have an *organic solidarity* with Adam. There is an unbroken line of descendants through which each of us can trace their origins to Adam. But what is the physical counterpart of this organic solidarity? How was Adam's image passed on through each generation down to us? The answer is the human genetic code. DNA is the physical means by which God has enabled Adam's likeness to be passed faithfully on to each generation.

Of course, the biblical concept of being 'in Adam' implies much more than just possessing a particular genetic code, but nonetheless in the physical and spiritual unity which comprises a human being, it is the human genome which is the physical sign that we are Adam's offspring, that we are 'in Adam'. This particular configuration of DNA molecules is the physical counterpart of a human person, a physical sacrament which points to a hidden spiritual mystery. And it is at fertilization that the particular configuration of the human genome is created. It is at fertilization that the image of Adam is passed on to the next generation. Even the early embryo is a being 'in Adam'.

The thinking which draws a distinction between the embryo or early fetus and the later mature fetus tends to verge towards dualism. It implies that the early fetus is merely a physical being, and therefore of little consequence until the spiritual bit, the soul, or the responsive mind, enters. In other words, it splits the indissoluble biblical link between the physical and spiritual realities. A very early human being can be just a physical entity with no spiritual element. Since it is only the spiritual bit of humanity that really matters, the purely physical stuff of which the embryo is constructed may be regarded as disposable or used for research. I am increasingly convinced that we should resist the creeping philosophical dualism which splits the physical aspect of the fetus from the spiritual.

The second familiar biblical tension that we have to retain is the *tension between the 'already' and the 'not-yet'*. The embryo is just one example of the tension which runs through the whole of human existence. We are already human beings, but, in Christ, we are also becoming something else. We have not yet arrived at our final destination, which is to become fully human. We are becoming what we already are. John Stott quotes the words of ethicist Paul Ramsey, 'The human individual comes into existence as a minute informational speck . . . His subsequent prenatal and postnatal development may be described as a process of becoming what he already is from the moment he was conceived.'[18] Seventeen hundred years previously Tertullian had expressed the same thought, 'The future man is a man already; the fruit is already present in the seed.'[19] Again this is a familiar tension in Christian theology. We have been saved by God's grace, but in God's grace we have yet to experience the full reality of that salvation. It is the same tension which holds together the two biblical senses of the image of God. All human beings are made in God's image, but Christ himself is the unique image of God. We are already made in God's image, but in God's grace we are being transformed to become like Jesus, the image of God. We are becoming what we already are.

Even the language we use reflects our understanding. The language of the scientist and clinician is that of the 'human embryo'. Embryo is the noun and human is the adjective. There are human embryos, monkey embryos, mouse embryos and fruit fly embryos. And guess what? They all look the same under the microscope. They are embryos.

But if we talk about 'embryonic humans' the focus changes. There are embryonic humans, fetal humans, adult humans, geriatric humans and resurrected humans! And guess what? They are all human beings in the process of becoming what they already are. It's another illustration of the power of language in moral discourse.

The language of potentiality, when applied to the embryo, tends to be confusing rather than helpful. What does it mean to be a 'potential person'? When used by philosophers it tends to mean 'not yet a person'. Because the fetus is not yet a person, we don't have to treat it as if it was a person. This kind of thinking cuts between the 'already' and the 'not yet'. It breaks the biblical understanding of human life, that all human beings are in a process of becoming what we already are. In the embryo, we encounter something which is the same as ourselves, although not yet the same. But why should this be so? Why should human beings be caught in an indissoluble link between the already and the not yet? The answer lies in the grace of God. In John Stott's words, 'It is God's grace which confers on the unborn child, from the moment of its conception, both the unique status which it already enjoys and the unique destiny which it will later inherit. It is grace which holds together the duality of the actual and the potential, the already and the not yet.'[20]

Using the human embryo in medical research

Professor Gareth Jones has argued that the sacrifice of human embryos in the best interests of the wider community may be justified within the context of Christian reasoning about a 'just war': 'Take Alzheimer's disease for example. This war is against an undefeated foe that wreaks immeasurable pain and suffering on its enemies, and currently defeat is imminent and death is inevitable.'[21] He argues that there is both a moral and a strategic necessity to use embryonic stem cells to try to develop new therapies for incurable degenerative diseases. Professor Jones also argues that surplus human embryos created during IVF cannot be regarded as 'innocent', because they will be destroyed anyway, whether used to create stem cells or not: 'The notion of innocence should not be viewed as an isolated value, but in relation to other lives we wish to save and benefit.'

The argument is complex and there isn't space to address it in detail here. But I find the analogy with warfare unconvincing. It is not possible to make a neat comparison between the 'war against disease' and the 'war against Hitler'. In my view, there is neither a moral nor a strategic *necessity* to use embryonic stem cells for medical research. It is an *option* which we as moral and thoughtful people should weigh and balance.

It is possible to imagine a fantasy scenario in which this argument might be relevant. Suppose a new worldwide pandemic infection threatens literally to wipe out humankind from the face of the earth. All possible research options are futile. The only possible therapy might be derived from research on human embryos. Would it be justified in this extreme emergency to go down the route of sacrificing embryos? Well, possibly. But the current situation with regard to new treatments for degenerative conditions is so far from this emergency scenario, that it is surely inappropriate to use the arguments based on military emergencies.

Human intuitions about abortion

In my own quest for a Christian understanding of the unborn child, it is not only the theological and biblical arguments which have influenced me. I have been deeply struck also by the profound intuitions about abortion which many people in our society reveal, including many who have no Christian or religious faith. I spoke some time ago to a BBC producer who was making a major television documentary about abortion. She had interviewed a considerable number of women and doctors by way of background research. She told me in private that she had been struck by the fact that when talking about abortion, the doctors and other professionals were careful to use medical language such as 'termination of pregnancy', in order to avoid giving offence. By contrast nearly all the women she had spoken to had talked about 'killing their babies'. In her view, the women were much more honest than the doctors about the emotional implications of medical abortion.

In a foreword to their book *A Silent Sorrow: Pregnancy Loss – Guidance and Support for You and Your Family*, American bereavement counsellors Ingrid Kohn and Perry-Lynn Moffitt, writing from an entirely secular perspective, discuss the language they have chosen to use:

> This book was written to provide guidance, comfort, and hope to all parents who have experienced an unwanted pregnancy loss, including those who have ended an impaired pregnancy. We considered using terms such as 'fetus' and 'embryo' when discussing abnormal pregnancies and abortions, realising this language was more in keeping with a pro-choice stance. In the end, we continued to refer to the 'unborn baby'. We felt compelled to acknowledge this common grief: *no matter what the cause of their loss, bereaved parents mourn for someone who was dear to them, someone who was supposed to be their 'baby'* [my emphasis]. If the words we chose are imperfect, they still represent our sincerest attempt to give expression to this universal sorrow.[22]

Elaine Storkey, in her meditation on the experience of Mary, the mother of Jesus, expresses the intuitive sense of wonder and the emotional demands of pregnancy from the mother's perspective:

> Pregnancy is itself a symbol of deep hospitality. It is the giving of one's body to the life of another. It is a sharing of all that we have, our cell structure, our blood stream, our food, our oxygen. It is saying 'welcome' with every breath, and every heartbeat. And for many mothers that welcome is given irrespective of the demands made on one's own comfort, health or ease of life. For the demands of this hospitality are greater than almost any of our own. And the growing fetus is made to know that here is love, here are warm lodgings, here is a place of safety. In hiding and in quiet the miraculous growth can take place . . .
>
> This is one of the reasons why the decision for abortion is such a painful and heavy one. Of course there are those who have been taught by our culture to present themselves to the clinic with barely a second thought, accepting the sterile terminology of the hospital for what they are about to do: 'a termination of

pregnancy'. Yet for many other women who have had an abortion there has been anxiety and grief and a sense of loss. In spite of all the reasons which directed them to take this step some feel guilty of a deep betrayal of trust. They could not find within themselves the hospitality that was needed to sustain this life.[23]

Whenever we contemplate abortion for a malformed or unwanted fetus, we are sending a message of rejection. We are saying that we don't wish to accept this new other, to offer basic human hospitality. Although the desire to spare a child from suffering is motivated by genuine human compassion, the act of abortion is the opposite of a loving unconditional welcome; it seems a sub-Christian act. The sense of unease is frequently expressed by mothers who plan to undergo an abortion in these circumstances: 'Once you get the results, every day your baby moves, you are dying inside.' This, of course, is why disabled people such as Marsha Saxton and Christy Nolan, react so violently to the practice of genetic screening and therapeutic abortion of affected fetuses. It strikes at the heart of our intuitions about humanity and human community. By contrast, Joseph Pieper helpfully defines the essence of love: 'Love is a way of saying to another person, "It's good that you exist; it's good that you are in this world."'[24]

I therefore find myself driven by the thrust of the biblical material, by theological arguments, and by the undeniable reality of widespread human intuitions about abortion, to the conclusion that we owe a duty of protection and care to the embryo and the early fetus as much as to the mature fetus and newborn baby. Even the earliest stages of human development deserve respect and protection. There is no point from fertilization onwards at which we can reliably conclude that a human being is not a member of the human community, one who is known and called by God, one with whom we are locked in community.

Fetal screening

I have argued that the destruction of even an impaired or abnormal fetus is inconsistent with a Christian worldview. As a result, I think that we should resist the tendency, noted in chapter 4, for modern pregnancies to become 'tentative'. The very existence of fetal screening and the availability of abortion until even late in pregnancy tend to imply that the commitment of parent to child is tentative or conditional. In some ways, it seems to me that fetal screening offers a false hope, a technological mirage. It seems to offer anxious parents the possibility of the security and confidence that my baby will be 'all right'. But the sad and unpalatable truth is that no technology can offer this confidence to parents. No technology can guarantee that unpredictable problems and dis-abilities will not arise after birth. As B. K. Rothman put it, 'The possibility of spending the rest of one's life caring for a sick or disabled child can never be eliminated by prenatal testing. I worry about women who say that they only dare have children because prenatal diagnosis is available. Motherhood is, among other things, one more chance for a speeding truck to ruin your life.'[25] Anxiety about our children is, sadly, a reality of being a parent which no amount of technology can assuage. It is part of the human condition.

But if, in my view, abortion for fetal abnormality falls short of genuine Christian compassion, does this mean that all fetal screening is valueless? What about the argument that fetal screening is helpful because it allows us to prepare ourselves psychologically for a disabled baby? This argument sounds good in theory, but in practice it may be less valuable than it seems. Certainly my own clinical experience is that the weeks of waiting for the birth of a baby who is known to be impaired may cause increasing anxiety and psychological distress rather than benefit. In some cases, it seems as if the medical knowledge provided by fetal screening has harmed the normal relationship between parents and newborn child. Why is this? I would like to speculate that in the original creation order, we are designed so that we start to love our unborn baby as a mysterious unknown, as a gift given in secret, before we meet them face to face at birth. Gilbert Meilaender expressed this perspective well: 'Perhaps the time of pregnancy will be better spent learning to love the child we have been given, before we evaluate and assess what our child is capable of.'[26]

I want to emphasize that this does not mean, of course, that all fetal screening and antenatal care is valueless. On the contrary, many of the tests offered by obstetricians and midwives, including antenatal ultrasound, congenital infection screening and antibody tests, allow treatable problems to be identified, so that the fetus can be helped and supported. What I feel deeply uneasy about are the tests for fetal conditions when the only available 'treatment' is abortion. Many pregnant women do not realize that they are being tested for conditions such as Down's syndrome for which the only option is abortion. They need to ask for information before the tests are performed and make clear their wishes to the hospital staff.

Hard cases

Of course we cannot escape the hard cases, the extreme and rare examples where there seems to be an overwhelming argument in favour of abortion. What about the dying mother, the rape victim, the conjoint twin, or the twelve-year-old pregnant child? In Western obstetric practice it is, thankfully, now very rare for the life of the mother to be actively threatened by a pregnancy. However, in these cases, it has been argued that death has already entered the pregnancy. It is not a matter of deciding whether a death should occur, but rather deciding whether death should strike the fetus, or both the fetus and the mother. In this extreme example it seems that an abortion may be acceptable, although deeply painful. As Meilaender put it, 'We cannot require a mother to build the human race by destroying herself.'[27] In practice, it may well be possible to delay termination of the pregnancy until the twenty-fourth or twenty-fifth week, when the fetus can then be delivered and offered a reasonable chance of survival with modern neonatal intensive care.

In the tragic case of the rape victim, again we can perceive a terrible conflict between fetus and mother. Although the fetus has, of course, no personal responsibility, its continued existence within the woman may constitute for her an embodiment of the original attack upon her person. There may be an understandable and overwhelming desire to get rid of any vestige, any reminder of the assault. Surely an abortion is the loving and Christian response? Even in this painful case there is an argument for continuing the pregnancy. To perform an abortion may be perceived, emotionally and unconsciously, as the perpetration of yet another assault on a woman who has already suffered terribly. To the long-lasting emotional consequences of rape are added the complex emotional traumas of deliberate abortion. How can the healing love of Christ be brought into this terrible agony?

Heather Gemmen was a mother of two who was violently raped in her own home by an anonymous intruder. She became pregnant and agonized over the decision whether or not to have an abortion. In the end she refused an abortion and loved and accepted into her family her beautiful mixed-race daughter Rachael. The book she wrote, *Startling Beauty*, is honest, shocking and profoundly Christian:

> Rape is ugliness at its basest form. Rape destroys innocence and cultivates bitterness, it steals security and extends fear, it kills hope and fosters shame . . . Rape takes too much. But I for one have gained more than I have lost. I have been startled by beauty in places it doesn't belong. I see it on a bloodied cross, and bitterness loses its power. I see it on the face of the man who keeps his vows to me, and fear loses its grip. I see it in the graceful dance of a child who was so unwanted, and hope revives its song.[28]

My wife and I have been involved, at first hand, with a similar story of extraordinary grace. Ruth was a single student who became pregnant following unconsensual sex. An abortion was arranged, but at the last moment she found she was unable to go through with it. Alone and desperate, by chance she found the leaflet of a local Christian crisis pregnancy centre. With the emotional support and practical help of volunteers, she found the strength to continue the pregnancy, and baby Jonathan was born. Now he has become the joy and light of her life, expressed in a simple poem she wrote: 'The love we share will always be there my son. Mother's love you will see . . . That's between me and thee, Jonathan.' Through this experience, Ruth's childhood faith was reignited. She has found a loving and caring community at a local church, and has resumed her studies, as a single parent. Through this painful experience, Ruth has not lost her sense of self-respect. So many women who seek help following an abortion, present with low self-esteem and loss of self-respect. In contrast, by God's grace, Ruth has found a new confidence; a sense of purpose, meaning and joy in parenthood. She freely admits that her experience has not been easy, but, in her words, 'I have something to show for it – my son.'

In Deuteronomy 30:19, God set out a dramatic choice for his people: 'I have set before you life and death, blessings and curses. Now choose life, so that you and your children may live.' It is not just Jonathan who has found life, but Ruth also.

Finally, there are rare and distressing hereditary conditions in which medical treatment seems unable to save children from appalling and uncontrollable suffering and progressive deterioration which is heart-breaking to watch. If the diagnosis can be made by DNA analysis before birth, is abortion always wrong? How can the love of Christ be demonstrated practically for parents confronted with these painful dilemmas?

The book *Shaming of the Strong* describes the experience of Sarah Williams, whose unborn baby was diagnosed in 2004 as having the very rare lethal abnormality called <u>thanatophoric dysplasia</u>.[29] Despite strong pressure to have an abortion from the medical staff, she decided to continue the pregnancy. Her book recounts in moving detail the experience of diagnosis, pregnancy, the naming of their unborn baby as Cerian 'loved one', Cerian's death during labour, and the painful process of grieving in the months and years that followed. Sarah's experience is a testament to the value and significance of an unseen and tragically deformed life, and the power of God to transform despair and bring hope in the strangest of circumstances. I'm afraid her book is also a painful indictment of virtually all the medical professionals she met, in a major UK centre of excellence, who appeared to fail at a most elementary level to demonstrate sensitivity, empathy and compassion.

Practical alternatives to abortion

My own personal belief, strengthened by my clinical experience, is that *nearly* *always* there is a better alternative than abortion for the unwanted or abnormal pregnancy. It is the way of practical support for the mother and for the unwanted child. This way is costly, emotionally, practically and financially. It is not an easy way because the truth is that there is no quick and pain-free technological fix for the ultimate dilemmas of the human condition. Practical, supportive caring is not an easy alternative. But I am convinced that it is a better way. It is also an essential response if we Christians are not to be guilty of hypocrisy. Unless Christians are in the forefront of providing practical care and support for those with unplanned pregnancies, and for parents struggling with the implications of bringing up a disabled or impaired child, then our supposed commitment to the sanctity of human life is deeply suspect.

One of the most remarkable developments in this field is the rapid expansion of crisis pregnancy centres, particularly those under the leadership of the Christian organization CareConfidential.[30] There are now more than 160 centres affiliated to CareConfidential throughout the UK. Each centre aims to provide free pregnancy testing, skilled and compassionate counselling from trained volunteers, clear information on all the options available, practical support and help, and time to explore all the conflicting emotions and long-term implications which an unplanned pregnancy brings. Instead of condemnation and judgment, they offer compassion and empathy, 'grace and truth'. Help, support and counselling is not restricted to those with unplanned pregnancies, but is also made available to those who have experienced abortions or suffered other forms of pregnancy loss, such as miscarriage or stillbirth. The centres are almost entirely staffed by female volunteers, many of whom have been personally affected by abortion and its consequences. A national telephone helpline has been established, and confidential advice and counselling is also available via the internet. Phil Clarke, a GP who has played a leading role in the development of the centres, provides a moving description of their work in his book, *Heart of Compassion*.[31]

The centres represent a wonderful Christian response to the problem of the unplanned pregnancy. At their best, they demonstrate all the qualities of authentic Christian caring: practical, costly, down-to-earth, realistic, unglamorous, empathic, respectful, sacrificial. Every year many thousands of people are touched by contact with these centres. Yet much more could be achieved with greater involvement of the wider Christian community, which represents a vast and still largely untapped resource for caring in our society. Here is an unparalleled opportunity for ordinary lay Christian people to demonstrate the practical reality of the gospel to hurting people in our midst.

Postscript

Maybe someone reading these words is oppressed by feelings of guilt or failure from a past experience. It is not my intention to judge others who have felt compelled to request, or to perform, an abortion in extreme circumstances. Maybe you pressurized your partner, your friend or your child to have an abortion. Maybe you were confronted by the existence of a terribly malformed baby and felt there was no alternative to abortion. I am painfully aware that many people carry deep burdens of secret pain and, maybe, guilt, in this area – burdens which they may feel completely unable to share with others. If this refers to you, then please get help from a trusted source.[32] Remember that human beings do not divide up into the guilty and the innocent. We are all guilty. No, human beings divide into the forgiven and the unforgiven. In Christ we can find a new beginning. Maybe, in God's grace, your painful experience can be transformed slowly, and miraculously – redeemed by God's power – so that it becomes a source of help and healing for others.

8. THE DYING BABY: DILEMMAS OF NEONATAL CARE

The effects of advances in medical technology are nowhere more obvious than in the development of intensive care for newborn babies. The survival of extremely preterm infants born at twenty-four to twenty-five weeks' gestation, almost four months before term and weighing just 500–700 grams (1 to 1½ pounds) is now a commonplace occurrence. Many babies with profound, and even bizarre, congenital malformations, (such as exomphalos, in which the bowel grows outside the abdomen), may be surgically treated at birth, leading to healthy survival into adulthood. But medical advances such as these are not bought cheaply, either in personal, social or financial terms. For parents and family there is the trauma of watching helplessly as their child struggles week after week under the burden of intensive-care procedures. For the National Health Service, the bill can be up to £1,200 or more, per baby per day. In 2006, the total cost to the public services of preterm infants in England and Wales was estimated to be a staggering £2.9 billion, and hospital care after birth accounted for 92% of the costs per preterm survivor.[1]

Ambivalence towards abnormal or premature babies

Those of us who care for newborn babies are frequently aware of an uncomfortable ambivalence which many people feel towards the abnormal or preterm infant. On the one hand, our society is highly sensitized towards the needs of babies and children. Charities and individuals donate hundreds of thousands of pounds to buy intensive-care equipment. Prominent publicity campaigns feature dramatic pictures of babies surrounded by life-saving equipment. Newspapers and television run prominent articles on the newest 'gee-whizz' medical technology, as well as heart-warming human-interest stories about the latest child survivor. Parents and visitors to neonatal units are frequently moved to tears by the sight of tiny babies struggling for life, and the concentration of resources and expertise devoted to their care. Behind this public interest and support lies more than sentimentality. Babies, especially those who are sick and vulnerable, are seen by many as infinitely precious beings, unique and defence-less individuals who are to be nurtured, cared for and protected.

But an entirely contradictory view towards the abnormal or preterm baby is also widespread, although frequently unspoken. According to this perspec-tive, however we may be moved by the abnormal baby's plight, we have to realize that he or she is in reality one of 'Nature's rejects', the unfortunate consequence of a complex biological process which is frighteningly fallible and prone to accidents. If Nature in her wisdom has decided that this particular baby has no viable future and should be discarded, who are we to use the panoply of modern intensive care techniques to thwart her wishes? Why waste scarce financial resources and emotional energy on this individual? Far better to ensure that the baby does not survive, and suggest to the parents that they try to have another.

This view has several hidden assumptions. First, the implication is that sick or abnormal newborn babies are disposable, unlike adults or older children who require medical care. In other words, there is no fundamental duty upon the rest of society to preserve their lives. Secondly, in distinction to adults who have a unique character and life-history, the sick baby has no genuine individuality or personality. 'It' cannot be regarded as a person, and so each baby is viewed as fundamentally *replaceable*. Another infant can always be conceived to substitute for the abnormal and unwanted one. Thirdly, there is the implicit acceptance of what might be termed a eugenic biological imperative, a desire to preserve the human gene pool and eliminate harmful genes. To believe that 'Nature knows best' is to believe that only the fittest should survive. The parents may have a 'selfish' wish to ensure the survival of their sick or abnormal baby, and this is understandable, but from a strictly biological perspective it may be against the best interests of humanity as a whole. From this perspective, the whole enterprise of neonatal intensive care for abnormal or premature babies can be seen as misguided, wasteful of scarce resources and ultimately futile. It is 'against Nature' – a modern version of medical *hubris*.

As we have seen, some bioethicists, such as Peter Singer, reinforce this attitude by arguing that newborn babies are not full members of the human community and that their lives may be painlessly brought to an end, if this seems to be in the best interests of the community as a whole. It would be misleading to suggest that all, or even the majority of, current medical ethicists would give whole-hearted support to the positions of Singer or Harris. They represent an influential but extreme position within the spectrum of attitudes amongst contemporary philosophers. Nonetheless, their views seem logically consistent with their basic philosophical presuppositions, and demonstrate the radical implications of a rigorously utilitarian approach to the newborn baby.

Neonatal euthanasia

In 2005 the prestigious *New England Journal of Medicine* published the 'Groningen protocol', a procedure for regularizing the euthanasia of newborns in the Netherlands.[2] The protocol describes three groups of infants in whom deliberate life-ending procedures could be taken: those with no chance of survival, those with a poor prognosis who are dependent on intensive care, and those with a 'hopeless prognosis who experience what parents and medical experts deem to be unbearable suffering'. A national survey in the Netherlands suggested that euthanasia was carried out in fifteen to twenty newborns each year, but reporting has been much lower. The Groningen protocol has aroused considerable con-troversy, but it has received strong support from a number of medical ethicists.[3]

In 2006, the Nuffield Council on Bioethics convened a working party to address ethical issues in neonatology and fetal medicine. Their report[4] explicitly addressed the issue of neonatal euthanasia, but concluded that the law should not be changed to allow neonatal euthanasia, even when the life of the newborn was seen as limited and even 'intolerable'. The working party rejected the view that intentionally ending a life was morally equivalent to the withdrawal of life-sustaining treatment. They argued that if it became legal to end the life of a newborn on the basis of their own best interests, then it was illogical not to kill an incompetent child or adult under similar circumstances. They also defended the generally accepted ethos of the medical profession to preserve and protect life wherever possible, arguing that allowing doctors to kill newborns would weaken the level of trust in the profession. The working party concluded that 'the moment of birth was the significant moral and legal transition for judgements about preserving life'. They supported the current UK practice of late feticide for fetal abnormality, whilst opposing a move to legalize neonatal euthanasia.

The issue remains a matter of active discussion and debate, and there appears to be a minority of paediatricians who would, if it was legalized, support the intentional killing of newborns who are perceived to have a 'poor quality of life'.

Treating babies with respect

Mother Teresa used to describe the work of her sisters of charity in the slums of Calcutta. Every day the sisters would scour the streets to pick up the dying beggar, the abandoned baby found in a dustbin, the leprosy victim. She described in graphic detail the appalling degradation of those she found, the maggots living in the wounds, the stench, the pathetic courage. Where did the sisters find the motivation which drove them to this level of caring? Was it pity for these miserable scraps of humanity? This is what she once said: 'It is more than pity motivates us, it is compassion mingled with *respect*.'

Here again is the theme of respect which we noted in chapter 2. But how can you possibly respect a being who has sunk to such degradation and filth? Mother Teresa used to give a spiritual answer to this down-to-earth question. She quoted the parable of the sheep and the goats in Matthew's Gospel: '"I was hungry and you gave me something to eat, I was thirsty and you gave me something to drink, I was a stranger and you invited me in, I needed clothes and you clothed me, I was sick and you looked after me . . . " "Lord, when did we see you hungry and feed you . . . ?" "I tell you the truth, whatever you did for one of the least of these brothers of mine, you did for me."' (Matthew 25:31–46)

Mother Teresa was saying, in effect, 'This is Jesus.' Jesus was present, in what she used to call 'a distressing disguise'.[5] When we care for the abandoned and rejected of society, we are ' tending the wounds of Christ'. That is why we respect them, and treat them with dignity. 'Here on the streets, in the unwanted children, in the broken body of the leper, in the dying beggar, we see Christ, we touch him and we care for him.' A Hindu social worker once described the difference between their official activities for the poor and those of Mother Teresa:. 'We do it for something, but you do it for someone . . . '[6] That is the heart of Christian caring. It's the reason for the note of respect which I believe is the hallmark of authentic Christian compassion.

Mother Teresa's thought has affected me deeply as I have reflected on my work as a paediatrician. I have come to realize that I am called to treat this tiny little body, struggling for life, covered in tubes, attached to complex machinery, with the same tenderness, the same sense of wonder, the same *respect*, that Mary and Joseph showed as they cared for their little bundle in a stable two thousand years ago. The Christian doctrine of the Incarnation teaches that Jesus was a baby – not a sentimental sugar candy, Christmas card cherub but a real baby, who dribbled down his front and had dirty nappies, a baby who fitted with the medical definition: ' a gastrointestinal tract with no sense of responsibility at either end'.

Christian caring for babies cannot be sentimental and airy-fairy. It must be down to earth, realistic and practical. It must be rooted in the stuff of our physical humanity. Yet, at the same time, it should display the distinctive qualities of the way that Christians should care for all members of the human community: wonder, respect, empathy and protection.

Advocacy for the vulnerable

Treating babies with respect means that we cannot treat even the extremely premature baby as less than a full member of the human community. Babies are our neighbours, who deserve 'respect-love' with all its sacrificial demands. Instead of a eugenic concern that only the fittest should become members of society, we should be concerned to ensure the survival and the protection of those who are the most vulnerable. The risk of exploitation can come from parents and relatives who may put their own interests above those of their child, from doctors or managers who may wish to use their patients to increase power or academic status, or from health-care purchasers who wish to redirect funds to other patient groups because of political expediency or utilitarian convictions. Our duty as Christians is to act as an advocate on behalf of all the weak in our society, to ensure that their voice is heard and their interests are preserved.

When should intensive treatment be withdrawn?

Treating babies with respect does not mean that we are obliged to provide intensive treatment in every conceivable condition, to attempt to prolong life even when there is no prospect of recovery. An extreme example is provided by the tragic story of Samuel Linares.[7] He was a young infant who was receiving life-support treatment in an intensive care unit in Chicago. The doctors had concluded that there was no chance of Samuel's recovery, but for legal and ethical reasons they felt unable to switch the machines off to allow death to occur. For eight months his parents pleaded for the doctors to switch the machines off. Then, one day, Samuel's father appeared on the intensive care unit carrying a gun. Holding the nurses at bay, he disconnected the life-support equipment, and cradled his son in his arms until he was certain that Samuel was dead. He surrendered to the police, who took him away and charged him with murder.

It seems obvious that this case represents a terrible failure of modern medical care. It was a failure on the part of Samuel's doctors, whether from fear of litigation or for some other reason, to recognize the point where medicine had changed from a source of healing and restoration and instead had become a technological monster, even a strange form of child abuse. Treating babies with respect means that we must learn to let go. We must learn to recognize the point where medical treatment becomes futile and abusive, or where the burdens of treatment exceed the benefits.

How do we balance the burdens and benefits of intensive medical treatment? If it is apparent that there is no hope of meaningful long-term survival, and that intensive support is merely prolonging the process of dying, withdrawal of medical treatment, following full discussion and with the agreement of the parents, is most consistent with a genuine respect for the dignity of the individual. Diagnostic techniques, such as ultrasound or magnetic resonance scanning of the brain, can give vital information about the severity of brain injury, in the critical few hours and days after delivery. Although it will never be possible to foresee the long-term outlook with complete reliability, medical technology does provide ways of predicting the neurological consequences for any individual. How should this information be employed?

Again, I have no precise or logically watertight way for balancing the burdens and benefits of intensive treatment in any individual case. But it seems to me that a Christian perspective on human life places special importance on the value of relationships. We are not 'vitalists', believing that biological survival, the maximum prolongation for a beating heart and respiring lungs, is the primary goal of medical treatment. As we saw in previous chapters, it is the human capacity for relationships which is at the heart of our identity. We are constituted by our relations. So, as we try to assess the consequences of brain injury, in my view the critical issue is not the degree of physical handicap which may result, but the likely capacity to enter meaningfully into relationships; relationships with family and friends, with the community, and ultimately with God himself.

Brain injury which causes impaired mobility or loss of vision or hearing, but in which sufficient brain function is retained for some capacity for loving human relationships, does not constitute in my view adequate justification for the withdrawal of intensive care. The benefits of medical treatment are likely in most cases to outweigh its burdens. On the other hand, brain injury of such severity that no capacity for meaningful relationships is apparently possible, can be regarded as reducing human life to mere biological survival. This is likely if there is global destruction of cortical and subcortical structures in both cerebral hemispheres. In a similar category, come brain malformations involving a generalized failure of development of the cortex or subcortical connections. While the presence of such brain injury would not prevent the infant from being regarded still as a human being, worthy of respect and dignity, it does raise questions about the appropriateness of prolonging survival by intensive medical and technological support.

Intensive life-support treatment has a purpose, a goal: it is intended to restore an individual to health. But in the case of profound and permanent brain injury, the benefit that treatment can bring is virtually nil; it cannot bring any degree of restoration. In other words, in this situation it is open to question whether the burden to the individual of invasive and unpleasant intensive care out-weighs the possible benefit that such treatment can bring. Provided there is a consensus between health-care staff and parents, it seems appropriate to withdraw intensive treatment with the realization that death is very likely to follow. The intention is not to end life, however, but to withdraw futile treatment, although doctors and parents can foresee that death may occur as a result of this action. (The important distinction between intention and foresight is discussed further in chapter 10.) If, as sometimes happens, the baby does not die as a result, then compassionate caring, provision of feeds and symptom relief is continued.

The decision to withdraw intensive treatment does not mean that we have accepted that the intrinsic value of a baby's life is reduced because of severe brain damage. This would be a contradiction of the basic Christian stance that we have defended earlier. Nor do I believe that we are justified in withdrawing life-support treatment because we believe that a baby's life 'is not worth living'. We are in no position to make a judgment on the value of another person's life. But as medical professionals we can, and must, make judgments about the value of medical treatment. We cannot withdraw life support because a *life* is not worth living, but we must decide if a *treatment* is not worth giving.[8]

The case of Jodie and Mary, outlined in the Introduction, illustrates how complex and difficult it can be to balance the relative burdens and benefits of treatment, especially in the extremely rare case of conjoint twins. If no surgery was undertaken, both twins would die, but palliative care could be provided, allowing a peaceful and pain-free death. If invasive surgery was undertaken, one twin would almost certainly die during the surgical procedure, and the other would be subjected to a major surgical insult with an uncertain outcome. Death in the post-operative phase would be a major risk. The parents and doctors could not agree about the right course of action, and ultimately the Court decided that surgery was justified.

I have had the privilege of caring for several sets of conjoint twins in my clinical career, and the precise nature of the fusion between the bodies is different in every case. Although the ethical principles are unchanged, the judgment about whether invasive surgical treatment is justified depends critically on the precise clinical details, as well as on the views of the parents and the many specialists involved. In some cases, there seems to be no obviously right answer; we must do what seems best, recognizing the terrible stakes involved, and the uncertainty of the outcome.

Techniques like brain scans, which allow the extent of brain injury to be assessed, do not of course solve the painful ethical dilemmas concerning the appropriateness of intensive care for a malformed or critically sick newborn, but they provide objective information which can be discussed in detail with the parents and with other concerned individuals, and on which ethical decisions about intensive care can be based. In this way, respect for the dignity and worth of the individual baby, and concern for his or her best interests, can be translated into practical decisions about medical care.

Care of the dying baby

When health professionals and parents recognize the point that intensive treatment should be withdrawn, it is important to realize that, although medical treatment may stop, caring must never stop. In essence, we must provide the highest quality of palliative care for dying babies, just as we should provide palliative care for every dying adult. In my view, every baby deserves a minimum level of care by virtue of their birthright as a human being.

First, we must provide adequate pain and symptom relief. We have a duty to use medical and nursing care to ensure that not only pain is adequately treated but also distressing symptoms such as breathlessness and convulsions are controlled. Secondly, except in extreme cases where there is no possibility of absorption through the bowel, we should provide food and fluids. Allowing babies to die from starvation and dehydration is not compatible with treating them with respect. Finally, and equally important, we must ensure that the dying baby receives 'TLC', tender loving care. Cuddles, where possible from mother or other close relative, are a physical demonstration of the wonder, respect and empathy which we owe to each baby. All other treatments, such as antibiotics and intravenous nutrition, are optional. They should only be given if the likely benefits will exceed the burdens of the treatment. But the short list of symptom control, food and TLC is the minimum that every baby deserves. This is what respect means when translated into clinical practice.

Christopher's story

Alan and Verity are close friends from my local church, All Souls, in the heart of London's West End. My wife Celia and I have known them for many years, and as two couples we have shared our lives together. In the spring of 1996, as we enjoyed an evening together, Verity told us that she was expecting a baby. We discussed the news with anticipation and excitement. But only two weeks later, the outlook had changed. A routine ultrasound scan at twenty weeks showed major abnormalities. The diagnosis was <u>Edwards syndrome</u>, a tragic and rare chromosomal disorder which causes multiple malformations, severe mental impairment and a uniformly fatal outcome. In this condition nearly all obstetricians will recommend abortion. What possible point can there be to continuing a pregnancy where there is no hope of long-term survival? Yet, after agonizing and heartfelt discussion, Alan and Verity decided not to have an abortion but to continue the pregnancy. What follows is the transcript of an interview in which Nick Page asked them to talk about their experience:

Nick: Why did you choose not to have an abortion?

Verity: I think by the time we'd reached twenty weeks, we'd already seen the child on the scan, seen his features, his limbs, known every condition that he suffered from. By then he'd already become a real person and it seemed terrible, the thought of ending a life that was already, in our opinion, so complete.

Nick: Looking back, what would you say was the legacy of Christopher for you two as a couple?

Verity: I think it was the chance to be a parent, one that we would have been denied completely if we'd have had an abortion. Each of us was able to be as normal a parent as we could be with a child with that condition, with all its joys, and with a lot of the normal things associated with parenthood. And the other thing is the way we were able to connect with him as a human being. I mean we didn't know the extent of his handicap, to what degree he would recognize us, but we really connected with him. He communicated with us and we did with him. And that ability to create a relationship with another human being is . . . wonderful.

Nick: The impact Christopher had, not just on yourselves but on everyone around you, was very interesting. Why do you think that was?

Verity: He seemed to have the ability to draw love out of people in quite a unique way. People were able to hold him. He was a very peaceful baby, but he seemed to melt the coldest heart and to make people really love him.

Alan: Verity sometimes used to visit the local hospice, St. Christopher's in Sydenham, and take Christopher round the wards. Here there were people who were dying and yet they were able to hold a baby who was also dying and in need of terminal, palliative care. And somehow that shared experience between a baby who was dying and an adult who was dying was quite remarkable.

Verity: One of the patients, Beatty, who was dying of leukaemia, was especially fond of Christopher, and one day when I visited her, she said, 'Now, Christopher, I don't know who's going to die first, whether it's going to be you or me, but I'll be waiting for you in Heaven with my arms open ready to welcome you when you arrive.'

Nick Page asked Richard Bewes, then rector of All Souls Church, to talk about the effect that Christopher's life had had on the church congregation.

Richard: His life exercised a most extraordinary ministry. There he was, the smallest little shrimp within the congregation. Here was the weakest member among us, easily the weakest member, and yet he did exercise a strong, strange hold upon us. Indeed, in a real way, we shared him among the congregation. He became, in the end, almost public property. His parents would be one side of the room, and he would be shared amongst people the other side of the room. People would take it in turns to cuddle him, and then to learn from his own life and from the attitude of his parents, Alan and Verity. They themselves were quite obviously growing through that experience in trust, in faith and, I think, in service too. So the three of them exercised a strong hold in those precious, very short, seven months that will live indelibly with us, all those of us who were members of the church at that time.

When Christopher was born he was the smallest member of the church, and when he died, seven months later, he was still virtually the same size. A friend summed up his influence: 'Although Christopher was unable to grow, he helped others to grow.' Christopher died in the summer of 1997. Yet his influence still carries on. I don't want to imply that there was no sadness. There was, and still is, a deep sense of grief, pain and loss at Christopher's disability and untimely death. Alan and Verity and their family have known tears and heartache, and those feelings carry on. But behind it all is the Christian conviction that even the weakest and most malformed human being has a life of unique value. Christopher in his way was a Godlike being, a masterpiece. His life was an example of Christian theology in practice, and it was a privilege to know him.

God's broken image

Here is a strange paradox. Sometimes we see the image of God most clearly, not in the perfect specimens of humanity, not in the Olympic athlete or the Nobel prizewinner. We see Christ in the broken, the malformed, the imperfect. It is an example of the Easter mystery. God is revealed, not in glorious majesty but in a broken body on a cross. This is the vision of the L'Arche communities founded by the French Catholic Jean Vanier. Vanier developed a way of caring for the profoundly disabled individuals who are so often rejected and abandoned by society. He saw them as in some way representing the presence of Christ in our midst. 'The person perceived by society as a problem, useless, a burden, we see as a source of life, drawing us towards truth, towards Jesus and the gospel . . . For me to follow Jesus is to be with those who have been cast aside and to meet him in and with them.'[9]

Is this just sentimentality: life denying sugar-sweet religiosity of the worst and most mystical kind? I can imagine the responses of the cynical clinician, the radical philosopher and the hard-bitten health economist. But no, it is not sentimentality. It is a vision of caring which fits with the Christian worldview, and the biblical revelation. I am increasingly struck at how this vision of caring also makes sense to ordinary people in our society. It 'rings bells'; it fits with the deepest intuitions of our hearts.

Over the years, I and my professional colleagues, especially Anthea Blake, senior nurse on the Neonatal Unit at University College Hospital, have had the privilege of caring for many dying babies. We have found a way of caring for them, and for their families, that recognizes the unique value and dignity of even a dying baby. Under Anthea Blake's leadership and together with the hospital chaplaincy team, we have developed an interdenominational Christian service for parents who have lost babies at our hospital, either as a result of neonatal death or stillbirth. Once a year, we invite bereaved parents and their families to a simple service in a local church. The content of the service is chosen entirely by parents. Often they contribute poems, either of their own or gleaned from other sources. At the climax of the service, the children, brothers and sisters of those who have died, bring cards to the front, each card bearing the name of a baby who died, in a simple act of dedication.

It is always a weepy and intensely moving experience. It may sound rather sentimental and even maudlin. Yet we have been struck by the depth of commitment which many bereaved parents have shown to this service, many of whom would claim no Christian or other religious faith. Some parents and families come year after year to remember a baby who lived maybe for only a few hours. Many parents have written to tell us how helpful and healing the experience has been. Why do so many people come to this simple service? Why do they see this straightforward act of commemoration as so important? I suggest it is because the service represents a public recognition of the unique significance and worth of their dead baby. It says that their baby was not just a nonentity, but a unique person – valued, grieved and missed. It fits with the deepest intuitions of a parent's heart.

I have tried to summarize what I have learned over the years about the intuitions of the many parents whose babies I have cared for. 'My baby is a unique individual with a history, an identity and a name. My baby is a person, not a thing: a "he" or "she" not an "it". My baby must be treated with gentleness and respect by those who are caring for him or her. My baby can never be replaced although I may have other babies in the future. If my baby's outlook is hopeless, then it may be the most compassionate act to withdraw treatment and "keep her comfortable" knowing that she may die. Withdrawing treatment and allowing my baby to die is not the same as deliberately killing her. If my baby does die, I need to have permanent reminders and mementoes of her short existence, to honour her memory as a unique person, my beloved child.'

It's obvious from my clinical experience that the intuitions of most parents are light years away from the philosophy of Peter Singer. To nearly all of us, babies are not 'non-persons'. They are unique, vulnerable and precious members of the human community. I am continually struck by the fact that the deepest intuitions of ordinary people, parents and families, in our pluralistic and multifaith society, are so often similar to the convictions of orthodox Christian theology. When we put forward a Christian perspective about the disabled and dying baby, we are not defending a sugary sentimentality. We are telling it like it is. The biblical Christian worldview works: it fits with reality.

In the next chapter we continue our progress from the beginning of life to its end, by addressing the controversial issues of euthanasia and assisted suicide.

9. A GOOD DEATH? EUTHANASIA AND ASSISTED SUICIDE

'Death like the sun should not be stared at.' So said the French philosopher, quoted in the Introduction. Yet advances in medicine force us to do just that. Of course, all generations have discovered that human beings cannot evade the reality of death. But, if we are going to develop an authentic Christian response to the issues of euthanasia and medically assisted suicide, we need to stare at death with renewed intensity. We need to stare at its mystery and awful finality, at the questions and fears that it raises, and at our own mortality. As with the other issues in this book, death and dying are not just 'out there' as abstract theoretical issues. Death is here in our midst. You, the reader, carry your future mortality with you as you read these words. To be a little over-dramatic, I am writing as a dying man to dying people.

According to the cynic, 'Life is a sexually transmitted degenerative condition with a mortality rate of 100%.' As I get older, my own death becomes a matter for reflection. How would I like to die? What will happen, who will be there, who will care for me? How will I spend my last days, my last hours, my last moments? Will I die well, or in pain and distress?

'It's not that I'm afraid of death, it's just that I don't want to be there when it happens.' The words of Woody Allen ring true. On balance, we don't want to be there when it happens. The problem is that we have little choice in the matter. As we shall see, it is the drive for choice, for control, for personal autonomy, which is at the heart of current moves towards the legalization of euthanasia which are taking place across the world.

The drive for euthanasia legalization

When I wrote the first edition of this book, the debate about euthanasia was focused on people dying in terrible uncontrollable pain, especially those with terminal cancer. Ten years later, the debate is still raging, but now the issues are strikingly different. Now the central question is the right to self-determination, and the diseases in focus are not cancer, but chronic debilitating neuro-degenerative conditions such as motor neuron disease (as in the case of Diane Pretty).

In the introduction we looked at the case of Dr Anne Turner which was publicized widely by pro-euthanasia activists. She was a professional with a degenerative disease who had a horror of becoming dependent on others. By objective criteria, she was only mildly disabled and she probably had a life expectancy of at least three to five years. But she had clearly expressed a wish to die. Why on earth should she be forced to travel to Switzerland in order to end her own life?

Another case which caused great public sympathy in the UK was that of Daniel James. He was a promising young rugby player who had played for the national youth squad, but in 2007, at the age of twenty-two, he suffered a spinal-cord injury while playing rugby, and was permanently paralysed from the chest downwards. A year later, accompanied by his parents, he received medically assisted suicide at the Dignitas centre in Switzerland. His parents said their son had tried several times to kill himself before he 'gained his wish'. They were quoted as saying, 'His death was no doubt a welcome relief from the "prison" he felt his body had become, and the day-to-day fear and loathing of his living existence . . . This is the last way that the family wanted Dan's life to end, but he was, as those who know him are aware, an intelligent, strong-willed and, some say, determined young man.'[1] Although there was widespread sympathy and support for Daniel and his parents, some saw this case (involving neither terminal illness nor severe pain) as an example of the 'slippery slope' which threatens all euthanasia legislation.

Definitions

Words are slippery things, and in this debate, phrases such as the 'right to die', a 'merciful death', 'relief of suffering', and 'assisted dying' are often used loosely, leading to confusion and misunderstanding. An old Chinese proverb states: 'The beginning of wisdom is to call things by their proper names.' The phrase 'the right to die' sounds so reasonable and yet it can mean at least five different things to different people: (1) the right to refuse life-sustaining treatment which is burdensome or futile; (2) the right to refuse life-sustaining treatment for any reason; (3) the right to commit suicide for 'rational' reasons; (4) the right to obtain help in committing suicide; or (5) the right to be killed by a doctor at your request.

Of these, the first is both legal and accepted as a basis of good medical care, the second and third are not illegal, whereas the last two are both illegal in most jurisdictions in the world. When we enter into the debate about euthanasia, we must challenge people to use words accurately and carefully. The term 'euthanasia' means literally 'a good death'. But here is a more precise definition: 'Euthanasia is the intentional killing by act or omission, of a person, whose life is thought not to be worth living.'

First, this definition puts emphasis on *intentional* killing, a deliberate and pre-meditated act to take life, to introduce death into a situation. Secondly, it implies that euthanasia may be performed either positively by deliberate act, or negatively by omission. It is the *intention to kill* which is central to the definition. In the past, the phrases 'active euthanasia' and 'passive euthanasia' have been widely used, but most ethicists now agree that they are ambiguous and should be dropped.

Euthanasia can be divided into *voluntary* euthanasia, killing carried out at the patient's explicit request, and *involuntary* euthanasia, where no immediate or unambiguous request has been given, although a previous willingness to be killed may or may not have been expressed. (Some have added a third category 'non-voluntary euthanasia' where the patient is not competent to express a wish.) In the Netherlands, the word 'euthanasia' is nearly always taken to imply an explicit request, so Dutch doctors say that 'involuntary euthanasia' is a contradiction in terms, and prefer the term 'life-terminating treatment'.

Under what situations has involuntary euthanasia been suggested? Here are some possibilities, although of course the list is not exhaustive. First there is the malformed or brain-damaged infant, whose life is considered to be worthless, or so limited due to disability that death is preferable to continued existence. As we saw in chapter 8, the Groningen protocol has been developed to provide a professional framework for neonatal euthanasia in the Netherlands. Then there is the child with a terminal disease who may have expressed a desire to die, although children are technically incapable of giving legally valid consent because of their immaturity. Thirdly, there is the comatose or unresponsive patient, such as a person in the persistent vegetative state. Fourthly, there is the confused or demented patient who may have previously expressed a wish to die, but is now incapable of understanding his or her current situation. Finally, there is the person with a severe untreatable psychiatric disease or personality disorder, who feels their life is worthless but is unable to give legally binding consent. In all such cases, euthanasia has been advocated, and has indeed been practised on occasion by doctors, on the grounds that it is a truly compassionate act.

It is important to distinguish euthanasia from two other clinical practices: the withdrawal of life-sustaining medical treatment which is regarded as futile or burdensome, and the giving of symptom-relieving treatment in order to benefit the patient, which may have the unintended side-effect of shortening life. Both of these are an accepted part of normal medical practice. In the next chapter, I shall argue that they are consistent with the Christian worldview, whereas euthanasia, intentional mercy-killing, is not. The case of Ms B, referred to in the Introduction, involved her refusal to consent to life-supporting treatment. After careful legal consideration, the treatment was withdrawn and Ms B died. This is an example, not of 'passive euthanasia', nor of intentional killing by omission, but of refusal of treatment – category 2 in the list above.

Physician-assisted suicide

If euthanasia is defined as intentional mercy-killing, its close relation is physician-assisted suicide (PAS) – the deliberate assistance by a physician in the suicide of a patient who intends to end his or her own life. It is intentional killing, but at one remove. The doctor provides the means – the drugs, the apparatus and the technical knowledge – explaining what to do and how to do it, but drawing back from the final act. The patient must take the tablets, put the bag over his or her head, or throw the switch. As in the rest of medicine, we should not be too surprised that technology has got in on the act. Now it is possible to perform physician-assisted suicide more 'cleanly', using computer-controlled infusion devices which inject lethal mixtures at the push of a button, or even at the blink of an eyelid.

Traditionally, both euthanasia and physician-assisted suicide were forbidden under almost every known code of law. Until recently, all accepted codes of medical ethics forbade them, although in fact, both have been known since ancient times.

The Hippocratic oath, which originated several centuries before Christ, specifically rules out both euthanasia and physician-assisted suicide: 'I will use treatment to help the sick according to my ability and judgement, but I will never use it to injure or wrong them. I will not give poison to anyone though asked to do so, neither will I suggest such a plan.'[2] As we shall see in chapter 11, the Hippocratic tradition was adopted by the early Christian church, and the Hippocratic-Christian consensus against euthanasia has held for more than 2,000 years.

But there is now an international move to legalize both euthanasia and PAS. At the time of writing, euthanasia is legal in the Netherlands, Belgium and Luxembourg. In the Netherlands, about 3% of patients die by voluntary euthanasia, and most family doctors can expect to be involved in a case every two or three years.[3] PAS is currently legal in the US states of Oregon and Washington, and similar legislation is being considered in several other states. In the UK and USA, PAS is seen as more acceptable to the public than euthanasia, perhaps because it fits with Anglo-Saxon preoccupations about individual liberty and autonomy. (See further information about euthanasia and PAS on the website.)

In the UK, the Voluntary Euthanasia Society has dissociated itself from the disreputable and 'dodgy' aspects of pro-euthanasia campaigning, such as DIY suicides using polythene bags and hoarded drugs. It now promotes the legalization of PAS and has a long list of distinguished and respectable patrons, including the eminent human rights lawyer Lord Joel Joffe.

A recurring theme in this book has been the sanitization of language to make ethically controversial actions more acceptable. It demonstrates how important language is to the way human beings make moral judgments. 'Killing' sounds so harsh, so blunt, so shocking. If we can find euphemisms like 'assisted dying', 'easeful death', or 'death with dignity', the same action will sound so much more acceptable. The euthanasia debate has been a classic example of this phenomenon ever since the Third Reich, whose Charitable Foundation for the Transport of Patients organized the transfer of mentally disabled people and Jews for 'special treatment' in the gas chambers, and the collection of payments for the treatment from their relatives.[4]

In 2006 the Voluntary Euthanasia Society changed its name to 'Dignity in Dying'. At the time of writing, their website studiously avoided straightforward words such as 'euthanasia', 'suicide', or 'mercy killing'.[5] Instead it used vague and euphemistic terms such as 'a dignified death where suffering is minimized', 'choice and control over how we die', 'assistance to die', and 'the choice to end suffering if it becomes unbearable'.

Not everyone has been convinced by this approach. A commentator in the *Daily Telegraph* said, 'It tells you something when an organisation has to refer to itself by a euphemism. The Voluntary Euthanasia Society now plans to call itself Dignity in Dying. Well, who among us does not want to die with dignity? It is hard to shake off the suspicion that euthanasiasts (*sic*) are shy of spelling out what they are really about, viz killing people.'[6]

A senior palliative care nurse responded to the use of the phrase 'assisted dying' for PAS. 'Midwives assist birth and palliative care nurses assist the dying with specialist palliative care. Assistance is not the same as killing. The use of the term "assisted dying" is offensive to those of us who are giving good care at the end of life. It is a deception to sanitize killing to make it more acceptable to the public. The implication is that you can only die with dignity if you are killed.'[7]

In 2006 Lord Joffe, strongly supported by Dignity in Dying, introduced the Assisted Dying Bill in the House of Lords.[8] Its aim was to legalize PAS under strictly controlled circumstances. In order to qualify for assisted suicide, the patient had to meet all the following criteria: a) be legally competent, b) have a terminal condition with an agreed life expectancy of less than six months, c) be suffering unbearably, which was defined as 'suffering, whether by reason of pain, distress or otherwise which the patient finds so severe as to be unacceptable', and d) have expressed a 'persistent wish to die'. The Bill was defeated by a vote in the House of Lords, but it seems highly likely that further attempts will be made to legalize PAS in the UK.

When the Assisted Dying Bill was first put forward, it included both PAS and voluntary euthanasia, but in order to make the Bill more acceptable to the public, the clauses concerning euthanasia were removed. However, some people who wish to die are almost totally paralysed and unable to perform any voluntary actions. Lord Joffe proposed that doctors could go to extraordinary lengths to assist suicide. The Bill stated that in the case of a patient for whom it was 'impossible or inappropriate' to ingest lethal medication orally, a doctor could give medicine by 'prescribing and providing' a means of self-administration. Thus a doctor could prescribe a lethal mixture of a muscle relaxant and an anaesthetic agent, draw up the drugs into a syringe, insert an intravenous cannula, connect the lines and set up a complex computer-controlled machine operated by button, or even by the patient's eye blink. But the doctor may not actually push the plunger or directly give an injection.

Is there genuinely a moral distinction between setting up the infusion and pressing the plunger? In both cases, the intention and the actions of the doctor are directed towards ending life. This is intentional killing, by any legal definition. And what happens if the doctor rigs up the infusion device, but the patient accidentally does not die, and suffers severe brain damage during the failed suicide attempt? Will the doctor now transfer the patient to the long-term neurodisability service, or will he or she feel a moral duty to finish the job cleanly by killing the patient?

A Dutch doctor with practical experience of both voluntary euthanasia and PAS said, 'Thinking that physician-assisted suicide is the entire answer to the question of ending of life of a suffering patient . . . is a fantasy. There will always be patients who cannot drink, or are semiconscious, or prefer that a physician perform this act. Experience has taught us that there are many cases of assisted suicide in which the suicide fails. Physicians need to be aware of the necessity to intervene before patients awaken.'[9]

In one Dutch study, it was found that in 18% of cases in which assisted suicide was intended, a lethal injection was given by the doctor because of complications. 'In most of these cases, the patient did not die as soon as expected or awoke from coma, and the physician felt compelled to administer a lethal injection because of the anticipated failure of the assisted suicide. In some cases, the physician administered a lethal injection because the patient had difficulty swallowing the oral medication, vomited after swallowing it, or became unconscious before swallowing all of it.'[10]

Fear – the heart of the debate

What then are the forces which lie behind the campaigning, the demonstrations, the vociferous propaganda for the legalization of euthanasia? I suggest that much of the debate is driven, not by *compassion* but by *fear*. Several years ago I had the opportunity to engage in public debate with a well-known and highly respected campaigner for legalizing euthanasia. I was struck by his words: 'Basically I'm afraid. It's not so much that I'm afraid of death, but I am afraid of the process of dying.' It seems to me that three fears lie at the heart of the debate.

Fear of pain

By 'fear of pain' I mean much more than merely physical pain. I am referring to what palliative care specialists call *total pain*. It is a concept which includes physical pain, but also emotional, relational and spiritual pain. Total pain is hard to define. It is distress which has many components. Take an elderly person dying from cancer. He is in physical distress because the disease has spread to the bones, causing a continual grinding discomfort. He is in psychological distress because he is frightened at what the future may hold. Will the pain get worse and worse until it is unbearable? Will he have to leave his home and be admitted to hospital? He is in relational distress because the family is putting on a brave face and refusing to acknowledge the reality of what is happening. He is in spiritual distress because he is confronting the ultimate reality of death without any sense of meaning or purpose. What has his life been for? What is there to hope for? This is total pain.

As a society, we have lost the belief that suffering can have any positive value at all. Pain is useless, futile, destructive, incomprehensible, terrifying. For many, the purpose of existence is to maximize personal happiness, and if we can't be happy then at least we can try to anaesthetize the pain.

Fear of indignity

With modern medical care, most people are not in great physical pain when they die. But to die with a tube in every orifice, to die with a rubber sheet on the bed in case we make a mess like a child, to require help even to have a shave or comb our hair, is not the way we want to live. It is undignified. When we look at the life of a person such as Tony Bland in the persistent vegetative state, we feel disturbed and distressed. As far as we can tell, such a person is not in pain. He is not suffering in any identifiable meaning of the word. And yet we feel his life has lost dignity.

These are the words of Ludovic Kennedy, a pro-euthanasia campaigner: 'For many people the fear of being snuffed out before our time has been superseded by a greater fear, that of suffering a painful and lingering death when all possibility of revival has gone, being kept alive but deteriorating all the time. It is not death that people fear most, but undignified dying.'[11]

I was struck by the wording of an Advance Statement form (sometimes known as a living will) which has been widely circulated: 'I wish it to be understood that I fear degeneration and indignity far more than I fear death. I ask my medical attendants to bear this statement in mind when considering what my intentions would be in any uncertain situation.' This is a deep anxiety as modern people face their mortality; fear of 'degeneration and indignity'.

Finally, there is the most deep-rooted fear of all, the fear of becoming dependent, and of losing our freedom.

Fear of dependence

These are the words of Friederich Nietzsche, one of the most formative influences on postmodern thinking: 'In a certain state it is indecent to live longer. To go on vegetating in cowardly dependence on physicians and machinations, after the meaning of life, the right to life, has been lost, that ought to prompt a profound contempt in society . . . I want to die proudly when it is no longer possible to live proudly.'[12] Ronald Dworkin, the legal philosopher, argues that any individual's way of death should fit with how that person has lived the rest of their life. Otherwise, a bad death might mar the whole story of a life, just as a bad ending can ruin a beautiful novel. If I have lived my life by choosing, taking responsibility for my own existence, telling my own story, then I must be free to end my life in my own way, in a way that fits. 'Death has dominion because it is not only the start of nothing but the end of everything, and how we think and talk about dying – the emphasis we put on dying with 'dignity' – shows how important it is that life ends *appropriately*, that death keeps faith with the way we want to have lived.'[13] He argues that we worry about dying in indignity because of the effect of life's last stage on the character of our life as a whole, 'as we might worry about the effect of a play's last scene, or a poem's last stanza, on the entire creative work'. 'People's views about how to live colour their convictions about when to die . . . There is no doubt that most people treat the manner of their deaths as of special, symbolic importance: they want their deaths, if possible, to express and . . . confirm the values they believe most important to their lives . . . None of us wants to end our life out of character.'[14]

People who have lived their lives as an expression of self-determination and self-reliance are horrified by the prospect that their death might express a completely contrary reality of dependence on others. Instead, they want to be free to die as they wish, even if that form of dying is not what others might wish. It seems clear that this was the fear which motivated Dr Anne Turner to kill herself: 'I don't want to be remembered by you as being totally incapacitated . . . I had this awful fall last night and could not get up. I thought then that this really demonstrates that what I am going to do is right.'

Ronald Dworkin argues that, even if we feel that our own human dignity is at stake if another person treats his or her own life as valueless, 'a true appreciation of dignity argues decisively in the opposite direction – for individual freedom, not coercion, for a regime of law and an attitude that encourages each of us to make mortal decisions for himself. Freedom is the cardinal, absolute requirement of self-respect: no-one treats his life as having any intrinsic objective importance unless he insists on leading that life himself, not being ushered along it by others.'[15]

John Harris draws the same conclusion: 'The point of autonomy, the point of choosing and having freedom to choose between competing conceptions of how, and indeed why, to live, is simply that it is only thus that our lives become in any real sense our own. The value of our lives is the value that we give to our lives.'[16]

This is a deeply rooted conviction for many people in our society, especially younger people who have grown up with postmodern concepts of radical individualism: 'I am master of my fate, captain of my boat. Others may not approve but it doesn't matter. I do it my way.' The idea of writing one's own script is a powerful one. I believe it is no accident that a leading international pro-euthanasia society chose the name Exit. It comes from the theatre. When the play is ended, when we reach the last page of the script, we will say, 'Thank you friends, goodbye and goodnight.' *Exit stage right.*

One way modern people cope with these deep-rooted fears is to hope for a rapid and unexpected death. It is fascinating that, whereas to many previous generations, sudden death was seen as one of the worst ways to die, now it has become the best. To be catapulted into eternity without preparation, without a chance of repentance, unable to say goodbye, was viewed with horror by our forebears. Some saw sudden death as evidence of God's judgment on a godless life. But to modern people it has become the ideal. The catastrophic accident, the explosion, the sudden cardiac arrest: 'Well at least he went quickly. Never knew what hit him, lucky beggar! I hope I go like that.'

But if we do not go quickly, if we have to face the ultimate horror of a slow, protracted dying, then we want euthanasia. That way, we do not need to be afraid. We can relax. Provided that euthanasia or assisted suicide is there as an option, we can face our death with equanimity. There will be someone there to help. Euthanasia seems to be the answer to our deepest fears.

If fear is the main force driving the euthanasia debate, there are other more sinister forces at work, though rarely acknowledged in public.

Social pressures in favour of euthanasia

First is the breakdown of traditional family structures, coupled with steadily increasing life expectancy. This means that modern societies contain increasing numbers of elderly people, many of whom are isolated and unsupported by relatives or children. How can we cope with the desperate problems of social isolation and ostracism? Some social planners see a nightmarish vision of the future, where large numbers of isolated and abandoned elderly people are kept alive to suffer a pointless and degrading existence, thanks to improvements in medical care. Dr Guy Brown, a former research colleague of mine, has written a book on death and ageing called *The Living End*.[17] It provides striking statistics on the rising number of dependent elderly people, together with rather bleak descriptions of decline in bodily function prior to death: 'Cancer patients normally have little functional impairment six months prior to death, then undergo a rapid and deep decline in functions such as moving, eating, dressing, bathing and using the toilet. Deaths due to heart disease and diabetes are preceded by a much slower decline in function extending over years ... Fatal illness is often accompanied by the following symptoms: pain, shortness of breath, digestive problems, incontinence, bed-sores, fatigue, depression and anxiety, confusion and finally unconsciousness.'[18] 'Dying is also increasingly lonely. Of those dying of stroke, 67% died in hospital, 24% in a residential or nursing home and only 9% at home. Fifty-nine per cent of dying women were widowed and 44% had lived alone in the year prior to their death . . . The elderly are increasingly isolated and have reduced sources of informal help and care to draw on as they endure old age and approach death.'[19] Wouldn't a liberal euthanasia and assisted suicide policy provide some kind of solution to this horror?

Secondly, there is the increasing pressure on scarce health resources. Every developed nation is witnessing a spiral of health-care costs which seem to be out of control. Every medical advance brings new and more expensive treatments. How can health planners find a way to control their runaway budgets? The truth is that high-quality multidisciplinary care for the terminally ill and chronically disabled is very expensive, whereas euthanasia is remarkably cheap.

Thirdly, there is the growing epidemic of Alzheimer's disease in our society. Alzheimer's currently affects about 11% of the US population over 65, and the percentage continues to rise. In 2007, the total number of people with dementia in the UK was estimated at nearly 0.7 million, and the number was predicted to rise to 1.7 million in 2050. The percentage of affected sufferers rises from about 6% between 75 and 80 years, to more than 25% over 90 years.[20] According to current predictions, someone born now has a one in three chance of developing some form of dementia before they die. Finding an appropriate way to care for Alzheimer's sufferers represents a major, and still partly unsolved, challenge for the medical and caring professions. Perhaps euthanasia will offer a solution?

Mary Warnock, in a 2008 interview, said, 'If you're demented, you're wasting people's lives – your family's lives – and you're wasting the resources of the National Health Service. I'm absolutely, fully, in agreement with the argument that if pain is insufferable, then someone should be given help to die, but I feel there's a wider argument that if somebody absolutely, desperately, wants to die because they're a burden to their family, or the state, then I think they too should be allowed to die.'[21] Her remarks created a furore, and were strongly opposed by the majority of those who care for Alzheimer's sufferers, but they reflect the unspoken thoughts of many.

Fourthly, there is the desperate shortage of organs for transplant. As transplant surgery techniques have improved, they offer successful treatment for an increasing range of severe medical conditions. But at the same time, to the intense frustration of medical specialists and patients alike, the supply of organs, coming mainly from accident victims, has steadily declined. Most natural deaths are prolonged, and the organs are unsuitable for transplant. But death by lethal injection offers the prospect of an almost limitless supply of valuable organs. Think of how much good we could do for other people!

In 1997, a distinguished working party known as the International Forum for Transplant Ethics suggested that sufferers in a persistent vegetative state should be killed by lethal injection, so that their organs could be used for transplant into other patients. Grisly reports have come out of South Asia that organs obtained from prisoners executed by lethal injection are widely available, at a price. These are the words of Gilbert Meilaender: 'There are circumstances in which we can save life only by destroying the kind of world in which we all should want to live. Perhaps if our noble desire to prolong life leads to such ignoble means, we need to be sent away to shudder.'[22]

Euthanasia by stealth

Although intentional mercy killing is outlawed in most countries, there are concerns that in certain circumstances medical staff may in fact be deliberately ending the lives of those who are regarded as having a 'poor quality of life', whilst concealing their actions under the cloak of normal medical practice. This may involve deliberately withholding nutrition or fluids from patients who are acutely ill, but not close to death, for instance those who are admitted unconscious following a stroke, or patients who are frail and elderly. Intentional killing by omission may also occur when life-saving interventions, such as a brief period of intensive care, are deliberately withheld in patients thought to have low quality of life; for example those with a chronic disability, with psychiatric illness or chronic neurological disorders.

One disabled, but very active, person with motor neuron disease told me that she was terrified of being admitted to hospital with an acute respiratory infection. Her acute fear was that she would be allowed to die in hospital, against her wishes, because the medical staff concluded that she had a 'poor quality of life'. Instead of places of safety, protection and care, some disabled people have a terrible, but understandable, fear that hospitals have become places where their lives may be terminated against their wills.

Euthanasia in the Netherlands

Euthanasia has been practised in Netherlands for many years, but it was formally legalized in 2001. Approximately 2,000 cases are reported to the authorities each year, although under-reporting of cases is thought to be common, and the true figure may be twice as high.[23] In addition, many more die from the increasingly common practice of terminal sedation, deliberately rendering a patient unconscious and withholding fluids and nutrition until death occurs. This practice does not require official reporting, but a recent report estimated that it accounted for 7.1% of deaths in 2005.[24] One Dutch parliamentarian, commenting on the rise in the practice of terminal sedation, said, 'Palliative sedation is easier for doctors. There is no control by the euthanasia committee, and it is emotionally easier, too.'

Although euthanasia is theoretically limited to adult patients who are legally competent, suffering unbearably, have a terminal illness, and who make a persistent request to die, in practice there is clear evidence that a significant number who receive life-terminating treatment do not meet these criteria. The Remmelink Report, an official report of deaths due to euthanasia in 1990, found that in about 1,000 cases deaths occurred where doctors had given drugs with the explicit purpose of hastening the end of life but without an explicit request from the patient.[25] Reasons given by doctors themselves for euthanasia included absence of any prospect of improvement, needless prolongation of life, the relatives' inability to cope, and low quality of life. Pain and suffering were only mentioned in 30% of cases. When the reasons that patients themselves gave for requesting euthanasia were analysed, 57% said it was 'loss of dignity', 46% 'not dying in a dignified way', 46% mentioned 'pain', 33% 'dependence' and 23% 'tiredness of life'.[26] (More detailed information about the Remmelink report is available on the website.)

Other reported cases of euthanasia in the Netherlands have included paediatric cancer patients, people with dementia, and those suffering from untreatable psychiatric illness. A report on medical life termination in 2005 stated, ' . . . the ending of life was not discussed with patients because they were unconscious (10.4%) or incompetent owing to young age (14.4%) or because of other factors (15.3%).'[27]

Oregon

The Death with Dignity Act became law in the state of Oregon in 1997, and by 2006 a total of 248 deaths had been reported.[28] The law allows a 'capable' adult patient who is a resident of Oregon, and has less than six months to live, to request voluntarily a prescription for lethal drugs. Physicians are encouraged to report cases, but the system is based entirely on trust. There is no regulatory authority, no resources are made available to ensure compliance with the law, and there are no penalties for doctors who fail to report assisted suicide deaths.

In published studies of PAS in Oregon, the most common reasons given were 'controlling the time of death', 'being ready to die', 'wanting to die at home instead of in a hospital', 'existence being pointless', 'losing independence' and 'poor quality of life'.[29] It is striking that severe or unbearable pain is an uncommon reason given for suicide.

One Oregon doctor commented, 'They are not using assisted suicide because they need it for the usual medical kinds of reasons, they are using it because they tend to be people who have always controlled the circumstances of their lives and they prefer to control their death in the same way.'[30]

The standard method for PAS in Oregon involves the oral ingestion of a massive overdose of barbiturates – sometimes as many as ninety tablets! Not surprisingly, there are case reports in which the suicide attempt has been unsuccessful because of vomiting. In fact, the Oregon approach has been opposed by Dutch euthanasia specialists. 'Taking 90 barbiturate tablets is not a harmless procedure: it causes vomiting; it tastes awful; it is painful. If you are going to have a quick and easy death from some kind of euthanasia or assisted suicide you have to have lethal injection.'[31]

As in the Netherlands, there have been reports of PAS occurring with individuals who don't appear to meet the strict legal criteria, including people with early dementia, depression and mental illness.[32]

The logic of euthanasia

Although euthanasia legislation is being strongly promoted around the world, there is a major logical inconsistency inherent within it. This argument has rarely been discussed in the public domain or in ethical debates, and yet I believe it provides a strong and purely logical reason for rejecting a change to legalize euthanasia. All proposed euthanasia legislation states that intentional mercy killing, or assisted suicide, should only be legal if all of four criteria are met:

1. There should be a terminal illness with a short life expectancy.
2. There should be 'unbearable suffering'.
3. There should be a persistent request to die.
4. The individual should be legally competent to take such a decision.

But it is impossible to mount a logically coherent justification as to why *all* of these criteria should be necessary before mercy killing may be carried out. On the one hand, if personal *autonomy* is a moral justification for killing people, then it is not logical to restrict mercy killing only to people who are about to die *and* in severe pain. What if I am suffering unbearably but do not have a terminal illness (like Dr Anne Turner or Daniel James)? Or suppose I have a terminal illness and express a persistent wish to die, but I'm not actually suffering pain – I just believe my life is futile. On logical grounds, why do I lose the right to be killed? Dr Richard Nicholson, a well-known medical ethicist, commenting on the case of Daniel James, said that, from an ethical point of view, he could not see much difference between the case of Daniel and that of an older person with a terminal illness, provided they were of 'sound mind'.[33]

On the other hand, if severe *suffering* is a moral justification for killing people, then it is not logical to restrict mercy killing only to people who can choose to die. If we see someone who is suffering unbearably, surely we should be prepared to kill them, even if they are not capable of expressing a wish to die? What if someone who is suffering terribly expresses a will to die while they are still competent, but then becomes confused before euthanasia can be performed? On what logical grounds could we say that they should not be killed out of compassion?

As one legal philosopher put it, 'If respect for autonomy requires assisted suicide for patients competent to request it, why does respect for beneficence not require euthanasia for those who are not?'

Here are the authors of an official report on euthanasia in the Netherlands: 'Is it not true that once one accepts euthanasia and assisted suicide, the principle of universalizability forces one to accept termination of life without explicit request, at least in some circumstances. In our view the answer to this question must be affirmative.'[34]

This is the logical basis for the slippery-slope argument. The proposed legislation does not have a consistent logical basis; it cannot withstand logical analysis. And hence, given the apparent demand for euthanasia, once it is enacted, it will be progressively challenged, extended and weakened. Once euthanasia is accepted as a moral and legal part of medical practice, it seems both logically and practically impossible to prevent the gradual extension to voluntary euthanasia of those who wish to die, even if they are not terminally ill, and involuntary euthanasia of those whose lives seem futile and pain-filled. To a number of observers of the Dutch scene, it seems that this progression down the slippery slope is slowly but inexorably taking place.

Practical risks of euthanasia legalization

But there are also other practical dangers from a change in the law to allow euthanasia. There is, first, the possibility of wrong diagnosis. Sadly, serious mistakes in diagnosis are not uncommon, even in specialist centres. The last few years have seen a number of public scares as major errors in diagnostic pathology laboratories have come to light. Most experienced clinicians can give individual examples of serious diagnostic errors. What if euthanasia was carried out in the mistaken belief that the patient was terminally ill, when in fact the disease was self-limiting?

Then there is the problem of predicting the future. Even when doctors make the right diagnosis, they are frequently wrong as they attempt to predict how long a patient will survive. Most medical prognostication in terminal illness is more akin to educated guesswork than scientific calculation. Yet euthanasia legislation assumes that the doctor can confidently predict both that the patient is terminally ill, and that death will occur within a matter of weeks or months.

There is the possibility of abuse by doctors and other health-care staff, who may be tempted to end the lives of patients for less than altruistic reasons, such as financial reward or managerial pressures or to conceal evidence of medical negligence.

There is the possibility of serious abuse by relatives, who see euthanasia as an opportunity to relieve themselves of a burden of caring, and preventing the dissipation of life savings on expensive nursing care. This is not to imply that most relatives harbour malevolent thoughts to the terminally ill. But their own emotional distress can be a major source of pressure for health carers. 'I can't bear to watch her in this state. Why can't you give her something to end it all?' Similarly elderly patients, seeing the financial burdens on their relatives, may feel that it is their 'duty', a matter of social responsibility, to request euthanasia. If there is no possibility of life termination, then I do not need to justify my desire to continue living. But once life termination becomes a 'treatment option', then, logically, I need to provide some justification for my desire to continue to live. How long will it be before the 'right to die' becomes a 'duty to die'?

There is the very real possibility that euthanasia legislation would increase anxieties for elderly and disabled people admitted to hospital, and erode trust in the actions and motivation of health staff. The patient-carer relationship would be unavoidably altered. Instead of a climate of trust, intimacy and pro-tection, vulnerable people in our health-care system might experience suspicion, distancing, and an exacerbation of their sense of defencelessness.

There is the psychological effect on doctors who have broken deep human intuitions and cultural taboos against the intentional taking of human life. There is clear evidence from the Netherlands that doctors find the experience of performing euthanasia 'emotionally traumatic'. Will the doctor who has just committed euthanasia fight as hard to save the life of her next patient? What are the psychological consequences for carers, when the duty of care includes a duty to kill?

Finally, there is the effect on society of legalized killing, and the existence of a specialized group of people who are authorized to kill under certain circumstances. Respect for human life is part of the glue which binds our communities together. Will legalized killing cheapen respect for human life in society as a whole?

The Nazi euthanasia programme

Before we turn to a Christian response in the next chapter, I want to refer briefly to the experience of the German medical profession under the Nazis. Understandably, the pro-euthanasia lobby is extremely sensitive to any comparison with the appalling crimes of the Nazi era. It is all too easy to use the Nazis to make cheap rhetorical points, and I do not want to fall into that trap. There is clearly no comparison between the legalized euthanasia activities of Dutch doctors and the hideous acts of the SS physicians and executioners.

Yet the whole terrible episode is of great importance for all doctors. It illustrates how a noble profession can become inexorably corrupted as a consequence of intense social and political pressures. The story is recounted in several sources including the book *Racial Hygiene: Medicine under the Nazis* by Robert Proctor.[35] Proctor and other historians point out that the terrible crimes against humanity performed by respectable and high-ranking German doctors started out with small beginnings, long before the outbreak of war. In 1920, Alfred Hoche, a professor of medicine, and Rudolf Binding, a professor of law, had published their book *Release and Destruction of Lives Not Worth Living*. They argued that the principle of 'allowable killing' should be extended to the incurably sick. The right to live, they asserted, must be earned and justified, not dogmatically assumed. Those who are not capable of human feelings – those 'ballast lives' and 'empty human husks' that fill our psychiatric institutions – can have no sense of the value of life. Theirs is not a life worth living and hence their destruction is not only tolerable but downright humane.[36]

By 1935, popular medical and racial hygiene journals carried charts depicting the costs of maintaining the sick at the expense of the healthy. One poster shows a healthy man carrying two disabled individuals. The caption reads, 'You are Sharing the Load! A Genetically Ill Individual Costs Approximately 50,000 Reichsmarks by the Age of Sixty.' A 1935 school mathematics textbook included problems where the average cost to the state of providing care for inhabitants of homes for the epileptic and institutions for the mentally ill were to be calculated by students. These calculations formed the basis of the euthanasia programme which was established by many of the German medical profession. Until the outbreak of war, the euthanasia programme was concerned entirely with the elimination of the mentally and physically disabled. It was after 1939 that the programme was extended to Jews. In 1945, detailed calculations of the savings achieved for the German state by one euthanasia centre, Hartheim, were found in a safe. The 'disinfection' or extermination of 70,273 individuals in the course of the operation at Hartheim had saved the German economy a total of 245,955 Reichmarks per day.[37]

In 1949 an American psychiatrist Leo Alexander, who had attended the Nuremberg War Trials, wrote an influential paper entitled 'Medical Science under Dictatorship', published in *The New England Journal of Medicine*.[38] In it he traced the historical roots of the Nazi euthanasia movement. How was it that respected doctors could have participated in such horrendous acts?

> It started with the acceptance by doctors of the idea, basic in the euthanasia movement, that there is such a thing as a life not worthy to be lived. This attitude in the beginning referred to the severely and chronically sick. Gradually the sphere of those to be included was enlarged to encompass the socially unproductive, the ideologically unwanted, the racially unwanted . . . But it is important to realise that the infinitely small lever from which this entire trend of mind received its impetus was the attitude towards the incurably sick.

'The life not worth living' is a concept at the heart of the modern euthanasia movement too: an idea promoted by ethicists, philosophers and health economists. For those with a sense of history, it is a phrase that has uneasy resonances.

The persistent vegetative state

As we saw in the tragic case of Tony Bland, the persistent vegetative state or PVS is an extreme case of severe brain injury, leading to loss of contact with the person. To many philosophers such as Peter Singer, the PVS sufferer is a prime example of a life 'not worth living'. The absence of normal cortical activity means that the PVS sufferer is a 'non-person', on the basis of 'ethically relevant characteristics'. In fact they are an 'it', rather than a 'he' or a 'she'; a being whose life has no personal value or significance, and who can demand no special duty of care or protection from the rest of us. The quality of such a being's life is so low that it is below zero – it is 'negative'. In other words, it is better for someone in Tony Bland's condition, and for the rest of us, if his life comes to an end. Our only duty to him is to end his life painlessly and cleanly. It would be an insult to Tony's memory, and a terrible waste of health resources, to allow his body to linger on. Here is the ideal case for involuntary euthanasia.

Singer does not explicitly state that all PVS sufferers should be killed, but leaves it as a veiled implication:

> Our decisions about how to treat such patients should not depend on lofty rhetoric about the equal worth of all human life, but on the views of families and partners who deserve consideration at a time of tragic loss. If a patient in a persistent vegetative state has previously expressed wishes about what should happen to her or him in such circumstances, they should also be taken into account. (We may do this purely out of respect for the wishes of the dead, or we may do it in order to reassure others, still alive, that their wishes will not be ignored.) At the same time, in a public health-care system, we cannot ignore the limits set by the finite nature of our medical resources, nor the needs of others whose lives may be saved by an organ transplant.[39]

Singer regarded the decision of the House of Lords, that artificial feeding could be withdrawn from Tony Bland, as a landmark move away from the traditional view of British law regarding the sanctity of life. Nonetheless, he denounces the intentional starvation and dehydration of PVS patients, while drawing back from killing them with a lethal injection, as irrational and indefensible.

Is the diagnosis right?

PVS is an extreme example of a clinical illness in which we have lost contact with the person. It is important to stress that PVS is totally different, both clinically and conceptually, from brainstem death. In brainstem death, there is no brain activity at all. The brain has permanently ceased any integrated function. The biological functions of the body are maintained purely by artificial life-support machinery. Nearly all Christian thinkers have accepted that brain-stem death can be regarded as equivalent to the death of the individual, and that artificial life support can be discontinued in such cases. (A few Christian doctors have raised concerns about the validity of the conventional diagnostic tests for brainstem death, and more information is available on the website.)

In PVS, however, the brain is working. Electrical activity in the cortex can be measured. There are periods of sleep followed by waking. The connections of the brain circuitry are deranged, but doctors don't know in detail what the effects on consciousness may be, nor if that derangement is permanent. There's something going on in there, but there seems to be no way to communicate, to access the experience of the individual.

Yet not all those who appear to be unresponsive are in fact so. In 2006, the journal *Science* reported the remarkable case of a twenty-three-year-old female with PVS following a road accident.[40] When placed in a magnetic resonance imaging scanner and asked to imagine playing a game of tennis, and then walking around her home, the scanner revealed brain activity in the same cortical regions as in healthy volunteers given the same tasks. Lead researcher, Dr Adrian Owen, said the results 'confirm that, despite the diagnosis of vegetative state, this patient retained the ability to understand spoken commands and to respond to them through her brain activity, rather than through speech or movement'. In future, it is likely that this form of brain scanning will become valuable in assessing other patients in profound coma.

On 8 December 1995, Jean-Dominique Bauby, the forty-two-year-old editor of *Elle* magazine in Paris was on his way home when he suffered a massive stroke and slipped into a coma. When he regained consciousness, three weeks later, he discovered that he was completely paralysed, speechless and only able to move one muscle: his left eyelid. Although this condition can be mistaken for PVS, in fact the diagnosis was very different; it was the rare condition known as 'locked-in syndrome'. Fortunately, the medical team made the correct diagnosis. Using a simple code, Bauby laboriously dictated his life story, letter by letter. The book was published in France in 1997, rapidly becoming a best-seller, and more recently was made into an award winning film. Entitled *The Diving Bell and the Butterfly*,[41] it is a moving account of the reality of an awake mind, an intact person, trapped in a paralysed body. He saw his inert body as a diving bell in which was trapped the butterfly of his soaring mind and imagination. An observer focusing solely on his motionless body might have viewed him as a perfect case for euthanasia. But Bauby was not asking to die: he was striving to live, to remember, to communicate, to reach out in love to his children and family.

At the heart of the diagnosis of PVS is the conclusion that the state of profound coma and unresponsiveness is *permanent*.[42] But a number of neurological experts have emphasized the difficulty of establishing the correct diagnosis and of predicting whether some degree of recovery may occur.

Dr Keith Andrews, a consultant from the Royal Hospital of Neurodisability in Putney, has probably more experience of caring for profoundly disabled adults than anyone else in the UK. He stresses the difficulties in the diagnosis of PVS, which requires considerable skill and prolonged assessment, sometimes continuing over months, and the variable severity of the condition. (Tony Bland's case was apparently one of the most severe examples of PVS.) According to Dr Andrew's report, published in the *British Medical Journal* in 1993, 42% of those referred to his hospital by other specialists were misdiagnosed as being in PVS.[43] Eleven out of forty-three patients diagnosed as PVS regained awareness, and ten out of the eleven were able to communicate with their carers. Four patients were able to feed themselves, and two became independent in daily activities. Dr Andrews argued that all patients with profound brain damage should be offered the opportunity of a specialist rehabilitation programme.

Is artificial feeding a form of medical treatment?

A further crucial issue in the care of PVS sufferers is the status of artificial feeding. PVS is quite different from many severe conditions, in that the sustenance of life is not dependent on major and invasive technology. PVS sufferers are able to breathe, metabolize food and excrete waste without medical assistance. They do not require life-support machinery, intravenous infusions or complex drug therapy. The only medical assistance they require is artificial feeding through a tube into the stomach. So does this form of feeding represent a medical *treatment* which can and should be withdrawn if its burdens outweigh the benefits? Or does it represent basic *nursing care*, which is part of the duty of care that we owe to all human beings, however damaged or disabled they may be? Some have argued that the artificial feeding equipment is conceptually no different from the adapted feeding apparatus, such as specially designed forks and spoons which some severely disabled people use. On the other hand, others have argued that the requirement for professional medical input in the insertion and management of feeding tubes demonstrates that this is a form of medical treatment. The debate continues with little sign of a consensus. (See website.)

What is the significance of the life of the PVS sufferer?

Within the framework of Peter Singer's philosophy, the significance and contribution of the life of the PVS sufferer seems negligible. But within the Christian worldview we must pause before we can accept this verdict. Ultimately the value of an individual life can be known only to God. But if we take seriously the belief that the value of human beings is intrinsic, in the stuff of their creation, rather than in their functioning or attributes, then we must conclude that even PVS sufferers have a prima facie case to be considered as members of the human community, persons to whom, for all their tragic disability, we owe wonder, respect, empathy and protection.

Although the legality of withdrawing feeds in PVS was established in the UK in 1993, in the period that has passed since then, only a relatively small number of cases have come to the courts, although it has been estimated that there may be many hundreds of PVS sufferers in the UK. Could it be that most carers have deep intuitions that the withdrawal of feeds is not the best way to express caring for these profoundly damaged individuals?

Dr Andrew's experience, and the recent evidence from scans of brain activity, should also give us reason to pause before we agree to stop artificial feeds. Are we sure that there is not an aware individual in that body? If we really want to express compassionate caring, perhaps we should be concentrating our attention on research, such as on new therapies which may limit damage and encourage brain recovery, and on attempts to find new ways to establish contact with brain-damaged individuals.

Dementia

Severe dementia, such as that which occurs in advanced Alzheimer's disease, is another tragic and debilitating condition in which communication is lost with the person inside. There are other causes for dementia, but Alzheimer's disease is the best known. The brain is active, but communication is disjointed and broken. Memories are distorted and fragmentary. The person expresses wishes and desires, but these change rapidly. One of the characteristics of dementia is that its severity may fluctuate, especially in the early stages. At times, people may have nearly normal memory and behaviour. At other times, they are profoundly confused and disorientated. This, of course, may add to the distress and feelings of terror, as the person may have periods of painfully accurate insight into their condition, and what the future holds for them. Dementia is deeply troubling, above all, because it threatens our understanding of personal continuity and identity.

> Often Mary was afraid, a nameless shapeless fear . . . People came, memories came, and then they slipped away. She could not tell what was reality and what was memory of things past . . . The tub was a mystery. From day to day she could not remember how to manage the water: sometimes it all ran away, sometimes it kept rising and rising so that she could not stop it . . . Mary was glad when her family came to visit. Sometimes she remembered their names, more often she did not . . . She liked it best when they just held her and loved her.[44]

Andrew Firlik, a medical student, wrote an article in the *Journal of the American Medical Association* following his meeting with a fifty-four-year-old Alzheimer's sufferer called Margo.[45] He visited her daily in her apartment.

Margo was always reading novels but 'her place in the book jumps randomly from day to day . . . maybe she feels good just sitting and humming to herself, rocking back and forth slowly, nodding off liberally, occasionally turning to a fresh page'. And yet, as Andrew Firlik commented, 'despite her illness, or maybe somehow because of it, Margo is undeniably one of the happiest people I have ever known'. She took endless delight in eating peanut butter and jam sandwiches! But where is the individual, when memory and personality seem so disconnected? As Andrew Firlik asks, 'When a person can no longer accumulate new memories as the old rapidly fade, what remains? Where is Margo?'

To Ronald Dworkin, as for many others from a secular liberal perspective, dementia is a horrifying and degrading reality. If the essence of our human existence is to create a personality by a series of autonomous choices – to write our own script – there can be few prospects so horrifying, so dehumanizing, as the loss of an ability to choose.

Dworkin argues that the right of individual autonomy 'makes self-creation possible. It allows each of us to be responsible for shaping our own lives according to our own coherent or incoherent – but in any case, distinctive – personality.'[46] But severe dementia strikes at the heart of this possibility of self-creation. If a demented person's 'choices and demands, no matter how firmly expressed, systematically or randomly contradict one another, reflecting no coherent sense of self and no discernible even short-term aims, then he has presumably lost the capacity that it is the point of autonomy to protect'.

Instead, Dworkin argues we must respect the *previous* autonomous wishes of the individual before they developed dementia. If, before she developed dementia, Margo had expressed a wish to die in this state, then the fact that Margo is now happy and enjoying her peanut butter and jam sandwiches is irrelevant. She no longer has any capacity for autonomy, and if she is allowed to carry on her existence, this will irrevocably mar the story of her entire life. Margo's previous wishes take precedence over her current experiences, even if the latter are enjoyable. To allow her to live on in a demented state against her previous wishes is to inflict a harm on her. We must allow her to die or even, if it is legally permissable, arrange for her to be killed. 'We cannot say that we would be showing compassion for Margo if we refused to do what she wanted when she was competent, because that would not be compassionate toward the whole person, the person who tragically became demented.'[47]

In response to Andrew Firlik's question, 'Where is Margo?' Dworkin answers, in effect, 'The *real* Margo has gone.' But although she has gone, we must respect her previously expressed wishes, much as we respect the wishes of the dead expressed in a will. We respect this being because of what she once was.

In the next chapter we will look at Christian responses to these painful and complex questions about the end of life and the challenge of euthanasia. Is there an alternative to mercy killing? It is not enough to defend abstract moral principles. What practical answers can we provide to the terrible modern fears of pain, indignity and dependence?

In this chapter we will respond to the challenge of euthanasia from the perspective of the Christian worldview. What insights can we gain from the biblical material we have already outlined? Can mercy killing be regarded as an act of compassion, a way to respect individual choices and personal integrity? Or is it a perversion of medicine and the start of a slippery slope? We shall look briefly at the responses of Christian carers to these dilemmas and at practical initiatives in the care of the dying, many of them pioneered by Christians.

Human life is sacrosanct because of the image of God

As we saw in chapter 2, the biblical worldview sees all human life as uniquely valuable because all human beings are made in God's image. In orthodox Christian thought, human beings, even when facing terminal illness like Diane Pretty did, suffering from dementia like Margo, or in the twilight state of Tony Bland, are Godlike beings. And any being made in God's image deserves a range of responses: wonder, respect, empathy, and above all *protection*: protection from abuse, protection from harm, protection from manipulation.

But some will argue that mercy killing can be seen as a way of protecting vulnerable people from harm. Isn't the deliberate ending of human life a way to protect an individual from suffering? No. Biblical thought always draws a line between removing *suffering* and removing *the sufferer*. In biblical thinking, human life is sacrosanct. We are not at liberty to destroy innocent human life, however noble may be the motive. Here again are the solemn words of the ninth chapter of Genesis in the *lex talionis*.

> Whoever sheds the blood of man,
>   by man shall his blood be shed;
> for in the image of God
>   has God made man.
> (Genesis 9:6)

As Dr Roy Clements pointed out, this ancient text combines two biblical themes. First there is the ancient blood taboo, a recognition of the special status of blood because it represents a spilled life, and secondly there is the condemnation of murder, the intentional destruction of innocent human life. To destroy human life is uniquely scandalous because it is a desecration of God's image, God's masterpiece. Clements put it like this: 'A human life is not just a gift of God's grace – it is a reflection of his person.'[1] The Christian view of life as a gift received from God is often caricatured by opponents. God is the slave-owner, and humans are his slaves and therefore God 'owns' each life. We are not free to dispose of our own life as we wish because God 'owns' it. But this is a distortion of the biblical view. We are not merely slaves. Human beings are special because of how they are made – because they are a mysterious expression of God's being.

This is why orthodox Christian thought has always been opposed, not only to homicide, the taking of another human life, but also to suicide. The deliberate destruction of one's own life is also a desecration of God's image. In many ancient cultures, suicide has been glorified as a noble way to die. The Norwegian warriors saw suicide as a path to heaven; in Buddhism, self-immolation is a prime example of the renunciation of desire; traditional Hinduism practised the suicide of bereaved widows; in Japan, until recently, hari-kari was a noble form of death; in ancient Greece, the Stoics encouraged the heroic suicide. But in all cultures influenced by the Judeo-Christian revelation, suicide has been opposed. It is never glorified in the Bible. Samson, that flawed and ambiguous character, is the only example of a heroic and desperate suicide whose act is, in some sense, approved. Samson's action is analogous to that of the suicide bomber, from which Christians instinctively recoil. In the rest of the Bible, suicide is associated with godlessness, for example in the tragic ends of Saul and Judas Iscariot. Despite this, it is interesting that suicidal thoughts are not uncommon in God's people. Elijah wanted to die, but was sent on a sabbatical instead. Job wishes he had never been born, but learns that God is in control of his life.[2]

In biblical thought, God gives human beings a wonderful and terrifying freedom of action. We are free to act and choose as responsible moral agents who are accountable to one another, and ultimately accountable to God. But there are God-given limits to our freedom as moral agents. The limits are part of the hidden moral order of the creation, the moral warp and woof of reality. And one of those limits which we must not transgress is to choose to destroy my own life or the life of another. 'Within the story of my life I have the relative freedom of a creature, but it is not simply my life to do with it as I please . . . Suicide . . . expresses a desire to be free and not also finite – a desire to be more like the Creator than creature.'[3] Self-destruction is a harm to be avoided, not a right to be assisted.

Yet there is a paradoxical character to Christian thinking about laying down one's life. After all, Jesus is the supreme example of a life deliberately laid down for others. To sacrifice one's own life for the good of others, or in the face of persecution, is seen as the height of Christian love. So what is the difference: sacrificing your life because there is something worth dying for is Christian martyrdom; sacrificing your life because there is nothing worth living for is suicide. The Christian martyr does not aim at death but aims to be faithful to God, foreseeing that death may occur as a result. 'Forbidding suicide and honouring martyrs, the early Christians recognised life as a real but not ultimate good – a great good but not the highest good.'[4]

Christians, then, view human life as sacrosanct: both intentional killing and suicide are contrary to the Christian worldview. Even when tempted to kill out of compassion, we come up against the limits of our creatureliness. It is not only those with an explicit Christian faith who sense a profound resistance to the taking of human life. The unease and distress expressed by many doctors and health-care workers who have participated in euthanasia or assisted suicide are evidence of profound intuitions about the sacrosanct nature of human life – intuitions which stem from our creation in God's image. When we assist in the killing of another human being, however compassionate and rational our motives might be, we damage our own humanity.

The human family

In Christian thought, not only is each individual human life special, but we are all part of the human family. We are created to be in community. Why do we try to prevent suicides in our society? Why do we try to prevent the prison suicide of wicked murderers like Harold Shipman? Why are brave police officers expected to try to save the life of a man attempting to jump from a high-rise block of flats, for example? Why on earth do they bother? If he wants to die, surely we should let him. Why risk the lives of valuable citizens attempting to save someone who doesn't value his own life? It is because our society, though penetrated by liberal individualism, is still deeply influenced by Christian thought. From a Christian perspective we are not autonomous individuals doing our own thing. We are locked together in community, bound together by duties of care, responsibility and compassion. Respect for life, and the prohibition of suicide, is part of the glue which binds society together. It is part of the moral order, the hidden moral grain which God has placed in the creation.

Imagine a society which quietly encouraged the depressed, the inadequate, the isolated or the disabled to take their own lives. Where doctors made available lethal mixtures for their patients, where suicides were left to get on with it. What kind of society would that be? Would we wish to be members of it? Instead, here is a Christian view of society, expressed in the well-known words of John Donne: 'No man is an island, entire of itself; every man is a piece of the Continent, a part of the main; if a clod be washed away by the sea, Europe is the less, as well as if a promontory were . . . any man's death diminishes me, because I am involved in Mankind. And therefore never send to know for whom the bell tolls; It tolls for thee.'[5]

Although the act of self-destruction is often born out of desperation and loneliness, suicide can have devastating effects on others. In fact, it can be a profoundly selfish and destructive act. Whether intentionally or not, the suicide strikes at all those in community with him, wounding and damaging them, often for life. When my loved one chooses to kill himself rather than carry on living with me, he points out the inadequacy of my own caring. Perhaps I didn't love him enough. We see this in the ambiguous and troubled reactions of the families of Anne Turner and Daniel James. 'Everybody had always told her not to go ahead with it because there were so many reasons to stay.' The relatives found themselves torn between loyalty to their loved ones, and a deep sense of their own failure. To commit suicide is to strike at the heart of what it means to live in community. As we saw in chapter 2, we are designed to be dependent on one another. It is part of the creation order. We are all called to share the burdens of the physical life which God has given us.

Death: an outrage and a mercy

Death as a consequence of the fall is an evil and an outrage to be fought against. In the same way, the evils of ageing – the loss of function, infirmity, the degenerative illnesses – are real evils. But old age itself is not an evil. It is part of the human narrative, a stage of life to be respected and honoured. And in God's providential care for fallen human beings, ageing and death may be, in C. S. Lewis's phrase again, 'a severe mercy'. Human lifespan is limited, not just as a curse, but out of God's grace. In God's providence, death may be a merciful release from an existence trapped in a fallen and decaying body. So, Christian attitudes to death must always reflect this strange ambiguity. Even though human death is fundamentally an evil to be fought against, a reality which can never be sought intentionally, it may also at times be accepted, even welcomed, as a sign of God's mercy.

Human suffering: a mystery of human dependence

In a modern secular worldview, suffering seems to have no ultimate meaning. It is pointless and destructive, the ultimate threat to individual human autonomy and self-direction. Therefore, suffering is an evil to be eliminated by whatever means are to hand. It is natural that the elimination of suffering has become, for many, the prime goal of medicine, as well as the fundamental motive behind all utilitarian philosophy. It is an easy step to accept that, in the name of eliminating the suffering, we are forced to eliminate the sufferer.

Yet, as we saw in the book of Job, suffering can never be meaningless in a biblical worldview, even if it has that appearance. Suffering is a painful reality which we are called to *accept* from the hand of a loving God. Dr Rob George, a consultant in palliative medicine in London, has pointed out that even the word 'to suffer' implies an element of passivity. It comes from the Latin *suffere* meaning literally 'to bear under', and hence 'to permit or to allow'. The original meaning of the English word was 'to put up with', and hence the root meaning of suffering is the idea of submitting or being forced to submit or endure some circumstance which is beyond our control. In the words of H. R. Niebuhr, 'Suffering is the exhibition of the presence of that which is not under our control.'[6] Suffering is a reality of our human condition which we can either accept or reject.

Here is the fundamental reason why suffering is regarded by secular philosophers as an affront to liberal ideas of individual autonomy. It is not so much that suffering impairs our ability to choose, but that suffering threatens our belief that we are in ultimate control. Suffering challenges our tendency to be control freaks. It challenges the widespread fantasy that we can be autonomous, choosing individuals. It emphasizes our deep and inescapable creaturely dependence. The suffering person cannot escape the reality of his or her profound dependence on others.

As Stanley Hauerwas points out, for most of us the initial reaction to witnessing suffering in another human being is to be repelled. Suffering tends to turn the other into a stranger. 'Suffering makes people's otherness stand out in strong relief.'[7] Yet suffering in another human being is a call to the rest of us to stand in community. It is a call to *be there*. Suffering is not a question which demands an answer, it is not a problem which requires a solution, it is *a mystery which demands a presence*. 'It is the burden of those who care for the suffering to know how to teach the suffering that they are not thereby excluded from the human community. In this sense medicine's primary role is to bind the suffering and the non-suffering into the same community.'[8] The sad reality is that, so often, modern medical and health-care systems have precisely the opposite effect. They isolate and marginalize those who are suffering and those who are disabled from the rest of the human community.

The duty of care that doctors and other professional carers are bound by is a moral commitment to *be there* for those who are ill, those who are suffering, those who are dying. The role that the caring professions are called to play in society is a practical demonstration of the covenant bonds of community. It is to say to the sufferer, 'We are the community's representatives and we promise to care for you, whatever will happen, whatever it may cost. We will walk this road with you to the end.'

As Hauerwas argues, this does not mean that we ought to welcome or enjoy suffering. This is to pervert Christian thinking into a form of masochism, an emotional pathology. Suffering is not to be sought, but it should, at least to some degree, be accepted. What medicine must attempt to do is, not to eliminate all suffering and death, but *unnecessary* suffering and *untimely* death.

Dissenting voices

Since the end of the Second World War there has been a remarkable consensus in opposition to euthanasia amongst Christians of all traditions, Catholic and Protestant, orthodox and liberal. In 1995, however, the distinguished theologian Professor Hans Küng from the University of Tübingen published *A Dignified Dying*, in which he and a fellow academic, Professor Walter Jens, argue passionately in favour of the legalization of voluntary euthanasia:

> There is no overlooking the fact that today there are more people than before who can no longer bear their already destroyed life, whose indescribable pain is not relieved even by the strongest sedatives of palliative therapy. They do not want to be made unconscious by means of psychotropic drugs and morphine,

and so be deprived of dialogue with family and friends. They want to say good-bye with a clear consciousness and die. And as they cannot die, they want effective help towards dying a dignified death.[9]

Speaking out of the painful experience of the death of his own brother from cancer in the 1950s, Küng argues for a Christian acceptance of human responsibility at the end of life. If Christians use contraception, recognizing that God has given us responsibility in the creation of human life, then,

> ... would it not be consistent to recognise that the same God now, more than before, has made the end of human life a human responsibility? This God does not want us to foist responsibility on him that we ourselves can and should bear. With freedom God has also given human beings the right to utter self-determination ... How can anyone presume to decide whether another person shall live or die and seek to compel him or her to go on living and suffering?[10]

Küng continues:

> As a Christian and a theologian I feel encouraged now to argue publicly for a middle way which is responsible in both theological and Christian terms: between an anti-religious libertarianism without responsibility ('unlimited right to voluntary death') and a reactionary rigorism without compassion ('even the intolerable is to be borne in submission to God as given by God'). And I do this because as a Christian and a theologian I am convinced that the all-merciful God, who has given men and women freedom and responsibility for their lives, has also left to dying people the responsibility for making a conscientious decision about the manner and time of their deaths. This is a responsibility which neither the state nor the church, neither a theologian nor a doctor, can take away.[11]

Professor Paul Badham, a liberal Christian theologian, makes a similar argument in his 2008 book *Is There a Christian Case for Assisted Dying?*. He argues that the greatest Christian commandment is that of love, summarized in the Golden Rule as a requirement to treat others as we wish to be treated ourselves. Since many doctors plan suicide for themselves, and the majority of the population appear to support legalized euthanasia, it must follow that doctors should be allowed to treat others at the end of life as they would wish to be treated.[12] Badham has even argued that assisted suicide could be incorporated into a Christian act of worship, a final act of deliberately laying down one's life.

These arguments are superficially persuasive, but ultimately it seems to me they ride roughshod over orthodox biblical thinking. There is no simple symmetry between the act of creating human life and the act of destroying a life. In biblical thought, God has delegated to human beings a degree of responsibility in the creation of human life, while reserving to himself the right to destroy human life, except in the specific circumstances of capital punishment, or possibly, defence of the vulnerable. This is part of the moral order of creation which cannot be supplanted. It is surely naive to argue that, after 2,000 years of Christian history, human beings have now reached a state of such maturity and wisdom that we are able to take on responsibility before God for the ending of our own and other people's lives. It seems to me that there can be no logically consistent 'middle way' between a secular libertarianism which allows individual autonomy to be pre-eminent at the end of life, and a Christian perspective which takes God's loving and sovereign rule and the hidden moral order of creation seriously. We are free to act as responsible moral agents, but only within the limits of the authority which God has delegated to us.

Practical responses in the medical care of the dying

So, if euthanasia is not an option, how can we relate an orthodox Christian worldview to practical medical decisions about the care and treatment of the dying?

Good medicine knows its limits

One of the driving forces for euthanasia is a type of modern medicine that doesn't know when to stop: medicine driven by fear, by inexperience or by medical machismo. We saw an example in the sad case of Samuel Linares, mentioned in chapter 8, and I am afraid that this kind of medical madness seems all too common in our hospitals. Sometimes it is a consequence of medical inexperience, fear of litigation or lack of empathy. I strongly believe that, as Christians, we need to stand out against it. Paradoxically, a recent survey in the USA has suggested that religious believers are more likely to request futile life-sustaining treatment continuing to the point of death, than are non-believers.[13] This suggests that there is much to do in educating Christian believers about care at the end of life. As we have seen, we are called to struggle against death, while recognizing the ultimate futility of our struggle. We must try to discern when active life-sustaining treatment becomes inappropriate, and when the dying process becomes a severe mercy. The temptation for modern doctors is to attempt to use medical means as a technological fix to ward off death and extend life indefinitely.

But doctors, above all, must recognize the limitations of their abilities and callings. 'Good physicians will know the limit of their art and they can help us to avoid the notion that there is any ultimate technological fix for the human problems of suffering and death.'[14] This mean that there are limits to what doctors can do to relieve suffering and death. 'A willingness to discern such limits as best we can – and, having discerned them, to act in accord with them – is deeply embedded in the Christian understanding of the moral life.'[15]

In fact, it can be argued that one of the primary roles of medical professionals in modern society is to teach modern people what the limits are that come from our physical nature. 'Medicine can be viewed as an educational process for both doctor and patient, in which each is both teacher and learner. It is from patients that physicians learn the wisdom of the body. Both physicians and patients must learn that each of them is subject to a prior authority – the authority of the body . . . medicine represents a way of learning to live with finitude.'[16]

In other words, the essence of being a good doctor is to know when 'enough is enough'. But how do we know when we should withdraw treatment, or withhold it? As discussed previously, the most helpful way of addressing this issue is, in each individual case, to try to balance the benefits against the burdens and risks of treatment. Treatment that is excessively burdensome, relative to its benefits, should be withdrawn or withheld. Doctors and patients together need to weigh up the burdens and the benefits. An obvious example is in advanced cancer. Is the burden of chemotherapy treatment, with all its unpleasantness, complications, risks, hospital visits, tests and expense, worth the benefit of, maybe, an extra three months of survival? The answer is, 'It all depends'. In different circumstances, and with different patients, the balance between burdens and benefits will change. In some situations, those extra three months might enable all kinds of 'unfinished business' to be completed: the reconciliation of long-standing broken relationships, the fulfilment of a long-cherished ambition, the chance to enjoy the presence of children or intimate friends. In other situations those three months may seem to bring little benefit compared to the burdens of invasive treatment.

It seems clear that if the burdens of any particular treatment outweigh the benefits, then that treatment should be withdrawn. However, there is a fundamental difference between making *treatment* decisions and *value-of-life* decisions. Doctors are qualified to make treatment decisions: to decide which treatment is worthwhile and which is not. But doctors are no better qualified than anybody else to make value-of-life decisions; to decide which life is worthwhile and which is not. In other words, doctors may determine whether a *treatment* is futile, but they can never determine whether a *life* is futile. When we withdraw or withhold treatment that is excessively burdensome, we are expressing a belief that the treatment is valueless, not that the patient is valueless.

Good medicine recognizes the difference between intention and foresight

The pro-euthanasia lobby ridicules the traditional view that doctors may give a drug to relieve suffering that may incidentally shorten life, but may not deliberately give a poison to end life. This is viewed as pure hypocrisy, as a deliberate attempt by doctors to cloak their life-terminating activities in a charade of respectability. Closely related is the widely disseminated propaganda to the effect that morphine is a highly dangerous and lethal poison, and that when doctors give morphine they are intending to kill but covering their tracks, to prevent prosecution. This is dangerous and misleading nonsense. Morphine and other opiates are highly effective pain killers, but in fact they are not dangerous, lethal drugs, unless used in massive overdose, as practised by the medically qualified murderer Harold Shipman. A few patients, particularly those with pre-existing respiratory pathology, are highly sensitive to the depressant effects of morphine and other opiates, but this is not common. When the euthanasia doctors want to kill, they do not use morphine. They use completely different drugs, like barbiturates and muscle relaxants. These are drugs of the anaesthetist, capable of inducing rapid-onset coma and muscle paralysis, not the drugs of palliative care. The propaganda about morphine is dangerous because, as a result, ill patients may refuse to take adequate amounts of opiates for pain relief, fearing that the doctor is secretly trying to end their lives.

Nevertheless, good medicine recognizes the difference between intention and foresight. This is the so-called 'principle of double effect'. Some years ago, as a junior doctor, I spent some time treating patients with cancer. Every day I used to inject terrible toxic poisons into people's veins. I knew all about the effects of the poisons I was injecting: they made the hair fall out; they damaged the bone marrow, the heart muscle and the bowel lining; they led to infections and weight loss, and they carried a real risk of death. Does this mean my actions were immoral and evil? No, my intention in administering these poisons was to heal, to treat various forms of cancer and leukaemia. When I gave the poison, I could foresee what the side effects might be, but they were not my intended goal. I was acting according to the principle of double effect. It is a fundamental principle on which many therapeutic decisions are based.

In the same way, in the treatment of the dying patient, my intention in withdrawing treatment such as intensive life support, or in giving opiates or sedation, is to relieve suffering, to bring benefit to the patient. I can foresee that my treatment decisions may shorten life, but that is not my intention. If it had been possible to use another drug to bring the same pain-relieving benefit, without any shortening of their life, then I would have used that. This is the way that the genuine intention of the treatment can be distinguished. If there had been an equally effective drug that did not have the unintended side effect, would I have used it? If my intention was to kill, then I would use the painkiller which was likely to end life. But if my intention was to prevent pain, then if there was an equally effective painkiller with no risk of ending life, I would use that. The truth is, however, that opiates such as morphine are, for most people, the most highly effective pain relievers known to medicine. In terminal cancer, their benefits outweigh their burdens.

The principle of double effect enshrines the difference between intention and foresight. It is, in fact, exactly the same principle which encompasses the Christian acceptance of martyrdom, but not of suicide. The Christian martyr does not aim at death but aims to be a faithful witness to God, foreseeing that death may occur as a result. Martyrdom transforms into suicide, when the intention changes from faithfulness to God and becomes instead the achievement of death itself.

Behind the principle of double effect lies a contrast between two ways of thinking about the actions of a moral agent. To many secular philosophers, human beings are totally responsible for the consequences of their actions, whether they are intended or not. Thus if I perform action A and B results, I carry full responsibility for B, even if I intended C. If I give a therapy intended to heal, but my patient dies as a result, I am as responsible for their death as though I had intentionally murdered them. My intentions are irrelevant. It is the consequences which allow us to assess the morality of the act. It is as if the future is being constructed as a human artefact by my actions. The future is a product of my choices, good or bad (see further in chapter 12).

But the orthodox Christian way of thinking views the stream of world history as ultimately under God's providential control, not as a product of human choices. My responsibility as a moral agent is to *act wisely*. It is as if I am called to toss into the continually moving stream of history wise and moral actions which are intended to do good. Wise reflection and good intentions are important. But the eventual consequences of my actions, 'down-stream', are outside my control and ultimately part of God's providential rule of the universe. Sometimes I try to do good things and terrible consequences seem to result. Any experienced doctor will recount many cases in which their own well-intentioned acts have led to apparent tragedy. Provided my action at the time was wise, well-informed, thoughtful and genuinely motivated by good intentions, given the limited information available to me, then the consequences are not ultimately my sole responsibility. It is up to God. This does not, of course, absolve me from concern about the consequences of my actions. Part of acting wisely is to recognize the likely effects of my actions. But the ultimate consequences are not under my control. I must learn to live with the reality of my finitude.

Stuart's story

Stuart was a friend of mine who died well. I had known him for years as a fellow member of All Souls Church. We were both pianists, (he was a professional musician), and we shared common interests in music and harmonization. Stuart was quiet and rather shy. He was absorbed in academic musicology, researching a rather obscure and technical aspect of church music in the Reformation. Then, out of the blue, he developed an unpleasant form of disseminated cancer, a lymphoma. He spent weeks in hospital, receiving the full gamut of intensive chemotherapy and radiotherapy. His hair fell out. He became emaciated. The cancer retreated, then came back in a more aggressive form. The oncologists were talking about 'one more push' with a new experimental treatment. He was in pain, weak and distressed.

Stuart and I had several intense and painful conversations about his predicament, and about what the future held. It seemed to me that Stuart was much closer to death than he realized. We talked about the shift from curative medicine to symptom control, about recognizing that death was inevitable, about letting go from the desperate attempt to be cured. I suggested that perhaps he should think about refusing further aggressive cancer treatment and instead ask for referral to palliative care specialists. I remember asking him, 'If I told you that you could have three months of pain-free, useful life followed by death, how would you want to spend those months?' His reply surprised me. He had been talking about completing his thesis, writing up his research. Now he changed. When death was staring him in the face, his priorities were different. 'I want to tell people about my faith. I want to talk to the students at All Souls. I want to write letters to my friends, to my family, to my old contacts in the musical world. I want to tell them what is happening to me and share my faith.'

Stuart was transferred to a local community-based palliative care team, in central London. He started receiving effective pain relief and appropriate symptom control. He knew he was going to die, but he was determined to make the most of the time he had left. After his death Nick Page recorded an interview with Richard Bewes (then rector of All Souls), and Diane Baird (the leader of its student work).

Nick: Richard, how did Stuart react when he knew he was going to die?

Richard: It had to be with a mixture of emotions. There was wistfulness, deep wistfulness of what might have been. I remember him talking about the career that he had in front of him, the prospects, the plans, the hopes, the dreams. And all that was going to come to an end. He was changing his scenario. But he did so with a very wonderful and Christian equanimity of spirit, so although there was wistfulness, I must say there was no trace, honestly, of terror.

Nick: But there must have been more than wistfulness, there must have been deep sadness, the awareness of loss, tears.

Richard: Oh there were tears, of course there were. And naturally there was much prayer. So we would gather round him. Several of us did, for a short service of healing, when together we asked God as strongly and as unitedly as we could that God would touch him and make him well. Because we were quite sure that God had the ability to do that. Nevertheless, we also said that the ball was placed entirely in God's court. That was, to Stuart himself, a great relief.

Diane: Stuart had such a solid faith, it was breathtaking in a way. He was only thirty-nine years of age and yet he saw what many people don't see. He knew that beyond death there was something else, and he knew that when he died he was going to see Jesus. And that just gave him a steady calmness, I think, towards the end. And the confidence with which he faced death. It didn't hold fear for him.

Nick: So, those last few months weren't wasted?

Diane: Completely not. He touched more people in those last few months than I think he probably had done in the preceding fifteen years of his life. I mean, he said that. And certainly he affected my life and, I know, the lives of many, many students very deeply.

Nick: And, I think he wrote more letters in those last few months than most of the rest of his life.

Diane: He was constantly writing letters. He had a big list that he was working through. I think he wanted to share the confidence that he had in the face of death, with friends who didn't know Jesus and hadn't the same confidence – people he'd met over the years. He really was bursting to tell them about this hope that he had. He was always writing letters and he was always telling me who he had written to that day and who he needed to write to. And he hoped he wouldn't die before he'd got all these letters written. So there was always a bit of pressure there at the end of his life to get these letters in the post.

Nick: You said he affected the student group that you lead at All Souls. How was that?

Diane: Well, students are just starting off their lives. The time that he came down to speak to the students, you could have touched the atmosphere that night. Everybody was in tears, and they were, I think, just amazed at the bravery with which he was facing it. And just his strength and the assurance he had of where he was going. It really spoke to the students. Because we don't tend to think about our own death. But here was a young man who was absolutely struggling, I mean the sweat was rolling off his face that night as he spoke, and he could hardly get a breath. Yet the glory with which he spoke and the joy with which he spoke just filled the room. And people were absolutely kind of gob-smacked really with him.

Nick: And how did the church react to his impending death?

Richard: The whole church knew what was happening. He had visited the student group; he had met with the various groups in the church. And also, because he was one of our public musicians, a pianist, it meant that he was regularly on show. So it came to a head finally, the last service that I can recall him taking part in, was a massive communion service at which there was at least a thousand of us present. I was presiding and Stuart was playing the piano. And at some point in the service, just before the breaking of the bread, and the pouring out of the cup, I was able to say, 'It's wonderful we are all here from our different backgrounds. It's wonderful that here is Stuart playing the piano for us on this very important night.' And that meant there was a fellowship, a deep fellowship of prayer, and of suffering and of the cross. The cross was there at the centre and we felt that we were all gathered together with Stuart at the cross. Everybody knew that he was dying, and I suppose most of us knew that this was perhaps the last time we would see him among us. But there was fellowship in that too and a deep understanding.

Diane: I know he was often in a lot of pain, but the actual death itself, he was actually looking forward to it. 'The big sleep' he used to call it.

At his memorial service there were many people there who had received a special letter from Stuart: a letter in which he poured out his heart to them, in an unusually open and forthright way. And, sitting in that memorial service, I suddenly realized that, in a strange sense, I was envious of Stuart. He had had an opportunity to write those letters that most of us never write, to say those things to his friends that most of us never say. The truth is that most people do not die like Stuart. They die unexpectedly over a few days or weeks, without warning: a sudden shock. They have little or no opportunity to experience the intensity of dying that Stuart did. Stuart died well. Those last three months were a wonderfully rich, profound experience for him, as well as for his many friends and contacts.

The opportunities of dying well

Here is a strange paradox. Dying is a terrible mystery, but it is an opportunity for growth. Stuart was in many ways an ordinary person, not some superhuman saint. But during those last few months he grew emotionally, internally. While his body was deteriorating, his spirit was growing. Dying is an opportunity for personal growth.

Secondly, dying well is an opportunity for healing from the inside: for the restoration and reconciliation of broken relationships, twisted by years of bitterness and hurt. It is a never-to-be-repeated opportunity for forgiveness and starting again and for the re-establishment of family ties which have been severed.

Thirdly, dying well is an opportunity for letting go, for relinquishing tasks which will never be fulfilled, for accepting with grace that the myth of a life as a self-directed and controlling individual must be abandoned, for recognizing the element of passivity which goes with the true understanding of suffering, for opening a hand which is tightly grasped and self-centred.

Fourthly, dying well is an opportunity for re-ordering priorities, for expressing what is really important in life. I think Stuart was slightly surprised by his own reaction to his imminent death: when death was staring him in the face, music took a back seat in his life and his desire to tell other people about his Christian faith came to the fore. He learnt about himself, and about what was really important to him.

Finally, dying well is an opportunity to fulfil dreams. Many people have found that it is only when they are dying, that their lifelong dreams can come to the fore, and be recognized, acknowledged and, to some extent, fulfilled.

Growth, internal healing, letting go, reordering priorities, fulfilling dreams: that is what dying well can offer. Stuart experienced all of these, to some degree. Death does not have to be unrelieved gloom and doom. It is a Christian conviction – the hope that transcends the grave. Clement of Alexandria expressed it beautifully: 'Christ has turned all our sunsets into dawns.'

Dealing with fear

What then are the answers to the three fears of the euthanasia debate: fear of pain, fear of indignity, fear of dependence? What prescriptions do we have to offer from the perspective of Christian medicine?

Palliative care

The answer to the fear of pain is good palliative care. Until the middle of the twentieth century, there was very little answer to the pain, especially in cancer. It was as though doctors were confronted with an impossible choice: to watch their patient die in agony or to kill them out of compassion.

How should Christians react when confronted by two totally unacceptable choices? Should we simply look for the lesser of two evils? No. The answer is to invent a totally new alternative which reflects Christian values, concerns and obligations. That is what a group of remarkable pioneering spirits did, notably Dr Cicely Saunders of St Christopher's Hospice, London, who founded the modern hospice movement which led to a quiet revolution in the care of the dying.[17] I have become convinced that, as Christian carers, perhaps the single most important attribute we need is creativity. Often it seems that we do not lack compassion, expertise or resources. But we seem to lack the creativity, the originality, the ability to innovate, the perception to see a new way forward. Cicely Saunders provides a wonderful example of innovative Christian caring – caring that refuses to accept old defeatist attitudes.

Modern palliative care is a way of using specialized medical and nursing techniques, and a multidisciplinary team of carers, to treat the whole person in response to the 'total pain' of dying. It is a way of helping dying people to make the most of their lives. In the words of one of the slogans of the movement, 'Not only will we help you to die in dignity, but we will help you to live before you die.' It's a positive and practical alternative to euthanasia. It is not necessary to kill the patient in order to kill the pain.

A modern hospice is not a gloom-ridden place of death and shadows, but a place of hope and laughter as well as tears and pain; a place where people live before they die. And increasingly, palliative care is moving into homes, into mainstream hospitals, and into GP surgeries. It is a concept, a way of caring, rather than an institution. Dr Robert Twycross, another pioneer of the movement wrote: 'Palliative care developed as a reaction to the attitude, "There's nothing that can be done for you." This is never true. There's always something that can be done.'

But can all pain be controlled? Specialists say that, with appropriate expertise, pain can be completely abolished or dramatically ameliorated in over 95% of cases. In fact, physical pain in terminal illness is rarely a major problem for carers these days. The problem pain is spiritual pain, emotional pain, relational pain. This is the pain which doesn't respond to pain-killing drugs or palliative procedures. There is a deep-rooted agony in the hearts of many dying people in our society – the agony that goes along with being lonely and isolated. Mother Teresa once said that the worst disease in the world is not leprosy or tuberculosis, but the feeling of being unwanted, unloved and abandoned by everyone.

How can we respond to the pain of dying, to the internal, spiritual suffering? It is by Christian caring, above all by *being there*.

The story is told of a little girl who is going to sleep in the bedroom upstairs while her mother is working in the kitchen.

'Mummy, Mummy, I'm scared. It's dark in here. I need someone to cuddle me.'

'I'm sorry, dear, both Mummy and Daddy are busy and can't come now. Just remember that God is with you. He will look after you.'

Long pause,

'But Mummy, I need someone with skin on!'

People who are dying need to feel God's love physically. They need human contact. They need physical arms around them. They need the sound of a human voice. This is the way that God made us. The Christian prescription for the fear of pain is God's love expressed in a human presence.

Compassion and respect

The answer to the fear of indignity is 'compassion mingled with respect'. The fact that many people feel that medical care leads to indignity is a stinging indictment of our modern medical systems and our modern medical attitudes, both of which tend to distance and demean our patients. We desperately need to recapture a sense of 'respect-love', which recognizes and honours the unique dignity of every human being made in God's image, every flawed masterpiece. The strange dignity which Mother Teresa and her sisters were able to perceive, even in the dying leprosy victim with maggots growing in the wounds, is the dignity of humanness. It is the dignity derived from the image of Christ. This is the Christian prescription for the fear of indignity.

The Christian gospel

The fear of becoming dependent on others, and the desperate desire to remain in control is, in my view, the hardest fear for modern people to conquer. In one sense the answer is the Christian worldview. We have to learn for ourselves, and teach one another, that dependence on others is part of the human story. This is where the educative role of the health professional is most needed and most resisted. To learn dependence requires humility and maturity. It also requires trust, and for many people in our society, trust in others has been steadily eroded and ultimately destroyed. But how can we die well if we cannot trust anybody?

The answer to this deep fear is the Christian gospel. It needs recognition of the painful and liberating truth that we cannot do it 'our way', trapped in what Malcolm Muggeridge once called the 'dark little dungeon of the ego'. If we are to grow and develop as human beings, we have to relinquish our desperate attempts at self-sufficiency. We have to learn about grace (God's unmerited favour), and that the most valuable things in life come as a free gift.

Standards of palliative care

There is, then, good news for those facing terminal illness. Modern palliative care is a wonderful development in caring, invented almost entirely by Christians, which has taken much of the force out of the euthanasia debate. We should be thankful that we live at a time when, thanks to the ongoing contributions of many dedicated carers, it is possible for most people to die well.

Yet there is another side to the story. Decades after Cicely Saunders invented a better way of caring, people in Britain and around the world are still dying in agony. Thousands of terminally ill people die in pain, inappropriately cared for, with no treatment or the wrong treatment, with no support or the wrong kind of support.

A study on the care of dying patients in four large teaching hospitals found that 'basic interventions to maintain patients' comfort were often not provided, oral hygiene was often poor, thirst remained unquenched, and little assistance was given to encourage eating. Contact between nurses and dying patients was minimal; distancing and isolation of patients by most medical and nursing staff were evident; this isolation increased as death approached.'[18] When I read these reports, and see the evidence with my own eyes, I feel distressed and indeed, angry. The pain and distress of all those dying people seem so unnecessary. Is it any wonder that people fear death and wish to have the option of euthanasia?

In the ten years since the first edition of this book was published, the availability of palliative care for people dying from cancer has improved significantly and there has been widespread recognition, both within the NHS and internationally, that high-quality palliative care should be made available for everybody who needs it. But it was estimated in 2004 that cancer was responsible for only 13% of all deaths worldwide while other long-term conditions accounted for 47%. In the future, the majority of deaths will be from chronic conditions leading to organ failure and/or cognitive decline.[19] Although there have been a number of positive initiatives in the UK to improve the situation, at present palliative care is still massively under-developed.

There are many reasons for the current difficulties. First, training in palliative care for medical students, doctors and nurses is inadequate. Palliative care forms only a very small part of the modern medical curriculum. Much more emphasis is placed on the scientific and technological basis of medical practice than on practical methods of pain and symptom relief. Secondly, front-line clinical staff in hospitals are often over-stretched and poorly supported. High-quality palliative care requires high staffing ratios and the expenditure of significant health-care resources. But to health economists, the benefits of palliative care are largely invisible and impossible to quantify. Spending money to improve palliative care has little political return. Sadly, many health staff are poorly motivated to care for dying patients. The preoccupations of modern medicine are the high-technology, high-status treatments which save lives and make the headlines. There is little or no technology in the care of the dying patient. There are few academic or professional reputations to be made.

Finally, medical research into improved methods of pain relief and symptom control is very limited. Every year hundreds of millions of pounds are spent in research, trying to find new life-saving treatments for cancer and other diseases, many of them rare and exotic. In contrast, research to improve methods of symptom control for dying patients is seen as a low priority. In the pecking order of the medical profession, palliative care medicine comes somewhere near the bottom. And it is not just the health professionals who are to blame, we are all culpable. Members of the public support charities which pour vast sums into research into high-tech ways of prolonging life by a few months, and lap up documentaries about open heart surgery and dramatic television soaps about modern medical life. Medical managers respond to public pressure. Questions are asked in Parliament. Ministers jump to attention. Money is found. But people do not seem very interested in whether they will get proper pain relief when they are dying. Apparently it is not a matter of public concern. Yet only a few of us will require the wonders of extremely high-tech medicine, but every one of us is going to die.

Advance directives – living wills

In 2005, the UK Parliament passed the Mental Capacity Act, and this piece of legislation is likely to have a major impact on medical care at the end of life.[20] The Act allows all adults to make legally binding advance statements of their wishes with regard to life-sustaining treatments. Medical staff in the UK are now legally obliged to obey a valid advance refusal of life-sustaining treatment, even if they believe that this is not in the patient's best interests. Hence, a person may direct that if they were to become unconscious or develop severe dementia, that no steps should be taken to resuscitate them or provide any form of active medical treatment. The Mental Capacity Act also allows any adult to nominate in advance another individual to have a Lasting Power of Attorney (LPA). If specifically stated in the deed of authorization, this person would then have legally binding powers to take decisions about life-sustaining treatment on behalf of the patient when they lost legal capacity (see website).

The Act is intended to strengthen the rights of people to make their own decisions about the care they receive, when they are not able to express their own wishes. In principle, this seems a worthy and appropriate aim. But it is already clear that this legislation may have unintended consequences. In April 2009, the *Evening Standard* reported that the London Ambulance Service had set up a register to allow any member of the public to record their end-of-life wishes. Paramedics called to an emergency, including those involving crash victims, will be required to check whether an individual has registered a 'do not resuscitate' order before commencing any life-supporting treatment.[21]

Although advance statements refusing life-sustaining treatment seem, in general, unnecessary and downright dangerous, there may be some value in what has been called an advance statement of values. This allows a person who is facing serious illness or major surgery to express their beliefs and values, enabling doctors and relatives to make better-informed decisions about life-sustaining treatment. (An example of this form of advance statement, drafted by a distinguished Christian teacher, is available on the website.)

Dementia and severe brain injury

In the previous chapter we looked at the deeply distressing problems caused by dementia and the persistent vegetative state. If modern palliative care, combined with Christian compassion, can provide a better way than euthanasia for the dying patient with cancer, what about the person with these conditions? Surely here is an argument for mercy killing. The tragic realities of dementia and PVS indicate how fragile our brains are. If human worth and significance are located entirely in our ability to think and to choose, in the functioning of a few millimetres of brain cortex, then our very humanity hangs by a thread. At any moment our brain functioning may become impaired, by disease or accident. Within the secular worldview of Ronald Dworkin or Peter Singer, the essence of our humanity, the ability to exercise autonomous choices, may be destroyed at any moment. This is why dementia is regarded with such horror by secular philosophers and by many ordinary people.

How can I be sure who I am, and how can I respect myself, when my own identity and worth is so evanescent and fragile? Of course, Christian believers too recognize the terrible degradation of dementia and PVS. This is not what human life was meant to be. But we cannot, and must not, respond to the brain-damaged individual with a sense of horror and revulsion. The Christian perspective enshrines a holistic view of human identity as a body-mind-spirit unity within community. It teaches us to value human beings in their complex totality; to value human beings because of who they are, because of how they have been made and how they are known by God.

The Christian view of human nature created in God's image provides a stability of human identity and significance throughout the whole of life, whatever events may befall. Even if my cortex is damaged, or my brain starts to malfunction, or I become confused and disorientated, I will still be me, a unique person, known and loved by others, and ultimately by God himself. No-one and nothing can take my human significance from me. I will always be worth what God thinks of me. Even if I become disabled, demented and despised by others, I can retain my own self-respect, and I can retain the right to be treated with respect by others.

Just as it is pointless to expect biology to reveal conclusively the point at which God's covenant involvement with a human individual commences, so it is pointless to use neurological examination to decide whether a human person is present within a body that is clearly living. As we saw earlier, Oliver O'Donovan argues that we cannot demonstrate that a person exists by scientific testing for various attributes or capacities, such as rationality or responsivity. Instead 'we discern persons only by love, by discovering through interaction and commitment that this human being is irreplaceable'.[22] In order to know one another as persons, we must engage, not in objective scientific analysis, but in a covenant commitment of respect-love.

If respect and empathy are central to Christian caring, then they must be reflected in our attitudes to those with Alzheimer's disease. One of the arts of caring for people with dementia is the ability to enter into the world of the other, to empathize, to enter into their experience. It is by attempting to understand, that we can show respect and love. It is a fundamental Christian instinct. Of course, treating the Alzheimer's sufferer in this way, with practical, respectful and compassionate caring, is not a soft option. It is emotionally and, at times, financially costly. It is a calling which is unglamorous and frequently demeaned and disregarded by our society. It demands reserves of patience, fortitude, humour and compassion. It is easy for carers to feel isolated, ignored and demeaned.

Caring for people with respect does not mean that we are obliged to provide intensive and burdensome medical treatment to prolong life at all costs. As in all other clinical situations, the burdens of any proposed treatment must be weighed against its benefits. In severe and irreversible dementia, just as in terminal cancer, the benefits of medical treatment may be extremely small or non-existent. If infection or other life-threatening disease develops, it may be right to withhold treatment, such as antibiotics, or more intensive life-support measures, especially if they are unpleasant or invasive. But just as with the cancer patient, withdrawing or withholding medical treatment is not the same as intentional killing. We retain the basic attitudes of wonder, respect, empathy, and protection. In the words of Joseph Pieper which we looked at earlier, 'Love is a way of saying to another person, "It's good that you exist, it's good that you are in the world."'

It is not always right to withhold treatment in dementia. For instance, according to a senior specialist in Care of the Elderly, following a femoral fracture, hip surgery has become the best, kindest and most cost-effective treatment in most patients with dementia.[23]

In several centres across the UK and elsewhere, doctors and other professionals are developing innovative ways of establishing communication with severely demented sufferers. There are now outstanding examples of good practice where highly skilled care-givers, working as part of a multidisciplinary team in an appropriately resourced environment, are able to minimize the use of sedative medication and physical restraints.[24] Just as with palliative medicine, care of people with dementia must involve every aspect of the person: physical, psychological, relational and spiritual. With the appropriate quality of care, the experience of dementia need not be the bleak and terrifying experience which is often portrayed. So often it seems that ethical dilemmas are raised, not because of the condition itself, but because we are not willing or capable of providing the highest quality of care. Isn't this a better way to respond to the challenge of dementia than Ronald Dworkin's option of euthanasia by advance directive?

Sharon Fish Mooney, an experienced Christian nurse from New York, has written a practical and helpful book entitled *Alzheimer's*.[25] She speaks movingly from her own experience of caring for her mother as the disease slowly progressed, and of practical ways of establishing and maintaining communication. She writes of her own anger with God at the disruption to her personal life, and the degradation to which her mother was subjected. 'My own struggles revolved as much around my own frustrated plans and desires as they did around my mother's disease and the devastating effects it had on her and my father.'[26] Yet Sharon found spiritual healing and practical support in many areas, including with a Christian community that was able to accept her and her mother. The spiritual care of Alzheimer's sufferers is an essential component of the holistic caring that reflects the Christian worldview. Often people with Alzheimer's seem to retain spiritual insight and capacity, long after the ability to think rationally has been lost. We must not fall into to the trap of thinking that advanced cognitive ability is essential to genuine and profound spiritual experience.

A friend recently described an incident with her father who suffered from progressively severe dementia, and who had almost completely lost the power to communicate. A televised act of worship was being shown and on impulse my friend said to her father, 'Do you still pray, Dad?'

To her surprise he responded with a distinct 'Yes'.

'What do you say to God when you pray?'

'I say . . . (long pause) . . . Hello . . . '

No more was forthcoming, but no more needed to be said.

Robert Davis, a Presbyterian minister, has written of the experience from the inside in *My Journey into Alzheimer's Disease*: 'In my rational moments I am still me. Alzheimer's disease is like a reverse ageing process. Having drunk from the fountain of youth one is caught in the time tunnel . . . Cruelly it whips us back to the place of infancy. First the memories go, then perceptions, feelings, knowledge and in the last stage, our ability to talk and to take care of our most basic human needs . . . At this stage while I still have some control of thoughts and feelings, I must learn to take on the role of the infant in order to make use of whatever gifts are left to me . . . Perhaps the journey that takes me away from reality into the blackness of that place of the blank, emotionless, unmoving Alzheimer's stare is in reality a journey into the richest depths of God's love that few have experienced on earth. Who can know what goes on deep inside a person who is so withdrawn? At that time I will be unable to give you a clue, but perhaps we can talk about it later in the timeless joy of heaven. On second thought, all these heartaches won't really matter over there, will they?'[27]

Robert Davis' moving words direct us towards the future hope to which all Christian caring points. In Richard Dworkin's view, we should treat Alzheimer's sufferers with respect, solely because of what they *once were*. But Christians treat all human beings with respect, not only because of what they were, but also because of what they are now, Godlike and wonderful beings, and what, by God's grace, *they are to become*. It's a theme we will return to in the final chapter.

I finish this chapter with a sense of both optimism and frustration. There are practical and effective alternatives to euthanasia which reflect Christian values and priorities. There are ways of caring for dying and disabled people with respect and compassion, showing God's love in practical action. These are messages which modern secular people (and modern philosophers) need to hear. But so often, the Christian community does not seem to respond to the challenge. Where is the Christian voice in our society, arguing for better care of the dying and better education of professionals? Where are the professionals who will raise the status of palliative care, bringing new insights and fresh expertise to the problems of the dying patient and the Alzheimer's sufferer? Where are the Christian believers who are just prepared to be there, to give practical care and emotional support for the vulnerable, the severely disabled and the dying?

We now turn from the end of life to the future of medicine. What are the values of medicine which will guide health professionals as we move into the next decade?

11. THE HIPPOCRATIC TRADITION AND THE PRACTICE OF MODERN MEDICINE

Perhaps the most all-pervading reaction to technological advances in biology and medicine is a sense of unease, not just amongst members of the general public, but also amongst policy-makers and so-called opinion-formers. Increasing numbers in our society betray a mood of deep suspicion of biotechnological developments which, while offering the possibility of spectacular benefits, seem to change the fundamental givens of our humanity. It is a suspicion which seems both emotional and irrational – the 'yuk factor'. To many scientists and philosophers, it is a purely negative, atavistic and retrograde phenomenon, a modern equivalent of the Luddites, who waged a futile campaign against the might of the Industrial Revolution. But from a Christian perspective, the 'yuk factor' may have more positive aspects: an expression of profound moral intuitions about what it means to be a human being. It is remarkable how these moral intuitions are still deeply rooted within our society, despite the corrosive acids of secularism.

In this chapter we shall look at the history of medicine and the strange alliance which was struck up between an ancient pagan craft and the Christian church. But first we examine a prominent feature of modern thinking about ethics: the distinction between facts and values.

Core values and the facts/values distinction

At the heart of the view of the world which derives from the Enlightenment is the facts/values distinction. To most modern secular thinkers, it is self-evident that there is no connection between facts (what is the case), and values (what ought to happen). Facts are rooted in reality, but values are just 'made up'. They are a product of human storytelling. They float free, detached from the physical stuff of reality.

From this perspective, our moral task, individually, as professional groups and as a society, is to *choose* the values by which we want to live. But where do we find those values if we can't derive them from the facts, from the nature of reality which we perceive? Ultimately, values are regarded as expressions of personal preference. Whether or not we personally are in favour of doctors committing euthanasia, or selecting the sex of future children, is simply a matter of personal inclination. These are not topics on which rational discussion and debate are helpful or even possible.

If we can't argue for a particular set of values on a rational basis, where can we find them? Where can a secular society and a secular profession find ethical principles which will provide practical solutions to the agonizing dilemmas we face and which will fit with our deepest human intuitions? It's an issue which continues to trouble many thinkers and professional leaders. I wish to suggest three crucial questions which health professionals need to answer:

1. *Humanity*. What does it mean to be a healthy human being? We need a renewed vision of humanity.
2. *Medicine*. What are we trying to achieve? We need a renewed sense of the goals and purpose of medicine.
3. *Caring*. How can we show compassionate involvement within ethical constraints? We need new models of caring.

How can we find a way forward in addressing these issues? To revisit the words of Archbishop William Temple: 'If you don't know where you are going, it is sometimes helpful to know where you have been.' In the confusion of a postmodern age, history has a crucial role in ethics, providing insights as to how we got here in the first place. If we are going to find a way forward together as a society, we need to understand how the ethical debates of today find their roots in the past. A discernible trend in moral philosophy is a renewed interest in the history of ethical traditions. In the same way, Christians who find themselves living in a postmodern age need to develop a renewed appreciation of our Christian history, especially, in my view, the history of the Early Church, and how it met the challenges of the pagan age in which it lived. So I make no apologies for a brief foray into the history of medical ethics, and the ancient craft of Hippocratic medicine.

Hippocratic medicine: an ancient tradition

The Graeco-Roman world into which Hippocratic medicine appeared had plenty of healers. There were herbalists of various descriptions, including the practitioners of *pharmakeia*, referred to earlier – the professional abortionists and poisoners, whose dubious services could be obtained for a fat fee. In addition, various healers were attached to the mystery religions and cults, and there were philosopher-physicians, thinkers who dabbled in the healing arts. It was a common aphorism at the time that, 'the doctor is physician of the body; the philosopher is physician of the soul'.

As we have seen, Graeco-Roman society was often cruel and inhumane. But the Hippocratic physicians seemed to have had a different attitude to their fellow human beings. They were a professional sect: a craft, who traced their origins to the quasi-mystical figure of Hippocrates, an inhabitant of the Greek island of Cos around 400 BC. The Hippocratic band was a clique of skilled practitioners, passing on their mysterious and strange healing customs to carefully selected initiates, who were required to swear a solemn and pagan oath: 'I swear by Apollo Physician, by Asclepius, by Hygeia, by Panaceia and by all the gods and goddesses, that I will carry out, according to my ability and judgement, this oath.'[1]

The oath summarizes the essential features of the Hippocratic tradition. First, the oath emphasized an arduous and prolonged apprenticeship in the art of medicine: the new doctor swore a binding and life-long allegiance to his teachers. Secondly, it stressed a duty of care to help the sick, and a specific abjuration of harm: 'I will use treatment to help the sick according to my ability and judgement, but I will never use it to injure or wrong them.' Thirdly, there was a refusal to abuse medical skill by taking human life by poisoning or abortion: 'I will not give poison to anyone though asked to do so, nor will I suggest such a plan. Similarly I will not give a pessary to a woman to cause abortion.' Fourthly, there was an emphasis on the protection of vulnerable patients from abuse and from sexual manipulation: 'In purity and holiness I will guard my life and my art . . . Into whatever house I enter, I will do so to help the sick, keeping myself free from all intentional wrong-doing and harm, especially from fornication with woman or man, bond or free.' Finally, there was a duty of confidentiality to protect patients from the harm of scandal: 'Whatsoever in the course of practice I see or hear, that ought never to be published abroad, I will not divulge, but consider such things to be holy secrets.' The novel aspect of the Hippocratic tradition was the concept of a profession which married skilled technical abilities with a clear structure of moral values and commitments.

How did this esoteric and pagan guild of physicians become so significant in the development of Western civilization?

Trust

The genius of the Hippocratic band was that they recognized that *trust* was at the heart of the doctor-patient relationship. Historians have suggested that one of the reasons for the development of the oath was a widespread mistrust of physicians. The Romans, in particular, were intensely suspicious of those clever Greek physicians and their strange practices. They were known to have an extensive knowledge and access to lethal herbs and potions. They entered private bedrooms and performed intimate examinations and procedures behind closed doors. They were privy to the most extraordinary secrets and personal confidences. It is hardly surprising that physicians were regarded with some suspicion by their clients. As a distinguished medical historian put it: 'There would be little point in solemnly forswearing murder, euthanasia, abortion, and fornication with patients, if doctors had never been known to participate in such deeds.'

By formalizing and publicizing their professional code of conduct, the Hippocratic physicians managed to win the confidence of the public, and just as importantly, they differentiated themselves from the numerous quacks, herbalists and witch doctors of the time. Before patients put their life and welfare into the hands of a physician, they needed to know whether or not he was trustworthy. Therefore, to the Hippocratic band, ethical conduct ranked even higher than technical skill. 'It is better to be a good man devoid of learning than to be a perfect practitioner of bad moral conduct and an untrustworthy man.'[2]

Philanthropy

They based their professional art on *philanthropy*, rather than on pure financial gain. What the ideal physician exhibited was a disinterested love and concern, not just for the elite of society, but for humanity as a whole. 'Like a saviour god, let the physician make himself the equal of slaves and paupers, of the rich and of rulers of men, and to all let him minister like a brother, for we are all children of the same blood.'[3] In the Hippocratic writings there is clear evidence of a humane professional tradition which treated all human beings as brothers and sisters. I find it fascinating that a pagan Greek craft should have been founded on a view of humanity which was so similar to that of the coming

Christian religion: 'If the love of man (*philanthropē*) is present, love of art (*philotechnē*) is also present.'[4]

Separation of healing and harming

The Hippocratic tradition drew a clear distinction between healing and harming. Margaret Mead, the distinguished anthropologist, commented on the momentous significance of the Hippocratic tradition as follows:

> For the first time in the history of humankind there was a complete separation between killing and curing. Throughout the primitive world, the doctor and the sorcerer tended to be the same person. He with the power to kill had the power to cure. He who had the power to cure would also be able to kill ... With the Greeks, the distinction was made clear. One profession was to be dedicated completely to life under all circumstances, regardless of rank, age, or intellect – the life of a slave, the life of the Emperor, the life of the immigrant, the life of the defective child.[5]

By a quirk of history which is still not fully explained, the ancient pagan craft of Hippocratic medicine shared much in common with the radical Christian religion that was to spread throughout the Graeco-Roman world.

The Hippocratic-Christian consensus

As we saw in chapter 6 the early Christians, such as the writers of the *Didache* and the *Epistle of Barnabas*, attacked Graeco-Roman morality with its acceptance of the elimination of unwanted human life and its cruelty to the weak and despised. They found unlikely allies in the Hippocratic guild of doctors. The physician Luke became an important part of the early apostolic group, writing both a Gospel and the history of the Early Church (Acts). Paul took him on his missionary journeys, probably to act in his professional role as personal physician to the members of the party. Like Luke, it seems that most of the physicians of the Early Church found that the Hippocratic oath fitted in with their own Christian perspectives.[6] Jesus himself provided a model as a healer. His ministry had emphasized the importance of physical healing, and in the Gospel writings he had described himself as a physician to the morally diseased: 'It is not the healthy who need a physician, but the sick' (Matthew 9:12).

Thus a strange alliance grew up between the pagan craft and the rapidly growing Christian religion. 'The pagan enterprise of medicine became suffused with the distinctives of the Judaeo-Christian revelation.'[7] In a remarkable way the Hippocratic medical art fitted both with Christian anthropology and with the ethical imperatives of the Christian church. As Osei Temkin, a distinguished Jewish historian of medicine, wrote, 'What was to distinguish the sincere Christian doctor from the pagan one, was a new relationship to his faith and his church, rather than a fundamental change in his professional ethics.'[8]

Christian contributions to medical ideals

Christianity did not just coexist with the old Hippocratic ideal, it brought an enhanced radical vision of the medical task. Christian thinking emphasized, first, the importance of the natural order. In the universe God had created a physical order which extended to the physical structure of human beings. This is a theme which we addressed in chapter 2. By investigating how the body worked, Christian doctors were 'thinking God's thoughts after him', as Kepler put it, many centuries later. Not only that, but God had created the hidden *moral* structure of the creation, and, by treating human life with reverence and respect, physicians were practising in accordance with the moral order of the cosmos.

, Secondly, in the historical event of the Incarnation God affirmed the dignity and lasting significance of the human body. So Christian doctors treated the human body, for all its strange idiosyncrasies, with special wonder and respect because this was the form in which God chose to become flesh. When Christ was raised as a human being, God proclaimed his vote of confidence in humanity and the created order. Hence humanity was not demeaned as something which separated us from God. On the contrary, it was the means by which God was made known. Christianity provided for Hippocratic medicine a new anthropology, a way of thinking about human beings with wonder and respect as the bearers of the divine image, and as a universal family. It also provided an ethical framework in which personal integrity, truthfulness and covenant commitment were part of the moral order of the universe.

Thirdly, Christian thinking pointed to a deeper and richer reality beyond the physical. The material aspect of the universe is an important, but not the most important, part of reality. In Greek, the word *sozo* can mean both 'to save' and 'to heal', and it is hardly surprising that this word crops up much more frequently in Luke's Gospel than in the other three. Perhaps Luke was fascinated by the ambiguity and the subtlety of *sozo*. He recognized that in the ministry of Jesus, physical healing and spiritual salvation went hand in hand. They were two sides of the same coin. Jesus helped people not to *escape* from their humanity, but to become full human beings, human beings as we were intended to be. Christians thus affirmed the importance of physical healing, while recognizing that behind the physical body lay a deeper, a richer, an even more wonderful reality. The physical body was not the limit of reality, humans needed a deeper healing. Christianity affirmed and supported the importance and the dignity of the medical and caring professions, while at the same time relativizing their role.

Fourthly, Christianity provided a new definition of neighbourliness. The Old Testament law had taught about duties to the neighbour, and especially to the vulnerable and defenceless: orphans, widows, aliens, the poor. Yahweh, the mighty Lord, had proclaimed that he was their defender, and those who followed him should be their defenders too. Love for neighbour was part of the Jewish Torah: 'Do not seek revenge or bear a grudge against one of your people, but love your neighbour as yourself' (Leviticus 19:18). The rabbis had interpreted this instruction in a narrow, localized and parochial manner. My neighbour was the person next door, my friend, my compatriot, the one who was like me.

Jesus combined the Old Testament commands to love God and to love our neighbour (Mark 12:28–31). By doing so, he highlighted their inter-relationship: in loving and respecting our neighbour we are in fact honouring the God whose image he or she bears. But Jesus reinterpreted the command to neighbour-love in a startling, radical way, as recorded by Luke in his Gospel (Luke 10:25–37).

The passage is so familiar to us that it has lost its original extraordinary impact. The expert in the Torah who had engaged Jesus in debate had started with a typically rhetorical debating point. 'What must I do to inherit eternal life?'

Jesus responded with the question, 'What is written in the Law? How do you read it?'

He answered: 'Love the Lord your God with all your heart and with all your strength and with all your mind', and 'Love your neighbour as yourself.'

'You have answered correctly,' Jesus replied. 'Do this and you will live' (Luke 10:25–28)

But, according to Luke, the rabbi 'wanted to justify himself', so he asked Jesus, 'And who is my neighbour?' In response, Jesus told the story about the nameless traveller who was mugged on the way from Jerusalem to Jericho, the failure of the orthodox Jewish teachers to assist, and the practical, costly compassion of the hated and despised Samaritan, the half-Jew. Jesus comes to the punchline: 'Which of these three do you think was a neighbour to the man who fell into the hands of robbers?' (verse 36)

As a number of commentators have pointed out, the question has subtly changed. The rabbi asked, 'Who is my neighbour?' In other words, 'Which out of all my friends and contacts am I supposed to love? Who has a claim on me?' But Jesus turns the question around: 'Who out of these three in the story proved to be a neighbour, who acted in a neighbourly way?'. In other words, we discover who is our neighbour, to whom we owe a duty, when we act in a neighbourly way. The relation of neighbourhood between the Samaritan and the Jewish victim would never have become apparent if the Samaritan had not taken the initiative. Both the Samaritan and the Jew discovered that they were neighbours, because the Samaritan had first acted in a neighbourly way, by acting with compassion towards an anonymous victim. We discover the humanity, the dignity, the worth of our neighbour when we have a prior moral commitment to them.

> Turning the concept of the neighbour around and applying it to the agent rather than the object of the loving act, Jesus draws attention to the fact that neighbourhood is a *reciprocal* relation. 'Nobody can be a neighbour except to a neighbour,' commented Augustine. And by casting the story in the form of an adventure . . . Jesus emphasizes the *contingency* of the circumstances which can place us in an unlooked-for neighbourly relation with others. The Samaritan was discovered to be the Jew's neighbour, not by any judgement or evaluation on the Jew's part but because he 'turned out to be' a neighbour in the event.[9]

The Christian concept of the neighbour is a commonplace to us in modern Western societies, but we should try to recognize how strange and threatening it must have seemed at the time. The duty of love for others was not limited to my friend next door. Any stranger that I happened to come across in the accidental events of life could make demands on me. My neighbours included the riff-raff, the slave, the tax-collector, the hated Roman collaborator, the leprosy victim, the prostitute, the unwanted baby, the pathetic old crippled widow, the weak, the vulnerable, the despised. Even the fetus was a neighbour to whom I owed a duty of compassion, respect, and protection. Again, to the devout Jew it was obvious that God commanded us to act in a neighbourly way to those who deserved it, to the good and godly. But the radical nature of Christian love was seen in Christ's command to 'Love your enemies and pray for those who persecute you, that you may be sons of your Father in heaven. He causes his sun to rise on the evil and the good, and sends rain on the righteous and the unrighteous' (Matthew 5:44–45).

As Michael Gorman put it, 'Jesus' new definition of neighbour yielded an ethical stance unique to the Ancient World. All distinctions between people – Gentile and Jew, man and woman, adult and child, slave and free, rich and poor, guilty and innocent – were obliterated.'[10] My fellow human being, in whatever form I find them, has a claim on me simply by being human.

Of course, Jesus not only talked about the importance of the riff-raff, he lived it out as well. Luke, the Hippocratic physician, takes great delight in spelling out how Jesus was known for his practical compassion for society's outcasts. Luke records the lepers he touched, the prostitute who kissed his feet, the unclean woman with a hidden haemorrhage who defiled everyone she touched, and those pathetic little children who, for some unaccountable reason, the Son of God wasted his time on.

Christian influence on the development of medicine

As Christianity spread through Graeco-Roman society, it was seen to be different from the mystery religions with which the state was awash. And a central peculiarity of these Christians was that they *cared for the riff-raff*. Right from the start they set up distribution schemes to provide practical support for widows, orphans, the needy and the sick, referred to in several places in the New Testament (e.g. Acts 6:1–6, 2 Corinthians 8 and 9, James 1:27). They went round the rubbish bins, rescuing abandoned babies. Later they set up orphanages and hospitals for the dying. Practical care for the needy was the consistent teaching of the Early Church Fathers, as exemplified by Clement of Alexandria in words we looked at previously: 'It behoves you to give honour to the image of God which is man, in this wise: food to the hungry, drink to the thirsty, clothing to the naked, care to the sick, shelter to the stranger, and visiting him who is in prison, to help him as you can.' Clement also exhorted the rich to abandon the Roman custom of buying one's own soldiers for personal protection. Instead they were to form an 'army' of the poor and the weak by providing for their needs. 'Contrary to the rest of men, enlist for yourself an army without weapons, without war, without bloodshed, without wrath, without stain – pious old men, orphans dear to God, widows armed with gentleness, men adorned with love . . . '[11]

The Emperor Julian, who attempted to resist the spread of Christianity, complained about these fanatics, the 'atheists' as he called them: 'It's their benevolence to strangers, their care of the graves of the dead and the pretended holiness of their lives that has done most to increase their atheism . . . the impious Galileans support not only their own poor, but ours as well!'[12] In the great plague which followed a period of persecution in 250–251, wealthy pagans were fleeing the city of Carthage. Bishop Cyprian preached to his congregation from the passage about love for enemies in Matthew 5:43–48, 'urging them not to save their own lives, not even to seek the survival of their Christian community, but to love their enemies who had recently been persecuting them. This was an opportunity to show the love of Jesus by staying in the city and nursing pagan and Christian alike.'[13]

Thus, Christianity gave new life to the tradition of Hippocratic medicine – a new vision of the natural creation and of anthropology and moral order; a new sense of the significance of the physical body, whilst pointing towards a greater reality. Christianity redefined the obligations of neighbourliness enshrined in medical practice, and orientated it towards those on the lowest rungs of society's ladder. Primitive hospitals had existed before in several forms. They had existed in military establishments to keep troops healthy for battle. There were healing centres attached to temples of Saturn to which sufferers flocked. But when the Christian church and its physicians set up hospitals, they were different because they were based on the radical teaching of Jesus of Nazareth, the Good Samaritan. They concentrated on treating strangers, travellers and outcasts, the abandoned and the destitute.

Here are the words of the eminent Jewish historian H. E. Sigerist:

> The most important and decisive development in the special status assigned to the sick was introduced by Christianity. This new teaching, in contrast with the other religions which were for the healthy and the just, appealed to the sick, the weak and to the crippled. It spoke of spiritual healing, but it also spoke of bodily healing. The place of the sick in society was altered from its very foundation. Whereas disease in the entire history of medicine had sharply isolated the sufferer, in Christian times he was actually brought closer to his fellow men by the fact of his illness. To care for him was a Christian obligation. The birth-hour of large-scale organised care of the sick had come. The care of the ill is now the concern of the church. The Bishop is in charge, the deacons and the laity are his agents.[14]

The development of hospitals

It is not surprising that the early Christians built hospitals, including distinctly dangerous places, such as specialist hospitals for plague victims and leprosy sufferers. Even the word 'hospital' has Christian roots. It comes from the Latin *hospes*, meaning 'a guest'. A hospital is a place where we practise hospitality, neighbour-love to strangers, a bizarre concept first introduced by one Jesus of Nazareth. Nearly all the Christian hospitals were built within monasteries run by the church authorities, like that of St Basil who built a hospital of 300 beds for plague victims at Edessa. Not all Christians held a high view of the body, however, and the development of ascetic monastic communities in the third and fourth centuries encouraged a fanaticism which could be associated with a sense of loathing towards the physical body. Several of the Church Fathers opposed this tendency, emphasizing respect and a sense of awe towards the human body. Gregory of Nyssa wrote, 'Do not despise the wonder within you.'[15] It is an authentically Christian response to the body; a sense of awe and wonder at the mystery of humanness.

Many lay monks trained as Hippocratic physicians, and some of the religious sisters and brothers devoted themselves to the art of caring for the sick and dying, becoming specialized nursing sisters, and nursing brothers (the male nurse is not a recent invention!). The rules of the Benedictine monastic order emphasized the importance of hospital duties to all its monks: 'Care for the sick stands before and over all. Accordingly one must help them as one would Christ.' As the classical world disintegrated, the so-called Dark Ages descended and most of the ancient learning was lost, it was the Christian monasteries that preserved the ideals of the old Hippocrates tradition. It was Christian monks who translated, taught and developed the ancient precepts of the Hippocratic ideal.

Many of the historic monastic hospitals still survive. In London, St Bartholomew's Hospital, St Mary's Spital, which later became the Bethlem Hospital for the Insane, and St Thomas's Hospital, were all founded adjacent to the thoroughfares and bridges of ancient London. Their positioning was deliberate. They provided practical medical help for the travellers and pilgrims. They were the ancient accident and emergency departments, enshrining the ethical commitments of the good Samaritan. The decimation of the English monasteries by Henry VIII had a disastrous effect on medical care, leading to the destruction of many monastic hospitals and the disbanding of the medical and nursing brotherhoods and sisterhoods which cared for the poor. The eighteenth century saw a rapid growth of hospitals for the poor which, most historians agree, was influenced, at least in part, by the Christian evangelical revival and by a renewed practical concern for philanthropy.

Although a small number of British hospitals were founded with secular roots (such as my own institution, University College Hospital, established on the utilitarian philosophy of Jeremy Bentham), they were the exception. Most of the major British hospitals had profoundly Christian roots, and it was not until the inception of the National Health Service in 1948 that these proud, independent institutions were absorbed into the UK welfare state, and became an arm of secular government. The development of the modern hospice movement, outlined in the last chapter, continues in the same Christian tradition of care for the needy.

International spread

Internationally too, we find that medicine and nursing spread round the globe, driven largely by Christian ideals. This was especially true of the developing world of Africa and Asia. The great vision of missionary medicine came

only relatively late onto the scene. It was not until around 1850 that the idea
of Christian health professionals going from the West to care for the sick and
dying in developing countries came to fruition. At that time it was estimated
that there were only between twelve and fifteen Christian doctors working
in Asia or Africa. But in the following century, more than 1,500 doctors
went from Britain alone to work in developing countries, and thousands
more missionary nurses and paramedicals went where there were no doctors.
Wherever they went, they introduced the Hippocratic Christian ideal. I understand that, until the middle of the twentieth century, the only professional
nurses in the whole of the Indian sub-continent were linked to Christian
establishments.

An Asian Christian has written of the remarkable impact of Christian
missionaries: 'Many of the finest medical institutions still standing on the Indian
sub-continent were founded by Christians on their own initiative, often against
the wishes of the European colonial powers. The missionary contribution to
medical health in Asia and Africa has been nothing less than extraordinary, from
the treatment of leprosy and pioneering discoveries in epidemiology, to the
development of national health-care systems, the training of primary health-
care workers, and the setting up of educational institutions for women doctors
and nurses.'[16] And yet Asia has been the site of several major world religions,
especially Hinduism and Buddhism, stretching back thousands of years. Why
was it that devout Hindu or Buddhist believers had never set up a system of
practical medical and nursing care for the weak and disadvantaged, for the
leprosy victims, the outcasts, and the untouchables? Why did the development
of large-scale medical establishments in Asia depend on the influence of
Christian doctors, nurses and religious orders. Ultimately all this can be traced
back to the teaching and example of Jesus of Nazareth.

The historical dimension provides a different perspective on the current
debates about the future of medicine. When we look backwards to see the
historical roots of Western medicine, we find Christianity at every turn. The
improbable cross-fertilization between a pagan guild of physicians and a radical
Middle-Eastern religion led to 2,000 years of proud medical, nursing and health-
care history. Inevitably, the potted version I have provided oversimplifies the
story. There have always been tensions and strains in this alliance. Western
Hippocratic medicine has often lost contact with practical care for the disadvantaged, for example. In Western society, physicians have frequently espoused
a social position amongst the elite. The London Royal College of Physicians
was, and to some extent remains, a highly aristocratic institution. I suspect
there was a distinct preference for its wealthy fellows to hob-nob with royalty
and the aristocrats of Mayfair, rather than frequent the Poor Hospitals in the

East End of London, although there are outstanding examples of philanthropy amongst physicians to royalty. For long periods of our history, the poor could not afford a properly trained Hippocratic physician. They had to make do with the apothecary, the herbalist or the quack doctor. Despite this, in most Western countries, the Hippocratic Christian consensus remained fundamentally intact until the 1960s. This Christian way of thinking was so much a part of the axioms of medical ethics that it was almost invisible and unquestionable. But, as we have seen, over recent decades the consensus has been steadily coming apart at the seams. Each of the five trends we looked at in Chapter 1 has been quietly eroding the partnership of two thousand years.

Erosion of the Hippocratic-Christian consensus

Reductionism

Biological reductionism strikes at the heart of Hippocratic-Christian anthropology. If I'm caring for a being made in God's image, I might have a motivation for philanthropy, for enshrining the values of respect and compassion. But if I am caring for a survival machine, for 'robot vehicles blindly programmed to preserve the selfish molecules known as genes', then, logically, why bother? After all, if the mechanisms of this particular survival machine are grossly abnormal, and it lacks the right DNA for the future of the species, why should we not help it on its way to the rubbish heap? There are many better-equipped survival machines which could benefit from medical help.

Technology

Technology changes the values and the aims of the medical enterprise. We do not have to accept our bodies as they have been given to us: we can improve the structure. Of course, in the days of the old Hippocratic-Christian consensus, this wasn't much of an issue. Most of the therapies the medical profession had to offer were of little use. The lover of the human (*philanthropie*) could also be the lover of the art (*philotechnie*). But this was partly because the biological potential of the art was extremely limited. Today we have effective biological technology. We can really change the design. So, the concerns of the medical technologist become the concerns of the Lego constructer. Does it work? Is it safe? The original focus of Hippocratic medicine was on healing, and the ban on abortion and euthanasia prohibited many of the destructive possibilities of the medical art. With the development of technology, seen most clearly in the field of reproductive technology, the original purpose of healing is being supplanted by a vast range of manipulative possibilities.[17]

Consumerism

Consumerism changes the relationship between doctor and patient. In the past, Hippocratic medicine was a collaborative enterprise between the doctor and the patient. The relationship was frequently paternalistic and unbalanced, a parent-child relationship. But, despite this, the doctor entered into a covenant with the patient to act solely in the patient's interests, within the ethical constraints laid down by the tradition of medicine. In a paternalistic relationship, it was inevitably the doctor's values which were dominant. Now, in many cases, the relationship has been turned on its head. In a consumerist culture it is the consumer who is king. The enterprise becomes a client-technician relationship, and it is the client's values which become overriding. As we saw previously, the aims of prenatal screening have been officially described as allowing 'the widest range of informed choice to women and their partners'. This is a remarkable mission statement for modern health care. It represents the values of a modern service industry. 'Got to keep the customer satisfied', as Simon and Garfunkel sang. It's a slogan which the market traders have been chanting since the dawn of time. But now it's becoming official policy in the medical world. The hospital staff are no longer carers or healers but 'health-care providers'. Instead of patients we have 'health-care consumers'. Our role is to employ health-care resources to satisfy the demand, with both 'effectiveness' and 'efficiency' (vital elements of the jargon of modern medicine).

The modern concept of non-directive counselling also has affinities with the values of the service industry. Philosophically it is another example of the facts/values distinction. The professional's job is just to give you the facts: cold, neutral, objective. What you actually decide to make of the facts is up to you, the consumer. But genuinely non-directive counselling is a myth. We are all coming from somewhere. Whether atheist, Christian, agnostic or Buddhist, every health professional has some core beliefs, a worldview which influences their perspective and colours the advice they give.

Resource limitations

Resource limitations have eroded the Hippocratic ideal of healing without harming. In a society in which economics becomes increasingly the most influential way of assessing all human activity, the terrible truth of what I have dubbed the first law of health economics cannot be resisted. Antenatal screening and abortion will always be cheaper than medical and social care for the disabled. Euthanasia will always be cheaper than multidisciplinary support for the dying. If we, as a society, allow the monetary cost of caring to dominate our thinking, we will turn away from Christian ideals. Yet Christian caring must always be practical and realistic. We cannot ignore the ever-spiralling economic costs of health care. We must learn to enshrine Christian principles in the rationing and allocation of health-care resources.

Bioethics

As we have seen, some modern bioethicists are directly challenging the old Hippocratic-Christian consensus. Nigel Cameron has suggested that the very word, created in the USA in the 1970s, symbolized a wholly fresh approach to the values of medicine: 'What appeared at first to be an opening of medicine to scrutiny from outside . . . has rapidly been transformed into a field of reflection in which medicine itself can claim only a tangential place.'[18] It is certainly remarkable how the bioethical enterprise has increasingly been taken over by philosophers, ethicists and lawyers. Clinicians are generally regarded as having little to contribute to the development of the discipline! By cutting loose the discussion of ethical values from the constraints of the professional Hippocratic tradition, which is caricatured as obsolete and culturally bound, bioethicists are free to develop their radical theories unchallenged.

We should not be surprised if thinkers from non-Judeo-Christian religious traditions have rather different concepts of the significance of the body and, therefore, of medical ethics. The President of the International Association of Bioethics, Hyakudai Sakamoto of Nihon University, stated his support for genetic enhancement of human beings. Sakamoto said that in Asia, there is no fixed distinction between the natural and the artificial, and that in Buddhist thought, everything is constantly changing. Therefore, genetic engineering should be used for what Sakamoto called the 'artificial evolution' of humankind.[19]

Peter Singer has no illusions about the magnitude of the ethical change that is going on in our midst:. 'After ruling our thoughts and decisions about life and death for nearly 2,000 years the traditional Western ethic has collapsed. To mark the precise moment when the old ethic gave way, a future historian might choose 4 February 1993 when Britain's highest court ruled that the doctors attending Tony Bland could lawfully act to end the life of their patient.'[20] After describing several other landmark events, such as the approval of euthanasia guidelines by the Dutch parliament, Singer goes on in apocalyptic tone. 'These are the surface tremors resulting from major shifts deep in the bedrock of Western ethics. We are going through a period of transition in our attitude to the sanctity of human life. The traditional ethic is still defended by bishops and conservative bioethicists who speak in reverent tones about the intrinsic value of all human life, but once challenged, the traditional ethic crumples. Weakened by a decline in religious authority and the rise of a better understanding of the origins and nature of our species, that ethic is now being undone by changes in medical technology with which its inflexible structures simply cannot cope.'[21]

How can we communicate and defend the Christian perspective in a pluralistic society which has little time for religion as a source of ethical norms?

Defending a Christian worldview

In essence there are three fundamental answers to the question, 'Why should we as a modern secular society adopt a Christian worldview?' They are:

1. *'Because it is true'*. The Christian worldview fits with reality, with the way the world is made.
2. *'Because it works'*. Adopting the Christian worldview leads to beneficial consequences for individuals and for the community as a whole.
3. *'Because it feels right'*. The Christian worldview accords with the deepest intuitions of the human heart.

In developing a public apologetic, biblical Christians have concentrated to a very large extent on the first answer. They have engaged in arguments to demonstrate the truth of the Christian worldview on rational grounds. Arguments based on practical, social consequences of Christianity, or the nature of human intuitions, have often been downplayed. Of course, presenting a rational defence of the truth of the Christian worldview remains of vital importance. Yet in the all-pervasive mood of postmodernity, rational debate about absolute truth seems to founder, all too often, in a morass of relativism. I believe that, in addition to maintaining and developing arguments for the truth of Christianity, we urgently need to develop a public apologetic which enshrines both the consequentialist argument (the beneficial effects of Christian beliefs in society), and the appeal to fundamental human intuitions.

In response to the challenge laid down by Peter Singer, it seems to me there are at least seven lines of argument which may be developed in the public arena, in defence of a Christian understanding of the sanctity of human life. In outline, these arguments are as follows:

1. The Christian perspective enshrines a holistic perspective of human identity as a body-mind-spirit unity within community, as sketched in chapter 2. It teaches us to value human beings in their complex totality, whereas the secular alternative tends towards a reductionist and purely biological view. In place of 'speciesism' the new bioethics offers a new form of discrimination which might

be called 'corticalism' – human value is reduced to the efficient functioning of a layer of cerebral tissue.

2. The Christian view of human nature in God's image provides a stability of human identity and significance throughout the whole of life, whatever events may befall. As we saw earlier, even if my cortex is damaged, or my brain starts to malfunction, or I become confused and disorientated, I will still be me, a unique person, known and loved by others, and ultimately by God himself. No-one and nothing can take my human significance from me. By contrast, within the new bioethical framework, my identity depends on whatever happens to me, on contingent factors. It is desperately precarious, vulnerable and unstable. How can I be sure who I am, and how can I respect myself, when my own identity and worth are so evanescent and fragile?

3. The Christian worldview promotes social cohesion and mutual respect: we are a society of equals, because we are equal before God. A shared belief in the sanctity of human life provides protection for the weakest and most vulnerable within society. Respect for human life is part of the glue which binds society together. By contrast, the new bioethics creates a society in which we are ranked according to our functional abilities. It creates an arbitrary distinction between persons and non-persons, and places a range of human beings – malformed babies, Alzheimer's sufferers and other 'riff-raff' – outside the human community. Is this the kind of society of which we wish to be part?

4. The Christian concept of the sanctity of human life provides the basis for a consistent legal framework in which the life of all human beings is protected from destruction. The attempt to create a just and stable legislative framework, in which medical euthanasia may be safely allowed, has posed insuperable problems for legislators around the world. If the concept of mercy killing becomes legally acceptable, the entire legal framework designed to protect human life becomes weakened. Ancient Hippocratic medicine drew an absolute distinction between curing and killing. For two thousand years the distinction has remained a foundation of our ethical and legal systems. The new bioethics wants to blur the distinction again.

5. The Christian perspective of human life fits with very widespread intuitions about the nature of human relationships, especially those within families. In Singer's book, *Rethinking Life and Death*, there is a description of his meeting with several mothers who had given birth to infants with anencephaly, a rare and fatal abnormality in which the cerebral hemispheres fail to develop normally. Singer uses the anencephalic infant as an extreme example of a being who, although of human origin, has no rational ability and, hence, less intrinsic value than most sentient animals. Yet Singer movingly describes how one

mother, Judy Silver, had lovingly cuddled and bathed her anencephalic baby who died peacefully in her arms. "'It was nice," Judy Silver said, and if that sounds banal when written down, no-one who heard her say it thought so at the time. For this mother, an anencephalic baby was still her baby, and some kind of person, whatever the doctors or philosophers might say about its lack of capacity for consciousness.'[22] In my clinical work, I have been repeatedly struck by the way that a Christian perspective on the sanctity and value of human life 'rings bells' with ordinary people – in fact with nearly everybody in our society except philosophers!

6. The Christian view of human life provides motivation for sacrificial and empathic caring by professionals and by lay carers alike. Authentic Christian caring is not a vague sentimentalism; it is motivated by a tough-minded and practical respect for the image-bearers of God, for God's creation. The reductionism of the new bioethics tends to lead inevitably to contempt for any whose body is no longer functioning properly. It leads to the cynicism of the junior doctor who describes the elderly person under his care as 'just a bit of old crumble'. Most of us, when our elderly relative is admitted to the local hospital, confused, incontinent and bedridden, would prefer the staff to be motivated by different ethical principles.

7. Finally, the Christian worldview provides a safeguard against the abusive and manipulative possibilities of medical techniques in a period of unparalleled biotechnological advance. If the technological manipulation of vulnerable humans could provide a limitless supply of organs and tissues for medical use, this would have the potential of bringing enormous benefit. If we follow Singer's 'new commandments' it would be hard to find a logical reason to oppose such a development. The Christian understanding of the significance of all human life provides a way of resisting the potential manipulation of vulnerable human beings in order to benefit others.

These are merely the outlines of a Christian response to the challenges of modern bioethics, and others are better equipped than I am to develop and extend these concepts. It is possible to defend the traditional concepts of the sanctity of human life in our secular society, but only if we speak from a living community of faith, which not only argues for these convictions, but lives them out in practice. Here are the words of historian Gary Ferngren: 'The idea of the sanctity of human life will only maintain its influence in a pluralistic age so long as the Judaeo-Christian tradition that gave it birth continues to be a living force that is capable of relating its belief in the transcendent value of all human life to contemporary issues in biomedical ethics.'[23]

Christian perspectives on the core values of medicine

Christianity can provide answers to the three crucial questions I raised earlier. First, what does it mean to be a healthy human being? In place of the Lego-kit model of humanity, we must defend a biblical anthropology, illustrated by the analogy of the flawed masterpiece. In this way health-care professionals can help to recapture a sense of wonder at the mystery and dignity of each individual human life.

Secondly, what is medicine for? What are we professionals trying to achieve? Are we scientists, are we technicians, are we secular priests, or are we social engineers? No, we are trying to be art restorers. We are aiming to protect flawed masterpieces from harm and restore them where possible. Our goal is to use our technological skills while respecting the creation order, the original artist's intentions. This means that we must also recognize the limitations of medicine. We have limited knowledge, limited resources. Our goals are limited. We can't solve all the problems of the world. We can't give everybody a perfect body or a perfect baby. We can't abolish suffering or make everybody feel happy and fulfilled. We can't help everybody live to 120. We have limited goals. Together with the rest of society, doctors need to relearn that there are no technological fixes to the ultimate mysteries of the human condition. Human ingenuity can provide no solution to the terminal consequences of that ancient curse – pain, futility, suffering, death. Instead medicine can provide a physical presence to help human beings face the mystery of suffering, and to 'bind the suffering and the nonsuffering into the same community'.[24]

Thirdly, Christianity provides new models of caring for patients.

Christian models of caring

The expert-expert relationship

As we saw earlier, the traditional form of medical interaction with the patient was paternalistic, a parent-child relationship. Modern consumerism and the emphasis on patient autonomy have tended to change it into a technician-client relationship. But both of these models are inadequate and inappropriate; we need a new model of health-professional relationships. There is an alternative paradigm which fits with Christian convictions: the expert-expert relationship. It is a collaborative relationship between patient and professional based on mutual respect and trust. Yes, the professional is the expert in the area of treatment options and possibilities, on medicolegal frameworks and ethical constraints. But the patient is also an equally valid expert, with specialist knowledge in his or her own personal concerns, history, family roots, philosophy and way of life. Expert-expert relationships can flourish only in an atmosphere of mutual respect. The professional must respect the areas of expertise of the patient, just as the patient must respect the professional's concerns and ethical codes. Instead of the manipulative possibilities of both paternalistic and autonomy-based approaches, expert-expert relationships should be a quest for consensus within a covenant of ethical commitment.

The expert-expert relationship emphasizes the centrality of respect. It seems to me there are fundamentally two kinds of love: 'Demeaning-love' and 'respect-love'. Demeaning-love may be very caring, very professional, and very active. But as it cares, it humiliates. It is based more on pity than respect. Listen to the words of Mother Teresa: 'I've found that practical help can actually put people down unless it is done with respect-love. No-one wants to have things done for them, or to be done to. The greatest injustice done to the poor is that we fail to trust them, to respect them. How often we just push and pull.'[25] There is the authentic note of Christ-like caring, respect-love. It is love that treats each person as an individual. In Mother Teresa's words again, 'I never take care of crowds, only a person. If I stopped to look at the crowds, I would never begin.'[26]

The example of Christ

But the Christian vision gives us not only a theoretical concept of respect. In Christ we see a new way to practical action, the way of self-giving and empathy. Jesus entered into the human experience of pain, suffering, loneliness and emptiness, as recorded in some detail by the Gospel writers. Here is an example written by Luke:

> Soon afterwards, Jesus went to a town called Nain, and his disciples and a large crowd went along with him. As he approached the town gate, a dead person was being carried out – the only son of his mother, and she was a widow. And a large crowd from the town was with her. When the Lord saw her, his heart went out to her and he said, 'Don't cry.'
>
> Then he went up and touched the coffin, and those carrying it stood still. He said, 'Young man, I say to you, get up!' The dead man sat up and began to talk, and Jesus gave him back to his mother.
>
> They were all filled with awe and praised God.
> (Luke 7:11–16)

Jesus and the disciples had been confronted by a sad little procession, one that was all too common in an era of high mortality. A young man, an adolescent, had been struck down at the very outset of adult life. Yet this little cameo was even more poignant than usual. This was the only son, the inexpressible treasure of his mother's heart. She had already lost her husband, and now her child had been cruelly snatched away. Not only that, but in a society without any pensions or social welfare, the widow's son was her only hope of future financial security. Without him she might well face a life of destitution.

Tragic as the circumstances were, this human story was hardly unusual. Mortality was high, widows were common, life was hard. But Luke records a remarkable observation. Jesus was strangely moved by this chance meeting. Luke chose a technical word, *splanchnisthē*. In our reading it was translated 'his heart went out to her', in deference to modern sensibilities. Its literal meaning is much more visceral. It has the same derivation as our anatomical term 'splanchnic', meaning 'of the bowels, guts'. In modern slang it's an emotion that gets you by the guts. It's not the sort of word that a physician would use lightly, especially when referring to the Son of God. It sounds inappropriate, almost blasphemous, to our modern ears. Perhaps if we were writing an account of Jesus's reactions, we would have been inclined to sanitize the language. Yet Luke chose this powerful, earthy word to describe the way that Jesus was moved by a chance encounter with suffering. It was this strong visceral reaction that moved him to respond with tenderness, compassion and action.

Time and again, Luke and the other Gospel writers emphasize that Jesus was not a cool, disinterested observer of suffering and pain. He was deeply and emotionally involved. In this respect he was rather different from the old model of the Hippocratic physician. Jesus cared, even about the tragedy of an anonymous stranger. According to the Greek concept, God was unable to suffer. Suffering was part of an inferior human existence, but God was beyond this, remote and passionless. The Gospel writers, however, stress the theological profundity of the Incarnation. God, through Jesus, has entered fully into the human experience, and is totally and emotionally involved in the joys and the agonies of his creation.

Caring in the Christian community

As we have looked at Christian responses to the challenges of modern medicine, the importance of practical caring has been a recurrent theme. Christian caring needs always to be practical, down-to-earth, unsentimental, realistic, incarnational. It is a model of caring which the Christian community is uniquely equipped to provide. Christine Pohl, in an essay about abortion, expresses it well:

> The Christian community is called to model a hospitable welcome to the most vulnerable human beings even if it cannot require that welcome throughout

society. In its life together, such a community can demonstrate that suffering and sacrifice have meaning, can offer welcome to unexpected strangers, and can provide networks of love and support that sustain women and families through difficult pregnancies and difficult child-rearing. In so doing, Christians offer a vision of a transformed community in which the most vulnerable have a safe place. In such a community, the reality of God's sacrificial welcome is lived as it is proclaimed.[27]

At the heart of Christian caring is Christ. We are called to *see* Christ in those we care for. We are called to *be* Christ to those we care for.

Empathy and the cost of caring

The key emotion of the Incarnation, the visceral emotion that Jesus displayed was *empathy*. Empathy breaks down the divide between the professional and the patient. Paternalism says, 'I am the doctor, you are the patient.' 'I am the professional, you are the client.' But empathy says, 'We are the same you and I. We are both human beings. I want to stand alongside you. I want to be there with you.' Christian love is self-giving love and this concept derives ultimately from the doctrine of the Trinity. Within the mystery of the Trinity God gives himself. In some mysterious sense, God's ultimate being is found not in glory, not in power, not in authority, but in self-giving. So this is how we express our created nature; how we find ourselves, as beings made in God's image – not in getting, but in giving. And if I may put it boldly, this is why the Christian carer is close to the heart of God himself.

The key emotion of the cross is empathy. Christ entered into the agony of judgment which human disobedience deserved. In his book, *The Cross of Christ*, John Stott movingly reflects on the experience of Christ:

> I have entered many Buddhist temples in different Asian countries and stood respectfully before the statue of the Buddha, his legs crossed, arms folded, eyes closed, the ghost of a smile playing round his mouth, a remote look on his face, detached from the agonies of the world. But each time after a while I have had to turn away. And in imagination I have turned instead to that lonely, twisted, tortured figure on the cross, nails through hands and feet, back lacerated, limbs wrenched . . . plunged in God-forsaken darkness. That is the God for me!'[28]

Jesus demonstrated a new shape to caring. Authentic Christian caring is *cruciform*. If we want to care for people as Jesus cared for people, we have to give ourselves, we have to pay a price. We have to enter into the pain of the other, and ultimately we must experience a kind of death – death to self in order to give oneself in love for others. That is the cost of being a carer. This is why we must respect and support the carers in our community, both professional and lay.

Challenges for Christian professionals

There are particular tensions for Christian professionals in certain areas of medicine, particularly obstetrics, infertility medicine and genetics. They are confronted on a daily basis with many of the complex ethical issues which we have addressed earlier. How do they reconcile their professional responsibilities to provide a specialist medical service within the NHS, with their personal Christian beliefs and perspectives? Is their Christian integrity compromised by exploring a range of treatment options with their patients, recognizing that some patients will choose to act in ways that may not be consistent with Christian values?

These are perplexing questions, and it is all too easy for those on the outside to criticize Christian professionals who struggle with these dilemmas at 'the coalface'. A sense of ostracism and misunderstanding from other Christians can only add to the stress of their position. Understandably, there has been a tendency for Christian believers to avoid entering areas of medicine where the ethical tensions are greatest. But if this trend continues, and certain specialties become 'no-go' areas for biblical Christians, the effectiveness of Christian influence in the profession will be seriously diminished.

Instead, as a Christian community we must encourage believers to enter these complex professional areas and provide the theological, practical and pastoral resources to support them in their role. At the same time, Christian professionals need to recognize that they cannot address these problems by themselves. They must put aside a tendency to professional isolationism and instead be prepared to learn humbly from the perspectives and insights of other members of the Christian community.

If health professionals are to retain their Christian integrity, they must attempt to recognize the point at which their involvement in ethically questionable procedures (such as abortion, fetal screening or surrogate pregnancy, for instance) compromises their witness to Christian principles. It may be that different individuals will discern this crucial point of compromise at different places. For instance, some may conclude that it is wrong for them to have any involvement in counselling patients where abortion is one of the options. Others will conclude that giving accurate information in a balanced way, and allowing each patient to take responsibility for their own decision, is an appropriate Christian response. The Abortion Act legislation enshrines the right of doctors to refuse to participate in abortion on the grounds of conscience, although in practice an appeal to the 'conscience clause' may raise considerable practical difficulties. The right of conscientious objection for Christian believers practising medicine has been under sustained attack recently from a vocal minority, who argue for a completely secular profession. It will become increasingly important for Christians to make the argument that the right of conscientious objection is an essential safeguard of the personal ethical integrity of every professional.

The Christian community must find new ways of caring for, and supporting, the carers in its midst. For not only are the patients made out of dust, so also are the carers, health professionals and lay people alike. This should make us more gentle with one another, more supportive, encouraging one another like our heavenly Father: 'As a father has compassion on his children, so the LORD has compassion on those who fear him; for he knows how we are formed, he remembers that we are dust' (Psalm 103:13–14).

The mystery of the cross

A recurring theme in this book has been the strange but wonderful way that the evil, pain, distress and agony of human suffering is capable of being gradually transformed, by God's grace, into something of profound beauty and lasting significance. Think of the stories of rape, stillbirth, lethal abnormalities, young death and dementia that we have encountered. What could a 'Devil's Chaplain' make of those? And yet Heather Gemmen, Sarah Williams, Alan and Verity Mitchell, Stuart, Ruth and many others would all say that their lives were immeasurably enriched by their tragic encounters with inexplicable evil. It is not that the suffering was eradicated. Far from it. But in the encounter with suffering, something of startling significance gradually emerged. As I have reflected on this recurring mystery I have concluded that these human stories, our human stories, are meant to be small cameos, reflections of the big story.

Behind the blessings, richness and joy of the natural order of creation, in which our human bodies and lives are embedded, there lies an even greater and more wonderful story. This is what C. S. Lewis called 'the Deeper Magic from before the Dawn of Time'.[29] It is the story of inexplicable and all-pervasive evil which is overcome and transmuted into blessing, but only through profound suffering, the self-sacrifice of the Lamb of God. This is the big story of redemption, the deeper magic which lies hidden behind our space-time reality. In the four-fold biblical framework used in chapter 2, redemption comes after creation and fall, but I am becoming increasingly convinced that, as Karl Barth argued, in a strange way redemption comes before and stands behind creation.[30]

It seems that God's plan is to write small cameos, reflections of the big story into our lives. It is as though our own little story can become penetrated, inter-woven, caught up into the big story. Of course, this is not to say that our suffering is redemptive in the sense that Christ's suffering on the cross was redemptive. But in some sense, our experience reflects, and becomes interwoven with, the suffering and redeeming power of the Lamb of God.

This wonderful mystery doesn't happen automatically. Suffering can be destructive, instead of redemptive. It seems that it requires our consent, our willingness to submit and, in some sense, to accept and then to let go our suffering before it can be redeemed. But we do not accept suffering in a fatalistic sense, as merely capricious or malevolent, the 'clumsy, wasteful, blundering low and horridly cruel works of nature'. We accept it from the hand of a loving God. And the hallmark of Christian suffering, redemptive suffering, is that instead of leading to despair, it is penetrated through with hope. For suffering is not the end of the story.

In the last chapter we turn to the hope of Christian caring and the future of humanity.

A remarkable feature of contemporary culture is the impact of technology on the way we think. Politics is a way of *making* a better world or *fashioning* stronger communities. Psychologists advise us how to *build* stronger relationships. Business entrepreneurs *create* wealth. In the words of Oliver O'Donovan we looked at in the first chapter, 'When every activity is understood as making, then every situation into which we act is seen as a raw material, waiting to have something made out of it.'[1]

The Enlightenment project

This is what some have called 'the Enlightenment project': the goal of building a better world through a combination of human ingenuity, science and reason. Right at the origins of the European Enlightenment in the eighteenth century was a dream of extending progress across the final frontier of the human body. In a visionary article called 'Dreaming with Diderot', James Hughes, executive director of the Institute for Ethics and Emerging Technologies, refers to a series of essays written in 1769 by the French *philosophe* Diderot:

> Diderot proposes that, since human consciousness is a product of brain matter, the conscious mind can be deconstructed and put back together. Science will

bring the dead back to life. Animals and machines can be redesigned into intelligent creatures, and humanity can redesign itself into a great variety of types whose changes and whose future and final organic structure it is impossible to predict.[2]

Hughes claims that Diderot's prescient vision of the future is now coming close to fulfilment:

> In the coming decades, as pharmacology, artificial intelligence, nanotechnology, and biotechnology converge, life spans will extend well beyond a century. Our senses will extend to perceive sights, sounds and sensations beyond our current abilities. We will remember more of our lives, with greater fidelity. We will master fatigue, arousal and attention, and give ourselves more working intelligence. We will have greater control over our emotions, and be less subject to depression, compulsion and mental illness. Our bodies and brains will be surrounded by and merged with computer power which itself will become as, or more, powerful than our brains. As we merge machines into our minds we will indeed be deconstructed and put back together. We will use these technologies to redesign ourselves, our children and animals, into varieties of intelligent life impossible to predict.[3]

Hughes argues that the goal of human enhancement is not the idle utopian dream of a few technocratic mavericks. Rather, it is part of the mainstream of the Enlightenment project, allied with a liberal concern for the limitless extension of individual freedoms. For modern Enlightenment followers, the quest for freedom is conceived as freedom *from* the restraints of nature. The natural world is seen as a straitjacket which confines, restricts and limits our human possibilities. The goal of the Enlightenment project is to use technology to overcome the limits of the natural order which constrain our possible futures.

For transhumanists such as James Hughes and Nick Bostrom, to be human is to be subject to claustrophobic limitations and restrictions: limited lifespan, limited cognitive and sensory capabilities, fallible memory, vulnerability to disease, accident, progressive deterioration, ageing and death. Without enhancement technology our possible futures are constrained, inhibited, restricted and, ultimately, futile. Previous cultures have perceived these limitations as part of the human condition, to be accepted with stoicism, fortitude and resignation as part of the natural order. But we do not have to show such supine defeatism. Instead, we must harness the converging technologies of the twenty-first century to fashion and create new versions of humanity, to break free from the constraints of our evolved nature.

In its more extreme forms, it becomes clear that transhumanism has the features of religious belief. It is a secular form of eschatology, a future hope which inspires action in the present. It incorporates a potent vision of a new age, a new way of being which is achieved by human ingenuity and technological intervention. Not surprisingly, it is a vision of the future which is profoundly materialistic: the future world is composed, like the present, of matter and energy.

And yet some transhumanists dream of a novel means for transcending their physical limitations. One form of human future involves the uploading of our conscious awareness – which to the materialist must be merely a form of software – into computers, where it is replicated indefinitely within artificial neural networks. Long after my physical brain has decayed or been destroyed, the dream is that my disembodied conscious self will persist in computer circuitry. Here is a secular version of the Christian hope of a personal existence which transcends the grave.

So, what are the moral values which underpin this technological dream? Most transhumanists have stressed the liberal values of individual choice, freedom from coercion and violence, and peaceful coexistence. But if conscious choice and self-awareness are the factors which give us moral significance, there are of course implications for other members of the species *H. Sapiens*. Those who lack the capacity for conscious choice – the fetus, the newborn, the brain-injured, the demented and the psychotic – are relegated to an inferior moral status. And part of their inferior moral status is that they become in some sense at the disposal of the choosing agents. They become part of the raw material on which the technologists may act in order to achieve their goals. It seems an inevitable consequence of this technological hope that vulnerable human beings will be instrumental-ized – regarded as means for other people's ends. Although many secular bioethicists would dissociate themselves from the wilder excesses of the transhumanist dreams, they remain wedded to the Enlightenment project, the humanist belief in progress, and a view of the future as a product of human construction.

In the secular eschatology of the Enlightenment, the future is built block by block, frame by frame, from the choices we make here and now, in the present. There is no ultimate purpose or *telos* to nature, apart from that which we construct from the present. This brings a terrible, even crushing, responsibility. Every choice must be calibrated to ensure that the outcome is desirable. Unless we choose correctly, the future may become a hell on earth. The ultimate con-sequences of every choice, the utilitarian calculus, must become the supreme and only moral arbiter.

The radical philosopher John Gray writes:

> Humanism is not science but religion – the post-Christian faith that humans can
> make a world better than any in which they have so far lived. In pre-Christian
> Europe it was taken for granted that the future would be like the past . . . History
> was a series of cycles with no overall meaning. Against this pagan view, Christians
> understood history as a story of sin and redemption. Humanism is the
> transformation of this Christian doctrine of salvation into a project of universal
> human emancipation. The idea of progress is a secular version of the Christian
> belief in providence. That is why among the ancient pagans it was unknown.[4]

Gray provides an elegant critique of the Enlightenment project:

> Modern humanism is the faith that through science humankind can know the truth
> – and so be free. But if Darwin's theory of natural selection is true, this is impossible.
> The human mind serves evolutionary success, not truth . . . The conventional view
> that natural selection favours nervous systems which produce ever more accurate
> images of the world must be a very naïve view of mental evolution.[5]

Gray is making the same point as Charles Darwin when he confessed to his
'horrid doubt' (see chapter 1). If our minds have evolved merely to improve
our chances of survival on the African savannah, there is no reason to believe
that they will lead us to ultimate truth about the cosmos, or indeed about
anything. Gray goes on to argue that we should abandon all belief in the possibility of progress and return to the understanding of the cyclical nature of
history. In place of the naive liberal belief that human beings have a privileged
significance within the natural order (which Gray calls an irrational remnant of
Christian prejudice), he advocates the Gaia hypothesis, the belief that the world
is a self-regulating system which resembles an organism – 'for Gaia human life
has no more meaning than the life of slime mould'.[6]

A further consequence of this secular view of the future comes to those
members of society who are perceived as making 'bad' or 'irresponsible' choices.
If, through the exercise of your personal autonomy, you wish to continue with a
pregnancy even though the fetus has a serious disabling condition, then it is only
fair that you should be responsible for the adverse consequences. Some have
argued (with impeccable logic) that the state should not be obliged to pay the
lifetime costs for a disabled child whose mother has voluntarily refused an abortion.
If the future is being created by our choices, then those who create an undesirable
future should be prepared to pay for the consequences. Under the guise of 'social
responsibility' this secular eschatology has profoundly coercive implications.

A moral imperative to enhancement

Within the Enlightenment project, we have a moral responsibility to construct a future which is as good as possible. As we saw in chapter 1, John Harris has argued that, if technical enhancement of our children will bring greater happiness into their lives, there is a moral duty on us to enhance our children. To choose not to enhance our children is morally equivalent to choosing an intervention to make them disabled. In both cases, the total happiness in the world is reduced.[7]

Ronald Dworkin comes to a similar conclusion:

> There is nothing in itself wrong with the detached ambition to make the lives of future generations of human beings longer and more full of talent and hence achievements. On the contrary, if playing God means struggling to improve our species, bringing into our conscious designs a resolution to improve what God deliberately, or nature blindly, has evolved over eons, then the first principle of ethical individualism commands that struggle, and its second principle forbids, in the absence of positive evidence of danger, hobbling the scientists and doctors who lead it.[8]

Perhaps one of the most troubling recent suggestions is that we should use biomedical technology to enhance the moral behaviour and motivations of human beings.[9] The argument goes that enhancement technology may have profound dangers for humankind, because evil people may use their enhanced bodies and brains to wreak destruction on the rest of us. In a 2008 issue of the *Journal of Applied Philosophy*, several writers argued that, in order to address this threat, research into moral enhancement was mandatory: 'If safe moral enhancements are ever developed, there are strong reasons to believe that their use should be obligatory, like education or fluoride in water, since those who should take them are least likely to be inclined to use them. That is, safe, effective moral enhancement would be compulsory.'[10]

Here is another example of the coercive and manipulative possibilities which are raised when the Enlightenment project of progressive mastery over nature is applied to our own humanity.

New Age spirituality – an escape from physical reality

A very different vision of the future is seen in a great deal of conventional 'spirituality'. A popular anonymous poem read at many modern funerals and memorial services expresses this:

Do not stand at my grave and weep;
I am not there. I do not sleep.
I am a thousand winds that blow.
I am the diamond glints on snow.
I am the sunlight on ripened grain.
I am the gentle autumn rain . . .
Do not stand at my grave and cry;
I am not there. I did not die.[11]

It is not just New Age spirituality which puts forward this vision of escaping from the body into a higher order of immaterial being. It is remarkable that in popular science fiction writing and drama (think, for example, of *Star Trek*), the most advanced and sophisticated alien life forms are nearly always immaterial, residing in strange ethers or hyperdimensional orders of reality! By comparison, carbon-based and other embodied life forms turn out to be rather low down on the cosmic scale of importance. As we saw above, even some avowedly materialistic transhumanists aspire to a future disembodied and deconstructed self – residing as software within a computer network.

The ethical implications of this form of thinking are clear: what happens to human bodies is of little or no importance. It is the mind, consciousness, Universal Spirit, or the immortal soul that is the essential part of our humanity. Popular Christian teaching frequently seems to collapse into this worldview: 'If it's all going to burn, why worry? Let's concentrate on the really important things – like saving souls.' Common pious expressions such as 'going to heaven when you die' reflect a half-formulated belief in the persistence of an immaterial soul after the death of the body. But in the words of Tom Wright, 'If the promised final future is simply that immortal souls have left behind their mortal bodies, why then death still rules – since that is the description not of the *defeat* of death, but simply of death itself.'[12]

Whilst this form of spirituality seems in many ways to be the mirror image of the materialist version, it may lead towards similar conclusions in current bioethical debates. Since the structure of the physical body is of little ultimate significance, it may be appropriate to manipulate or enhance human bodies if it serves a greater 'spiritual' end. If an embryo or fetus has no 'soul' or 'spirit', then the destruction of the partially formed being in the womb cannot be of great significance. If an elderly person is distressed and suffering, trapped in a deteriorating body, mercy killing may enable the immortal spirit to shed the husk of a physical existence which has become redundant.

A biblical understanding of future hope

The consistent biblical message is that the history of the physical universe does have a purpose, a meaning, a *telos*. But the future is not a construct of human activity, it is not an artefact of human ingenuity – rather it is a reflection of the loving purposes of God. It is as though there is a great river of God's providential purposes running through the cosmos. When we perform an action we launch it on the great river of history. What happens then is almost entirely out of our control. Our action may well have profound consequences downstream, but those consequences are not ours to control. We are called to act wisely, responsibly, within the limitations both of our knowledge and of our created humanity. And we are held accountable for our actions as responsible moral agents. But we have the humility to recognize the limits of our human responsibility. We are spared from the crushing God-like responsibility of the materialist. The future is not ours to fashion.

Karl Barth argued that, when God rested from his creative work on the seventh day (Genesis 2), he revealed his freedom over the creation he had made. Unlike an impersonal, evolutionary force, which was tied to an infinite and unceasing process of development and progress, the God of the Bible is free to rest from his creative activities. He sees that his work is very good. He has found the object of his love and has no need of further works. For Barth, the history of the covenant between God and humankind was secretly established in the Sabbath rest of the seventh day. And in the establishment of the weekly Sabbath rest, God gives to human beings the gift of regular cessation from their labour of subduing and filling the earth.[13]

Unlike the secular humanist, who can never be spared from the crushing responsibility of fashioning the future, Christians can dare to rest, and celebrate the goodness of the creation, sharing the rest, freedom and joy of their Creator.

The biblical eschatology, which starts in the creation narratives, finds its most powerful expression in the incarnation and resurrection of Christ. As we saw in chapter 2, the Creator God takes on a human body made, like all other bodies, from the dust of the ground. And after death on the cross, he is raised as a physical, touchable, recognizable human being who goes out of his way to demonstrate his physical reality to his bewildered disciples. The New Testament narratives are clear. The tomb was empty and remained empty. The physical molecules that had constituted Christ's incarnation were in some mysterious way incorporated into his resurrection body. The physical creation is not overturned but subsumed, or caught up, into a greater and richer reality. In Jesus, the Second Adam, we see both a perfect human being (what the original Adam was meant to be), and the pioneer, the blueprint for a new type of human being,

the one in whose likeness a new creation will spring, the firstfruits of those who
are to come (1 Corinthians 15:20). 'For as in Adam all die, so in Christ all will
be made alive' (1 Corinthians 15:22). The Christian hope is that, one day,
we will be 'conformed to the likeness of his Son' (Romans 8:29). If we over-
spiritualize the doctrine of the bodily resurrection, in an unconscious attempt
to make it more acceptable to modern sensibilities, we lose the force of the
biblical teaching. The redemptive work of Christ can come to fulfilment only
in the 'redemption of our bodies' (Romans 8:23). The passage from Romans is
of great significance for a Christian understanding of the future of humanity.

> I consider that our present sufferings are not worth comparing with the glory that
> will be revealed in us. The creation waits in eager expectation for the sons of God
> to be revealed. For the creation was subjected to frustration, not by its own
> choice, but by the will of the one who subjected it, in hope that the creation itself
> will be liberated from its bondage to decay and brought into the glorious freedom
> of the children of God.
>
> We know that the whole creation has been groaning as in the pains of
> childbirth right up to the present time. Not only so, but we ourselves, who have
> the firstfruits of the Spirit, groan inwardly as we wait eagerly for our adoption as
> sons, the redemption of our bodies. For in this hope we were saved.
> (Romans 8:18–24)

Only by the redemption of our physical bodies can the physical creation, of
which they are part, be ultimately liberated. Christian medicine, in its concern
and respect for the physical stuff of our bodies, provides a vital corrective to
the over-spiritualizing tendency which has repeatedly crept into the thinking
of the church. In its work of healing and the continual fight to hold back death
for a period, medicine anticipates the future resurrection. And in showing an
unbreakable commitment and respect-love for human beings, terribly malformed as a result of the fall, or suffering as physical degeneration and death
approaches, medicine again bears witness to the Christian hope.

The transhumanist dream is that our original humanity is an infinitely
malleable and improvable reality – it is the raw material from which we can
construct a better reality. In contrast, New Age spirituality leads inevitably to a
disregard for the physical nature of our humanity, since it is through the decay
and destruction of the physical body that the trapped 'life force' or spirit can
be released.

But biblical eschatology teaches us to respect, protect and treasure the original
human body, the form of physical humanity we have inherited. This kind of
physical reality, this form of embodiment, is the one that is vindicated in the

person of Christ. Because Christ's body is raised, all bodies are special. Instead of the divisive distinction between the conscious, choosing members of the species and those who are available to be manipulated and instrumentalized, the Christian hope teaches us that all members of the human race are special, to be valued, protected and loved. Because Jesus was an embryo, a fetus, a newborn, a lost child, a weeping, agonized figure, a dying man, we celebrate these forms of embodied humanity; we perceive their dignity and intrinsic worth.

If this kind of humanity was good enough for Christ, then maybe it's good enough for me too. It is not necessary to be enhanced – to have a greater intelligence, stronger muscles, better memory – in order to be fully human, to be human-as-it-was-intended-to-be.

In Christian thought, love is joined with the other virtues of faith and hope, as in 1 Corinthians 13:13: 'And now these three remain: faith, hope and love. But the greatest of these is love.'

They are virtues which all point to the future. To use theological jargon, they are eschatological virtues, pointing towards the end times. When we love someone in the present, showing practical, empathic, respectful, sacrificial caring, we are also pointing them to the future, to the hope of the resurrection. We are treating someone now *in the light of what they are going to be*. We saw an example of this in the previous chapter when we looked at the moving words of dementia sufferer Robert Davis. This is why we can still respect and treat with dignity even the most tragically damaged of human beings. The anencephalic baby, the person in the persistent vegetative state, the profoundly demented individual are those who may, in God's grace, be transformed to become a new creation. So practical Christian caring for those with a degenerative condition like dementia is not a sentimental nostalgic reaction, treating someone with respect just because of what they once were. We treat them with respect because of the God-like image which, in his grace, they will display in the future. In fact, Christian love can be intelligible only in the light of the Christian hope.

This hope, reflected in Paul's first letter to the Corinthians, is that though tongues will fail, prophecies will become unnecessary and partial knowledge will become complete, the acts of genuine *agape*-love will somehow remain – in some mysterious way they will become part of the new heaven and the new earth: 'Love . . . always protects, always trusts, always hopes, always perseveres. Love never fails . . . ' (1 Corinthians 13:6–8)

From an earthly perspective it seems that, all too often, love does fail. To show persistent, sacrificial love to a disabled child, a violent disturbed adolescent, or a demented adult, may seem pointless, futile, and meaningless. And from one perspective it is: 'If only for this life we have hope in Christ, we are to be pitied more than all men' (1 Corinthians 15:19). But Christian hope teaches, reminds and rebukes us – love never fails . . .

After a description of the future hope of physical resurrection in 1 Corinthians 15, Paul concludes with these well-known words: 'Therefore, my dear brothers, stand firm. Let nothing move you. Always give yourselves fully to the work of the Lord, because you know that your labour in the Lord is not in vain.' Because of the future resurrection hope, Paul says that our labour now, in this space-time physical world, is not in vain. In some mysterious way, the work we do now, work which is motivated and directed by Christian truth and love (labour in the Lord), will last into the new age. It will become part of the new heaven and the new earth. This is what Tom Wright has referred to as 'collaborative eschatology'.[14] We are called to collaborate with God in transforming the present in the light of the future.

To the secular philosopher, life starts from nothing. It rises to a peak, to a brief flowering of autonomy, of pleasure, of meaning in the middle of life. And then it gradually declines into decay, dissolution, and finally death. It rises to a crescendo and then slowly fades away into nothingness. But the Christian view of a human life transformed by God's power is totally different. It is a slow and growing crescendo. It is a journey, a pilgrimage, which starts from nothing but grows and grows: 'The path of the righteous is like the first gleam of dawn, shining ever brighter till the full light of day' (Proverbs 4:18).

I came across a picture recently which illustrated this verse. A pair of rock climbers had toiled through the night to the summit of a desolate peak in Alaska. Whilst they clung to the rock, one of them took a photo of the distant blush of the coming dawn on the far horizon. It is an image I've since reflected on several times. The day is coming – slowly, imperceptibly, inexorably, unstoppably. Our task is to live and work in the darkness yes, but darkness transformed by the ever-present reality of the first gleam of dawn.

In chapter 2 we looked at Paul's analogy of the seed and the flower. 'The body that is sown is perishable, it is raised imperishable; it is sown in dishonour, it is raised in glory; it is sown in weakness, it is raised in power' (1 Corinthians 15:42). It is a dramatic image encapsulated in the strange paradox of the seed packet. The contrast between the tiny brown specks of tissue on the inside, and the multicoloured splendour pictured on the outside of the packet is startling. If you had never witnessed the transformation, you would not think it was possible. Yet in those tiny and pathetic fragments of tissue is packed all the information (in the form of DNA) that is required to create the glorious blossom. Add water and stand back! The two entities, which in appearance are so dissimilar, share a common hidden identity. The seed is in the process of becoming what it already is. And so it is for human beings, too.

'Then the new earth and sky, the same yet not the same as these, will rise in us as we have risen in Christ. And once again, after who knows what aeons of the silence and the dark, the birds will sing out and the waters flow, and lights and shadows move across the hills and the faces of our friends laugh upon us with amazed recognition. Guesses of course, only guesses. If they are not true, something better will be. For we know that we shall be made like him, for we shall see him as he is.'[15]

This is the wonderful reality which awaits us. This is what Christian caring is pointing to. In the words of the old rock song: 'That's the way God planned it. That's the way God wanted it to be.'

GLOSSARY

Achondroplasia A genetic condition resulting in severely restricted growth, also described as dwarfism.

Alzheimer's disease A common neurological condition in which there is a gradual and progressive deterioration in mental function.

Amniocentesis A diagnostic procedure in which a small sample of amniotic fluid is taken during pregnancy to screen the unborn baby for genetic abnormalities.

Anencephaly A rare developmental disorder in which the cerebral hemispheres fail to develop, leading to death shortly after birth.

Beta thalassaemia major A genetic blood disorder causing severe anaemia and limited life expectancy.

Bioethics The academic discipline which concerns study of the ethical controversies brought about by advances in biology and medicine.

Brainstem death A legally accepted definition of death that refers to the irreversible cessation of all brain activity, including involuntary activity necessary to sustain life. It should not be confused with the persistent vegetative state (see below) in which some brain activity continues.

Chorionic villus sampling A diagnostic procedure in which a small sample of tissue is taken from the placenta during early pregnancy to screen the unborn baby for genetic abnormalities.

Cleft lip and palate A developmental abnormality in which the upper lip and palate fail to develop normally.

Cloning A procedure to create a cell or an organism with identical genetic material to another cell or organism.

Congenital A medical condition which is present from an early stage of life in the womb.

Cordocentesis A diagnostic procedure in which blood is taken from the umbilical cord of the unborn baby.

Cortex The layer of brain cells overlying the cerebral hemispheres which is mainly responsible for higher mental functions, including sensory awareness, voluntary muscle movement, thought, reasoning, and memory.

Cystic fibrosis A genetic condition which causes severe respiratory and digestive problems and which usually leads to death in childhood or early adulthood.

Dementia A general term for medical conditions which lead to progressive deterioration of mental function. Alzheimer's disease is one form of dementia.

Down's syndrome A congenital condition caused by the presence of an extra chromosome, associated with characteristic facial features and learning difficulties.

Edwards syndrome A congenital condition caused by the presence of an extra chromosome, associated with very severe malformations of the brain and other organs, and usually leading to death within the first weeks or months of life.

Embryo A developing human whose age is less than eight weeks after fertilization.

Feticide A medical procedure designed to end the life of the fetus in the womb. In the UK the procedure involves the injection of a lethal compound directly into the fetal heart.

Fetus The technical term for a developing human in the womb whose age is greater than eight weeks after fertilization.

Fibroblast cells A type of cell found in skin or connective tissue.

Fragile X syndrome A genetic condition caused by a mutation in the X chromosome which causes intellectual disability and behavioural problems in males but not usually in females.

Gametes A biological term for reproductive cells, that is either an egg cell or a sperm cell.

Haemophilia A genetic condition which leads to severe and recurrent bleeding in affected children.

Hominid The technical term for a primate of the family Hominidae, of which *Homo sapiens* is the only living species.

Human Genome Project An international scientific research collaboration to determine the complete structure of human DNA and understand its function.

Huntingdon's disease A rare progressive neurological disorder of genetic origin, which leads to movement disorders and progressive dementia. Onset of symptoms usually occurs in middle age.

Hypothyroidism A medical condition involving impaired secretion of thyroid hormone.

In vitro fertilization A medical procedure in which fertilization (the fusion of sperm and egg) occurs in the laboratory rather than in the woman's body.

Libido The force of sexual desire which is of central importance in Freudian psychological theory.

Living will Also known as Advance Statement, or Advance Directive. A declaration of a patient's wishes concerning the provision or withholding of future medical treatment, which may be legally binding in certain circumstances.

Motor neuron disease A progressive neurological disorder leading to paralysis and ultimately death.

MRI Magnetic Resonance Imaging – a form of medical imaging using strong magnetic fields.

Muscular dystrophy A range of rare genetic disorders leading to progressive muscle weakness and muscle loss.

Neurons Brain cells which initiate and conduct electrical impulses.

Palliative care Medical and nursing care for terminally ill patients which has the aim of relieving symptoms rather than achieving a cure.

PAS Physician-assisted suicide: a procedure in which a physician prescribes lethal drugs to enable a patient to commit suicide.

Paternalism The practice of treating people as a father would treat a child.

Persistent vegetative state A neurological condition found in patients with severe brain damage who are in an apparent state of wakefulness but without detectable conscious awareness.

PET Positron Emission Tomography – a form of medical imaging using short-lived radioactive tracer elements.

PGD Pre-implantation genetic diagnosis. A diagnostic procedure in which a single cell is taken from the early embryo in order to screen for genetic conditions or to enable the sex to be determined.

Photomicrograph A photograph taken through a microscope.

Progressive supranuclear palsy A rare progressive neurological condition leading to movement difficulties and deterioration in mental function.

Psychodynamics The study of the psychological forces that underlie human behaviour, with particular emphasis on unconscious processes.

Psychotic A severe form of mental illness leading to loss of contact with reality.

Sickle-cell disease A genetic blood disorder causing severe anaemia which is particularly common in people of African origin.

Thanatophoric dysplasia A rare and very severe form of congenital dwarfism which usually leads to death within the first days or weeks of life.

Thalidomide A sedative drug which was unexpectedly found to cause major fetal deformities when given to pregnant women.

NOTES

Introduction

1. J. R. W. Stott, *The Contemporary Christian* (IVP, 1992).
2. *Re A (Children) (Conjoined Twins: Surgical Separation)* [2001] Fam 147 (CA), see E. Jackson, *Medical Law* (OUP, 2006), pp. 980–987.
3. http://news.bbc.co.uk/1/hi/health/4625538.stm.
4. http://www.cps.gov.uk/news/press_releases/117_05/, R. Dobson, *The British Medical Journal* (2003), 327:1307.
5. *Re B (Adult: Refusal of Medical Treatment)* [2002] EWHC 429, [2002], 2, All ER 449, see E. Jackson, *Medical Law* (OUP, 2006), p. 928.
6. Clare Dyer, *BMJ* (2005), 330:1041. E. Jackson, *Medical Law* (OUP, 2006), pp. 847–852.
7. *R (on the application of Pretty) v. Director of Public Prosecutions* [2001] UKHL 61, [2002] 1 AC 800, see E. Jackson, *Medical Law* (OUP, 2006), pp. 916–921.
8. *Airedale NHS Trust v. Bland* [1993] AC 789 (HL).
9. P. Singer, *Rethinking Life and Death* (OUP, 1995), p. 68.

1. What's going on?

1. D. M. MacKay, *The Clockwork Image* (OUP, 1974), pp. 40–45.
2. R. Dawkins, *The Selfish Gene* (OUP, 1976), p. ix.
3. Ibid., p. 21.
4. R. Dawkins, quoted by M. Poole, *Science & Christian Belief* (1994), 6:57–58.

5.   *Third Way* magazine (April 1995).

6.   R. Dawkins, *The God Delusion* (Bantam Press, 2006), pp. 185–2001.

7.   http://www.darwinproject.ac.uk/darwinletters/calendar/entry-13230.html.

8.   Thielicke, quoted by D. G. Jones, *Brave New People* (IVP, 1984), p. 16.

9.   V. S. Ramachandran and S. Blakeslee, *Phantoms in the Brain: Probing the Mysteries of the Human Mind* (William Morrow, 1998).

10. http://www.thoughtsciences.com/.

11. J. A. Richeson et al., *Nature Neuroscience* (2003), 6:1323–8.

12. J. Monod, *Chance & Necessity* (Vintage Books, 1972), pp. 112–114.

13. R. Dawkins, *The Blind Watchmaker* (Penguin, 1988), p. 5; see also A. E. McGrath *Science & Religion* (Blackwell, 1998), pp. 99–101.

14. R. Dawkins, *A Devil's Chaplain* (Phoenix, 2004).

15. S. Adams et al., *Journal of Medical Genetics* (1993), 30:549–556.

16. R. Dawkins, *The Selfish Gene* (OUP, 1976), p. 215.

17. D. G. Jones, *Brave New People* (IVP, 1984), p. 33.

18. R. Dawkins, *A Devil's Chaplain* (Phoenix, 2004), p. 13.

19. L. Silver, *Remaking Eden* (Avon Books, 1997), p. 236.

20. O. O'Donovan, *Begotten or Made?* (OUP, 1984), p. 3.

21. Ibid., p. 5.

22. S. Hauerwas, *Suffering Presence* (T. & T. Clark, 1996), p. 64.

23. G. McGee, *The Perfect Baby* (Rowman & Littlefield, 1997).

24. B. Glass, *Science* (1971), 171:23–29.

25. http://www.ukpublicspending.co.uk/uk_health_care_spending_10.html; http://www.cdc.gov/nchs/data/hus/hus08.pdf.

26. http://www.nice.org.uk/.

27. H. S. Cuckle, *BMJ* (1995), 311:1460–1463.

28. Medical Aspects of the Persistent Vegetative State, *New England Journal of Medicine* (1994), 330:1572–1579.

29. T. L. Beauchamp and J. F. Childress, *Principles of Biomedical Ethics* (OUP, 2008).

30. B. Brock and J. Wyatt, *Studies in Christian Ethics* (2006), 19:153–168.

31. R. Dworkin, *Life's Dominion* (HarperCollins, 1995), p. 166.

32. Ibid., p. 239.

33. Ibid., p. 155.

34. Ibid., p. 167.

35. Ibid., p. 157.

36. Ibid., p. 150.

37. Ibid., p. 239.

38. John Stuart Mill, *On Liberty* (1859), chapter 1.

39. M. Charlesworth, *Bioethics in a Liberal Society* (CUP, 1993).

40. Ibid., p. 166.

41. Ibid., p. 42, my emphasis.
42. P. Singer, *Rethinking Life and Death* (OUP, 1995), p. 1.
43. Ibid., p. 189.
44. Ibid., p. 80.
45. Ibid., pp. 190–192.
46. Ibid., pp. 192–196.
47. Ibid., pp. 196–198.
48. Ibid., p. 210.
49. Ibid., pp. 198–200.
50. H. Kuhse and P. Singer, *Should the Baby Live?*, pp. 155–161.
51. P. Singer, *Rethinking Life and Death* (OUP, 1995), p. 201.
52. Ibid., p. 209.
53. J. Harris, *Enhancing Evolution* (Princeton, 2007), p. 16.
54. Ibid., p. 74.

2. Biblical perspectives on humanness

1. J. R. W. Stott, *Issues Facing Christians Today* (Zondervan, 2006), pp. 62–64.
2. H. Blocher, *In the Beginning* (IVP, 1984).
3. Quoted by Blocher, ibid., p. 77.
4. See, for example, R. J. Berry, *God and the Biologist* (Apollos, 1996), pp. 29–57.
5. See, for example, P. Johnson, *Darwin on Trial* (IVP, 1993), and J. Lennox, *God's Undertaker* (Lion, 2007).
6. A. Millard and P. Bordreuil, *Biblical Archeologist*, 1982; 45:135–141.
7. O. O'Donovan, *Resurrection and Moral Order* (IVP, 1994), p. 38.
8. V. Ramachandra, *Gods that Fail* (PaternosterPress, 1996), p. 70.
9. H. Blocher, *In the Beginning* (IVP, 1984), p. 82.
10. H. Thielicke, *Theological Ethics* (Fortress, 1966), p. 177.
11. G. Meilaender, *A Primer in Bioethics* (2nd edition) (Eerdmans, 2005), p. 2.
12. Romans 2:11; Ephesians 6:9; Colossians 3:25.
13. J. Zizioulas, *Being as Communion* (Darton Longman & Todd, 2004).
14. G. Meilaender, *A Primer in Bioethics* (2nd edition) (Eerdmans, 2005), p. 59.
15. S. Jones, *The Language of the Genes* (HarperCollins, 1993), p. 127.
16. R. Thomson et al., *Proceedings National Academy of Science*, 2000; 97:7360–5; J. K. Pritchard et al., *Molecular Biology & Evolution*, 1999; 16:1791–8; E. Watson et al., *American Journal of Human Genetics*, 1997; 61:691–704.
17. C. S. Lewis, *Prince Caspian* (Puffin, 1962), p. 185.
18. Romans 5:12.
19. C .S. Lewis, *Reflections on the Psalms* (Collins, 1961), p. 115.
20. http://www.churchinhistory.org/pages/booklets/chloroform.htm.
21. V. Ramachandra, *Gods that Fail* (Paternoster, 1996), p. 131.

22. O. O'Donovan, *Resurrection and Moral Order* (IVP, 1994), pp. 53–75.

23. G. Meilaender, *A Primer in Bioethics* (2nd edition), (Eerdmans, 2005), p. 28.

24. J. R. W. Stott, *The Cross of Christ* (IVP, 1986), p. 336.

25. O. O'Donovan, *Resurrection and Moral Order* (IVP, 1994), pp. 56–57.

26. I'm indebted to Paul Blackham for this image.

27. O. O'Donovan, *Resurrection and Moral Order* (IVP, 1994), p. 55.

3. Reproductive technology and the start of life

1. P. Moore, *Trying for a Baby* (Lion, 1996).

2. L. R. Kass, quoted in G. Meilaender, *A Primer in Bioethics* (2nd edition), (Eerdmans, 2005), p. 10.

3. L. Silver, *Remaking Eden* (Avon Books, 1997), p. 67.

4. European Society of Human Reproduction & Embryology. World Collaborative Report on Assisted Reproductive Technology (2002), http://humrep.oxfordjournals.org/cgi/reprint/dep098v1.

5. M. Warnock, *A Question of Life: The Warnock Report on Human Fertilisation and Embryology* (Blackwell, 1985), p 2.

6. M. Warnock, *Nature and Morality: Reflections of a philosopher in public life* (Continuum, 2003), pp. 98–99.

7. Ibid., p. 99.

8. Ibid., p. 65.

9. Reported in *BMJ*, 16 December 1989.

10. http://www.hfea.gov.uk/docs/Latest_long_term_data_analysis_report_91–06.pdf.

11. http://www.eggdonor.com/.

12. http://www.slate.com/id/104633/.

13. *Daily Telegraph*, 15 February 2009, http://www.hfea.gov.uk/docs/HFEA_ES_form.pdf.

14. O. O'Donovan, *Begotten or Made?* (OUP, 1984), p. 65.

15. http://www.timesonline.co.uk/tol/news/world/asia/article4543797.ece.

16. *Evening Standard*, 2 July 1997.

17. G. Pennings, *Human Reproduction* (2004), 19:2689–2694.

18. http://en.surrogacy-ukraine.com/.

19. http://www.londonwomensclinic.com/gen/lesbian_single.php.

20. A. J. Steel and A. Sutcliffe, *Human Fertilisation* (2009), 12:21–27.

21. A. McWhinnie, *Who am I? – experiences of donor conception* (Idreos Education Trust, 2006).

22. Ibid., p. 8.

23. Ibid., p. 9.

24. Ibid., p. 10.

25. E. Jackson, *Medical Law* (OUP, 2006), pp. 825–829.

26. J. B. Stanford et al., *Journal American Board Family Medicine* (2008), 21:375–384.

27. J. Ashley-Smith, 'The ethics of conservation', in F. Knell (ed.), *Care of Collections* (Routledge, 1994).

28. See, for example, R. Dawkins, *The Blind Watchmaker* (Penguin, 1988), p. 268.

29. O. O'Donovan, *Begotten or Made?* (OUP, 1984), p. 1.

30. Quoted by B. McCarthy, *Fertility and Faith* (IVP, 1997), p. 144.

31. *Donum Vitae*, 1987 and *Dignitas Personae*, 2008.

32. Quoted by B. McCarthy, *Fertility and Faith* (IVP, 1997), p. 155.

33. Ibid., pp. 156–161.

34. Ibid., p. 221.

35. G. Meilaender, *Bioethics – A Primer for Christians* (2nd edition) (Eerdmans, 2005) p. 5.

36. O. O'Donovan, *Resurrection and Moral Order* (IVP, 1994), p. 96.

4. Fetal screening and the quest for a healthy baby

1. See, for example, http://www.rcog.org.uk/womens-health/clinical-guidance/amniocentesis-what-you-need-know.

2. C. F. Wright and H. Burton, *Human Reproduction Update* (2009), 15:139–151.

3. http://www.tellmepinkorblue.com/.

4. J. C. Harper et al., *Human Reproduction* (2008), 23:741–755.

5. http://www.guardian.co.uk/science/2009/jan/10/pgd-baby-debate-breast-cancer.

6. http://www.timesonline.co.uk/tol/news/uk/science/article1706615.ece.

7. J. M. Green and H. Statham, in T. Marteau and M. Richards (eds.), *The Troubled Helix* (CUP, 1996), pp. 140–163.

8. T. Marteau et al., *Journal of Psychosomatic Research* (1988), 32:403–408.

9. J. M. Green and H. Statham, ibid., p. 146. and H. Statham et al., *Ballieres Clinical Obstetrics & Gynaecology* (2000), 14:731–747.

10. B. K. Rothman, *The Tentative Pregnancy* (Viking, 1986).

11. J. M. Green and H. Statham, ibid., p. 149 and H. Statham et al., *Ballieres Clinical Obstetrics & Gynaecology* (2000), 14:731–747.

12. J. M. Green and H. Statham, ibid., p. 143.

13. J. M. Green and H. Statham, ibid., p. 150.

14. R. Dodds, *The Stress of Tests in Pregnancy: an antenatal screening survey*, National Childbirth Trust (UK), 1997.

15. T. Shakespeare, *Disability & Society*, 13:665–681.

16. J. M. Green and H. Statham, ibid., p. 151 and H. Statham et al., *Ballieres Clinical Obstetrics & Gynaecology* (2000), 14:731–747.

17. Quotations from I. Kohn and P. L. Moffitt, *Pregnancy Loss, A Silent Sorrow* (Hodder & Stoughton, 1994), pp. 116–117.

18. T. Marteau and E. Anionwu, in T. Marteau and M. Richards (eds.), *The Troubled Helix* (CUP, 1996), p. 134.

19. I. Kohn and P. L. Moffitt, ibid., p. 113.

20. http://www.arc-uk.org/.

21. J. M. Green and H. Statham, ibid., p. 145.

22. T. Marteau and E. Anionwu, ibid., p. 135.

23. G. McGee, *The Perfect Baby* (Rowman & Littlefield, 1997), p. 93.

24. M. Pembrey, in J. M. Green and H. Statham, ibid., p. 78.

25. S. Shiloh, in J. M. Green and H. Statham, ibid., p. 86.

26. G. McGee, ibid., p. 93 and J. S. Wyatt, *J Medical Ethics* (supplement) 2001; 27 II:15–20.

27. T. Marteau et al., *J Psychosomatic Research* (1993), 11: 75–82.

28. Quoted in J. M. Green and H. Statham, ibid., p. 144.

29. A. O. Odibo et al., *Obstetrics & Gynecology* (2005), 106:562–568.

30. *The Guardian*, 29 April 1997.

31. T. Marteau and E. Anionwu, ibid., p. 135.

32. See E. Parens and A. Asch, *Prenatal Testing And Disability Rights* (Georgetown University Press, 2000), and T. Shakespeare, *Disability Rights and Wrongs* (Routledge, 2006).

33. Quoted in E. Parens and A. Asch, ibid., p. 14.

34. T. Shakespeare, ibid., p. 94.

35. S. Saigal et al., *The Journal of the American Medical Association* (1999), 281:1991–1997.

36. Hubbard, quoted in T. Shakespeare, *Disability & Society*, 13:665–681.

37. C. Nolan, *Under the Eye of the Clock* (Pan, 1987).

38. M. Stacey, in T. Marteau and M. Richards (eds.), *The Troubled Helix* (CUP, 1996), p. 345.

5. Brave new world: biotechnology and stem cells

1. http://www.genderselection.uk.com/home.html.

2. Amartya Sen, *New York Review of Books*, vol. 37, December 20, 1990; see also A. Sen, *BMJ*, 327:1297–1298.

3. http://news.bbc.co.uk/1/hi/world/south_asia/5264174.stm.

4. Quoted in BMA News Review, May 1994.

5. http://www.hfea.gov.uk/cps/rde/xbcr/hfea/PGD_document.pdf.

6. L. Silver, *Remaking Eden* (Avon Books, 1997), pp. 22–45.

7. I. Wilmit et al., *Nature*, 385:810–813.

8. A. Huxley, *Brave New World* (Chatto & Windus, 1932), p. 17.

9. A. Toffler, *Future Shock* (Random House, 1970), p. 197.

10. L. Silver, ibid., p. 113.

11. *Independent*, 22 April 2009.

12. R. K. Burt et al., *The Journal of the American Medical Association* (2008), 299:925–936.

13. http://www.telegraph.co.uk/news/1980250/Gordon-Brown-backs-animal-human-hybrids.html.

14. J. Picoult, *My Sister's Keeper* (Hodder, 2005).

15. C. S. Lewis, *The Abolition of Man* (Collins 1978), p. 35.

16. Quoted by L. Silver, ibid., p. 75.

17. Quoted by M. J. Sandel, *The Case against Perfection* (Harvard University Press, 2007), pp. 49–50.

18. G. Meilaender, *Bioethics – A Primer for Christians* (2nd edition) (Eerdmans, 2005), p. 44.

6. Abortion and infanticide: a historical perspective

1. Some of this chapter is based on previous published material (J. S. Wyatt, *Science and Christian Belief*, 8:2–30; J. S. Wyatt and A. Spencer, *The Survival of the Weakest* [CMF, 1992]); and on the detailed analysis of Michael Gorman, *Abortion and the Early Church* (IVP, 1982).

2. Quoted by G. F. Ferngren in R. C. McMillan et al., (eds.), *Euthanasia and the Newborn* (Reidel, 1987), pp. 23–45.

3. M. J. Gorman, *Abortion and the Early Church* (IVP, 1982).

4. M. J. Gorman, ibid., p. 15.

5. J. S. Wyatt, *Science and Christian Belief*, 8.

6. See D. W. Amundsen (1987) in R. C. McMillan et al., (eds.), *Euthanasia and the Newborn* (Reidel, 1987), pp. 3–22.

7. Ibid.

8. *Soranus' Gynecology* (John Hopkins University Press, 1991); text also available at http://www.pubmedcentral.nih.gov/articlerender.fcgi?artid=1888953 reprint.

9. J. S. Wyatt and A. Spencer, *Survival of the Weakest*, 1992.

10. G. F. Ferngren in R. C. McMillan et al., *Euthanasia and the Newborn* (Reidel, 1987).

11. J. S. Wyatt and A. Spencer, *The Survival of the Weakest* (CMF, 1992).

12. M. J. Gorman, *Abortion and the Early Church* (IVP, 1982), p. 48.

13. M. J. Gorman, ibid., pp. 49–50.

14. M. J. Gorman, ibid., pp. 58–59; G. F. Ferngren, in R. C. McMillan et al., *Euthanasia and the Newborn* (Reidel, 1987) p. 55.

15. G. F. Ferngren in R. C. McMillan et al., ibid., p. 55.

16. G. F. Ferngren in R. C. McMillan et al., ibid., p. 55.

17. Legalised Abortion, *BMJ* 2 April 1966, pp. 850–854; M. Potts et al., *Abortion* (CUP, 1977), p. 320.

18. http://www.independent.co.uk/opinion/commentators/david-steel-there-is-no-case-for-changing-the-abortion-act-818002.html.

19. http://www.dh.gov.uk/en/Publicationsandstatistics/Publications/
    PublicationsStatistics/DH_085508.

20. http://www.careconfidential.com/PeoplesStories.aspx.

21. C. A. MacKinnon, *Feminism Unmodified* (Harvard University Press, 1987) quoted
    by R. Dworkin, *Life's Dominion* (HarperCollins, 1995), p. 52.

22. Quoted by R. Dworkin, *Life's Dominion* (HarperCollins, 1995), p. 53.

23. See Dominic Beer, *Psychological Effects after Abortion* (CMF, 2006); http://www.cmf.
    org.uk/publications/content.asp?context=article&id=1850 psychological
    consequences of abortion.

24. N. Wolf, *Promiscuities* (Chatto & Windus, 1997).

25. N. Wolf, ibid., p. 197.

26. http://www.dh.gov.uk/en/Publicationsandstatistics/Publications/
    PublicationsStatistics/DH_085508 abortions stats 2007.

27. H. Statham, et al, *BJOG* (2006), 113:1402–1411.

28. RCOG report *Termination of pregnancy for fetal abnormality in England, Wales and
    Scotland,* Royal College of Obstetricians and Gynaecologists (January 1996).

29. J. M. Green and H. Statham, in T. Marteau and M. Richards (eds.), *The Troubled
    Helix* (CUP, 1996).

30. F. A. Chervenack et al., *British Journal of Obstetrics & Gynaecology* (1995),
    102:434–435.

31. H. Statham, et al., *British Journal of Obstetrics & Gynaecology* (2006), 113:1402–1411.

32. R. Dworkin, ibid., pp. 68–101.

33. Ibid., pp. 83–84.

34. Ibid., pp. 92–93.

35. Ibid., p. 101.

36. Ibid., p. 158.

37. Ibid., p. 159.

38. Ibid., p. 167.

39. P. Singer, *Rethinking Life and Death* (OUP, 1995), p. 211.

40. Ibid., p. 121.

41. Ibid., p. 214.

42. Ibid., p. 130.

7. When is a person? Christian perspectives on the beginning of life

1. J. R. W. Stott, *Issues Facing Christians Today* (4th edition) (Zondervan, 2006),
   pp. 389–417.

2. G. Meilaender, *A Primer in Bioethics* (2nd edition), (Eerdmans, 2005), p. 28.

3. R. J. Berry, *God and the Biologist* (Apollos, 1996), p. 73.

4. G. R. Dunstan, *Journal of Medical Ethics* (1984), 1:38–44; see also discussion in
   D. A. Jones, *The Soul of the Embryo* (Continuum, 2004).

5. M. J. Gorman, *Abortion and the Early Church* (IVP, 1982), p. 34.

6. D. A. Jones, *The Soul of the Embryo* (Continuum, 2004).

7. Quoted by G. R. Dunstan, ibid.

8. Ibid.

9. See detailed discussion in D. A. Jones, *The Soul of the Embryo* (Continuum, 2004).

10. See account in J. R. W. Stott, *Issues Facing Christians Today* (Zondervan, 1990), pp. 319–320.

11. D. G. Jones, *Brave New People* (IVP, 1984), pp. 174–184.

12. D. G. Jones, *Designers for the Future* (Monarch, 2005).

13. See detailed discussion in D. A. Jones, *The Soul of the Embryo* (Continuum, 2004).

14. O. O'Donovan, *Begotten or Made?* (OUP, 1994), p. 59.

15. Ibid., p. 66.

16. Ibid.

17. B. McCarthy, *Fertility and Faith* (IVP, 1997), p. 122.

18. J. R. W. Stott, *Issues Facing Christians Today* (4th edition) (Zondervan, 2006), p. 402.

19. Tertullian, *Apology*, quoted by J. R. W. Stott, ibid., p. 402.

20. J. R. W. Stott, ibid., p. 403.

21. G. J. Jones, *Designers for the Future* (Monarch, 2005), pp. 217–220.

22. I. Kohn and P. L. Moffitt, *Pregnancy Loss, A Silent Sorrow* (Hodder & Stoughton, 1994), p. viii.

23. E. Storkey, *Mary's Story, Mary's Song* (Fount, 1993), p. 34.

24. Quoted by G. Meilaender, *A Primer in Bioethics* (2nd edition) (Eerdmans, 2005), p. 48.

25. B. K. Rothman, *The Tentative Pregnancy* (Norton, 1993), pp. 252–253.

26. G. Meilaender, *A Primer in Bioethics* (2nd edition) (Eerdmans, 2005), p. 54.

27. Ibid., p. 34.

28. H. Gemmen, *Startling Beauty* (Kingsway Communications, 2004).

29. Sarah Williams, *Shaming of the Strong* (Kingsway Communications, 2005).

30. Care Confidential website http://www.careconfidential.com.

31. P. Clarke, *Heart of Compassion* (Authentic Lifestyle, 2006).

32. CareConfidential can provide contact details for local centres.

8. The dying baby: dilemmas of neonatal care

1. L. J. Mangham et al., *Pediatrics* (2009), 123:e312–327.

2. E. Verhagen and P. J. Sauer, *New England Journal of Medicine* (2005), 352:959–962.

3. B. A. Manninen, *Journal of Medical Ethics* (2006), 32:643–651; H. Lindemann and M. Verkerk, *Hastings Center Report*, 38: 42–51. See also Peter Singer, http://www.utilitarian.net/singer/by/20050311.htm.

4. http://www.nuffieldbioethics.org/go/ourwork/neonatal/publication_406.html.

5. Mother Theresa, *A Gift for God* (Fount, 1975), p. 87.

6. Ibid., p. 50.

7. See 'Family privacy and persistent vegetative state: a symposium on the Linares case', *Law of Medicine & Health Care* (1989), 17:295–346.

8. J. S. Wyatt, 'What's wrong with quality of life as a clinical tool?' *Virtual Mentor*, 2005. Available at http://www.ama-assn.org/ama/pub/category/14553.html.

9. J. Vanier, *A Door of Hope* (Hodder & Stoughton, 1996), p. 16.

9. A good death? Euthanasia and assisted suicide

1. http://www.timesonline.co.uk/tol/news/uk/article4969423.ece.

2. O. Temkin, *Hippocrates in a World of Pagans and Christians* (John Hopkins University Press, 1991), p. 21.

3. A. van der Heide et al., *New England Journal of Medicine* (2007), 356:1957–1965.

4. D. Welch, *The Third Reich: Politics and Propaganda* (Routledge, 2002), p. 89.

5. http://www.dignityindying.org.uk/.

6. http://www.telegraph.co.uk/comment/telegraph-view/3622559/Euthanasias-euphemism.html.

7. Quoted in I. G. Finlay et al., *Palliative Medicine*, 19:444–453.

8. http://www.publications.parliament.uk/pa/ld200506/ldbills/036/06036.i.html.

9. Quoted in J. Keown, *Medical Law Review* (2007), 15:126–135.

10. J. H. Groenewoud et al., *New England Journal of Medicine* (2000), 342:551–556.

11. *Evening Standard*, November 1992.

12. Quoted by R. Dworkin, *Life's Dominion* (HarperCollins, 1995), p. 212.

13. Ibid., p.199.

14. Ibid., pp. 211–212.

15. Ibid., p. 239

16. J. Harris, in J. Keown (ed.), *Euthanasia Examined* (CUP, 1995), p. 11.

17. G. Brown, *The Living End* (Palgrave Macmillan, 2008).

18. Ibid., p. 85.

19. Ibid., p. 76.

20. C. P. Ferri et al., *Lancet* (2005), 366:2112–2117, Dementia UK report; http://www.alzheimers.org.uk/downloads/Dementia_UK_Full_Report.pdf.

21. http://www.telegraph.co.uk/news/uknews/2983652/Baroness-Warnock-Dementia-sufferers-may-have-a-duty-to-die.html.

22. G. Meilaender, *A Primer in Bioethics* (2nd edition) (Eerdmans, 2005), p. 98.

23. H. Jochemsen and J. Keown, *Journal of Medical Ethics*, 25:16–21. See also J. Keown, *Euthanasia, Ethics and Public Policy* (CUP, 2002) and http://www.carenotkilling.org.uk/pdf/Keown_report.pdf.

24. A. van der Heide et al., *New England Journal of Medicine* (2007), 356:1957–1965.

25. P. J. Van Der Maas et al., *Lancet* (1991), 338: 669–674.

26. J. Keown, in J. Keown (ed.), *Euthanasia Examined* (CUP, 1995), pp. 266–289.

27. A. van der Heide et al., *New England Journal of Medicine* (2007), 356:1957–1965.

28. http://www.oregon.gov/DHS/ph/pas/docs/year8.pdf.

29. L. Ganzini et al., *Journal of Palliative Medicine* (2003), 6:381–390.

30. http://www.carenotkilling.org.uk/pdf/Keown_report.pdf.

31. http://www.carenotkilling.org.uk/pdf/Keown_report.pdf.

32. http://www.internationaltaskforce.org/orrpt6.htm.

33. http://news.bbc.co.uk/1/hi/health/7676813.stm.

34. Quoted in J. Keown (ed.), *Euthanasia Examined* (CUP, 1995), p. 287.

35. R. Proctor, *Racial Hygiene: Medicine under the Nazis* (Harvard University Press, 1988).

36. Ibid., p.178.

37. Ibid., p.184.

38. I. Alexander, *New England Journal of Medicine* (1949), 241:39–47.

39. P. Singer, *Rethinking Life and Death* (OUP, 1995), p. 192.

40. A. M. Owen et al, *Science* (2006), 313:1402.

41. J. D. Bauby, *The Diving-Bell and the Butterfly* (Fourth Estate, 1997).

42. See 'Medical Aspects of the Persistent Vegetative State', *New England Journal of Medicine* (1994), 330: 1499–1508.

43. K. Andrews, *British Medical Journal* (1993), 306:1597–1600. See also C. Schnakers et al., *BMC Neurology* (2009), 9:35.

44. R. Dworkin, *Life's Dominion* (HarperCollins, 1995), p. 220.

45. A. D. Firlik, *The Journal of the American Medical Association* (1991), 201:265.

46. R. Dworkin, ibid., p. 224.

47. R. Dworkin, ibid., p. 232.

10. A better way to die

1. R. Clements, *Cambridge Papers*, 1994; 3(1):1–4.

2. Ibid.

3. G. Meilaender, *A Primer in Bioethics* (2nd edition) (Eerdmans, 2005), p. 57.

4. Ibid., p. 67.

5. John Donne, 'Devotions upon emergent occasions', Meditation XVII, 1624.

6. Quoted by S. Hauerwas, *Suffering Presence* (T. & T. Clark, 1986).

7. Ibid., p. 25.

8. Ibid., p. 26.

9. H. Küng & W. Jens, *A Dignified Dying* (SCM Press, 1995), p. 19.

10. Ibid., pp. 30–32.

11. Ibid., pp. 37–38.

12. P. Badham, *Is There a Christian Case for Euthanasia?* (SPCK, 2009).

13. A. C. Phelps et al., *The Journal of the American Medical Association* (2009), 301:1140–1147.

14. G. Meilaender, ibid., p. 64.

15. Ibid., p. 64.

16. S. Hauerwas, ibid., p. 48.

17. S. Boulay, *Cicely Saunders* (Hodder & Stoughton, 1984).

18. M. Mills et al., *British Medical Journal* (1994), 309: 583–586.

19. World Health Organisation, *The Global Burden of Disease* (2004), http://www.who.int/healthinfo/global_burden_disease/2004_report_update/en/index.html.

20. Mental Capacity Act 2005; http://www.opsi.gov.uk/acts/acts2005/ukpga_20050009_en_1.

21. *Evening Standard*, 17 April 2009.

22. O. O'Donovan, *Begotten or Made?* (OUP, 1984), p. 59.

23. C. Swift, *Triple Helix* (Christian Medical Fellowship), Easter 2009.

24. R. Bullock, *Age and Ageing* (2007), 36:357–358; D. Jolley, *Age and Ageing* (2008), 37(2):237; see also *Dementia: guideline*, National Institute for Health and Clinical Excellence (2006), www.nice.org.uk/Guidance.

25. S. Fish, *Alzheimer's* (Lion, 2008).

26. Ibid., p. 163.

27. R. Davis, *My Journey into Alzheimer's Disease* (Tyndale House, 1989).

11. The Hippocratic tradition and the practice of modern medicine

1. Translated by Ludwig Edelstein, from *The Hippocratic Oath: Text, Translation, and Interpretation* (Johns Hopkins University Press, 1943); see http://www.pbs.org/wgbh/nova/doctors/oath_classical.html (1991).

2. O. Temkin, *Hippocrates in a World of Pagans and Christians* (Johns Hopkins University Press, 1991), p. 21.

3. Ibid., p. 72.

4. Ibid., p. 30.

5. Quoted by N. Cameron, *The New Medicine* (Hodder & Stoughton, 1991), p. 9.

6. See O. Temkin, ibid., pp. 126–145.

7. See N. Cameron, ibid., p. 4.

8. O. Temkin, ibid., p. 35.

9. O. O'Donovan, *Resurrection and Moral Order* (OUP, 1994), p. 240.

10. M. J. Gorman, *Abortion and the Early Church* (IVP, 1982), p. 24.

11. Quoted by M. J. Gorman, ibid., p. 84.

12. Julian epistle 22, cited by V. Ramachandra, *The Recovery of Mission* (Paternoster, 1996), p. 280.

13. Eusebius, cited by V. Ramachandra, ibid., p. 280.

14. Quoted by J. T. Aitken et al., *The Influence of Christians in Medicine* (CMF, 1984), p. 8.

15. Quoted by O. Temkin, ibid., p. 34.

16. V. Ramachandra, *Gods that Fail* (Paternoster, 1996), p. 216.

17. N. Cameron, ibid., p.10.
18. Ibid., p. 3.
19. *Genethics*, 1997; 17:9.
20. P. Singer, *Rethinking Life and Death* (OUP, 1995), p. 1.
21. Ibid., p. 4.
22. Ibid., p. 44.
23. G. F. Ferngren, in R. C. McMillan et al., (eds), *Euthanasia and the Newborn* (Reidel, 1987), p. 42.
24. S. Hauerwas, *Suffering Presence* (T. & T. Clark, 1986), p. 26.
25. Mother Teresa, *Contemplative in the Heart of the World* (Fount, 1985), p. 60.
26. Mother Teresa, *The Love of Christ* (Fount, 1982), p. 37.
27. C. D. Pohl, in J. F. Kilner et al., *Bioethics and the Future of Medicine* (Paternoster, 1995), p. 222.
28. J. R.W. Stott, *The Cross of Christ* (IVP, 1986), pp. 335–336.
29. C. S. Lewis, *The Lion, the Witch and the Wardrobe* (Fount, 1950), p. 142.
30. K. Barth, *Church Dogmatics*, III i (T. & T. Clark, 1958).

12. The future of humanity

1. O. O'Donovan, *Begotten or Made?* (OUP, 1984), p. 3.
2. J. Hughes, *Dreaming with Diderot*, http://ieet.org/index.php/IEET/more/1102/.
3. Ibid.
4. J. Gray, *Straw Dogs* (Granta, 2002).
5. Ibid.
6. Ibid.
7. J. Harris, *Enhancing Evolution: the ethical case for making better people* (Princeton, 2007).
8. R. Dworkin, *Sovereign Virtue* (Harvard University Press, 2002), p. 452.
9. T. Douglas, *Journal of Applied Philosophy* (2008), 25:228–245.
10. I. Persson and J. Savalescu, *Journal of Applied Philosophy* (2008), 25:162–177.
11. Sometimes attributed to Mary Elizabeth Frye, quoted by N. T. Wright, *Surprised by Hope* (SPCK, 2007), p. 16.
12. N. T. Wright, ibid., p. 22.
13. K. Barth, *Church Dogmatics*, III i (T. & T. Clark, 1958), pp. 213–219.
14. N. T. Wright, ibid., p. 57.
15. C. S. Lewis, *Letters to Malcolm* (Geoffrey Bles, 1964), p. 158.

INDEX